GATEWAYS

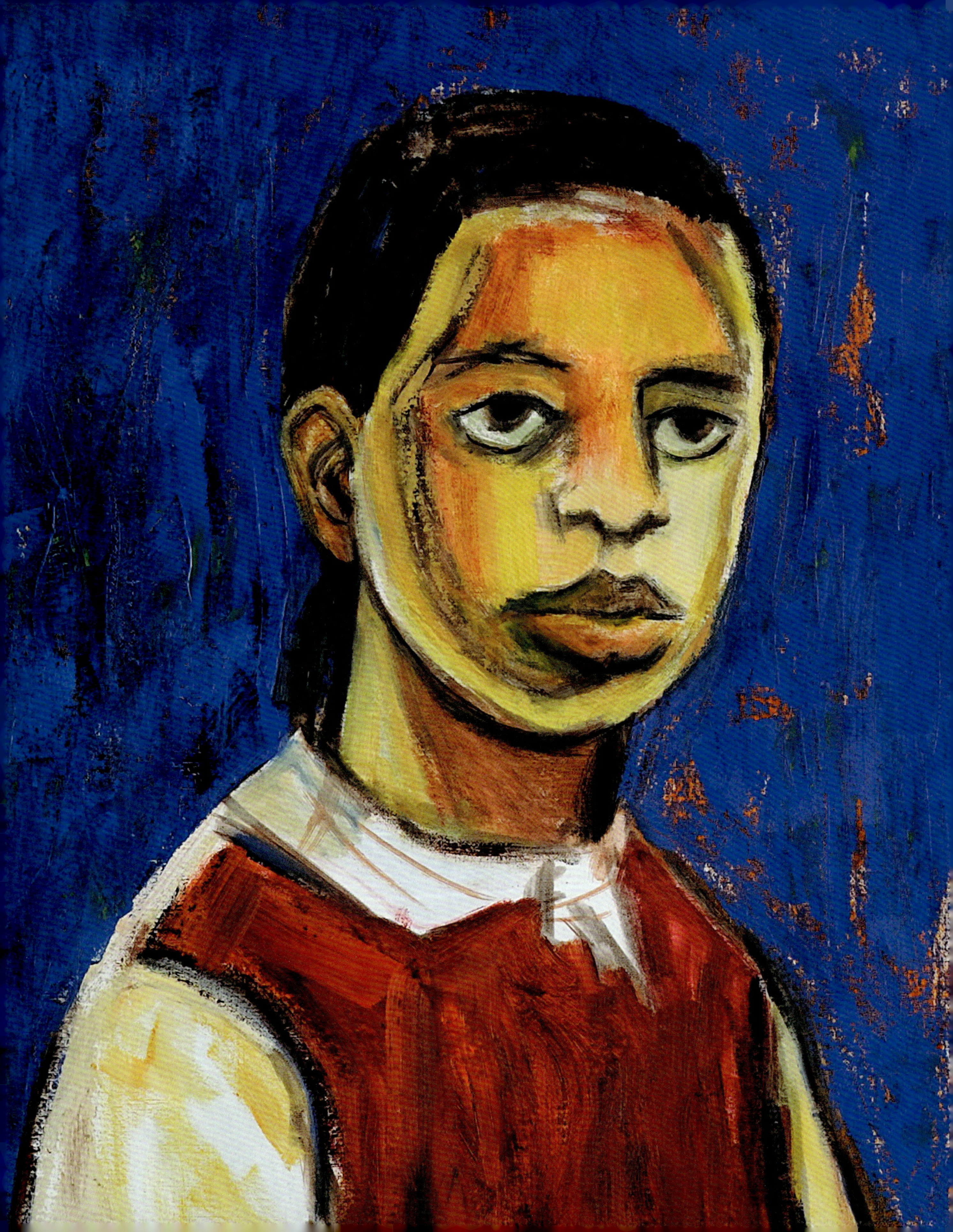

GATEWAYS

AFRICAN AMERICAN ART FROM THE KEY COLLECTION

Halima Taha and Adrienne L. Childs PhD

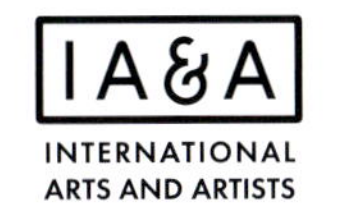

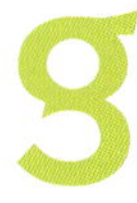

International Arts & Artists, Washington, DC in association with D Giles Limited

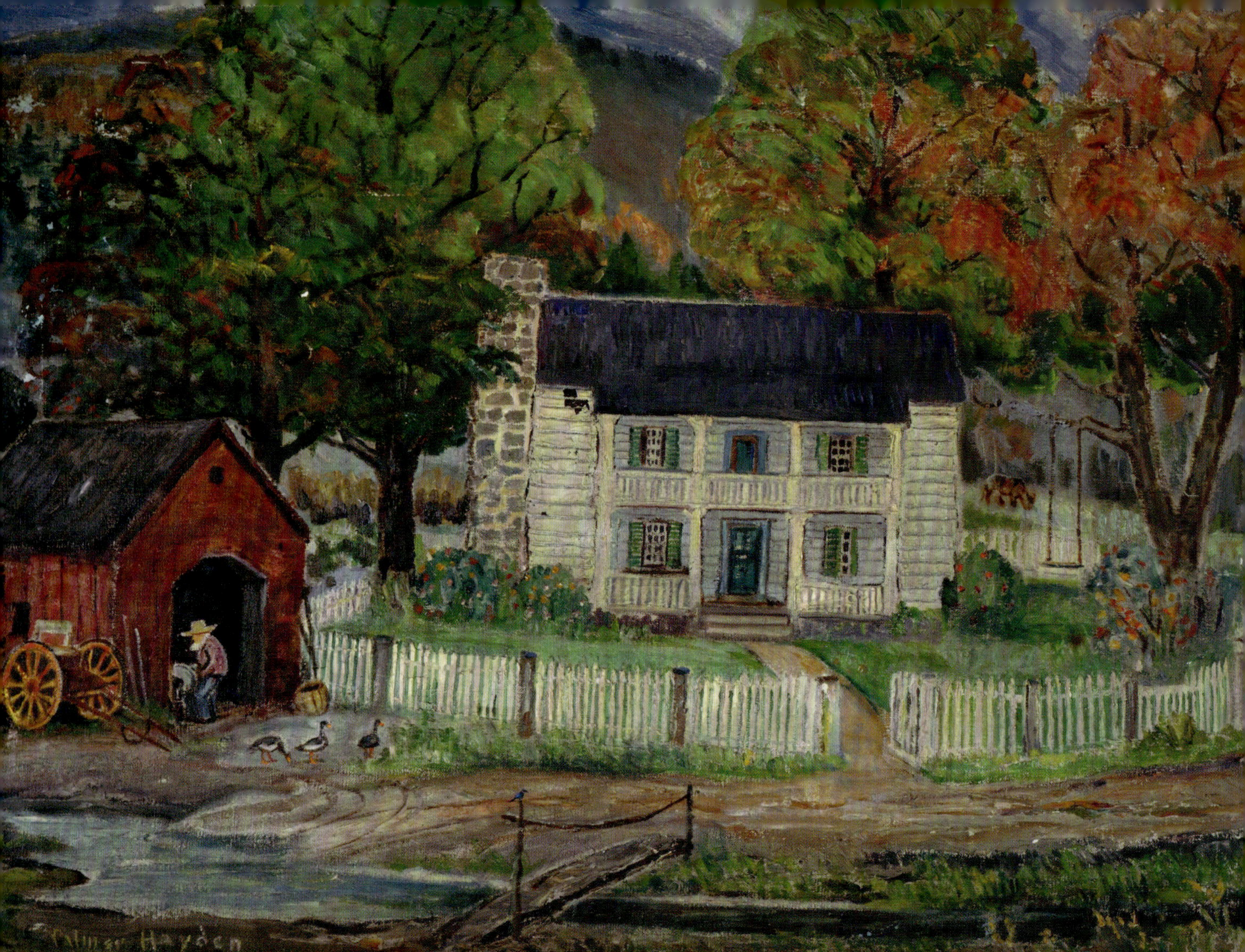

This catalogue accompanies the exhibition *GATEWAYS: African American Art from the Key Collection.*

Every attempt has been made to find the copyright owners of all illustrations. IA&A apologizes for any unintentional omissions and would be pleased to add an acknowledgment in future editions.

First published in 2024 by GILES
An imprint of D Giles Limited
66 High Street,
Lewes, BN7 1XG, UK
gilesltd.com

ISBN: 978-1-913875-66-4

Library of Congress Control Number: 2024937864

The exhibition was curated by Anthony Stellaccio, Eric Key, and Dr. Sarah Klein

For International Arts & Artists:
Nora van Trotsenburg, Exhibition Manager and Curatorial Assistant
Anthony Stellaccio, Former Director and Chief Curator of Traveling Exhibitions
Seth Dorcus, Exhibition Manager
Amie Geremia, Director of Traveling Exhibitions
Dr. Sarah Klein, Senior Curator
Gregory D. Houston, President and CEO
Copy-edited by David Walker

For D Giles Limited:
Proofread by Jenny Wilson
Designed by Alfonso Iacurci
Produced by GILES, an imprint of D Giles Limited
Printed and bound in China

All measurements are in inches; height precedes width precedes depth.

Front cover: Nelson Stevens, *Untitled (nude female)* (detail), 1980, Oil on canvas, 42" × 42" × 2", Courtesy of the Eric Key Collection, © Nelson Stevens
Back cover: Elizabeth Catlett, *Family*, 2022, Bronze, 15" × 5½" × 5", Courtesy of the Eric Key Collection, © 2023 Mora-Catlett Family / Licensed by VAGA at Artists Rights Society (ARS), NY
Frontispiece: Samella Lewis, *Untitled* (detail), 1999, Mixed media, 32" × 26", Courtesy of the Eric Key Collection, © 2023 Samella Lewis / Licensed by VAGA at Artists Rights Society (ARS), NY
Page 4: Palmer Hayden, *White House at Great Bend* (detail), 1940s, Oil on canvas, 22" × 30", Courtesy Hayden Family Revocable Art Trust and the Eric Key Collection, © Lisa L. Crane, Trustee, Hayden Family Revocable Art Trust.

CONTENTS

FOREWORD

The histories of African American art collectors across the late twentieth and twenty-first centuries reveal rich cultural networks, shaped by institutions, friendships, and aesthetic kinship. The Key Collection reflects these contextual factors and connections, providing a crossroads to remember, consider, and imagine future possibilities. Eric Key cultivated his appreciation and passion for the arts as a student at Hampton University, where his matriculation coincided with a cultural awakening in which African American history was emphasized across academic disciplines and art forms. The accessibility of Black cultural production and empowering representations at Hampton University directly influenced Key's desire to live in an aesthetic environment defined by his art collection. The artworks and prestigious art community at Hampton University, including former faculty and students, left an indelible impression on Key and informed his collection practice.

Thanks to Eric Key's friendships with artist Elizabeth Catlett and artist-scholar Dr. Samella Lewis, his collection bears the aesthetic influence of their artist-activist legacies. Today, Elizabeth Catlett is widely recognized as a pioneer in forging a Black Feminist visual art practice that centers the experiences of Black women.[1] Catlett's sculptures in Key's collection establish a conceptual frame

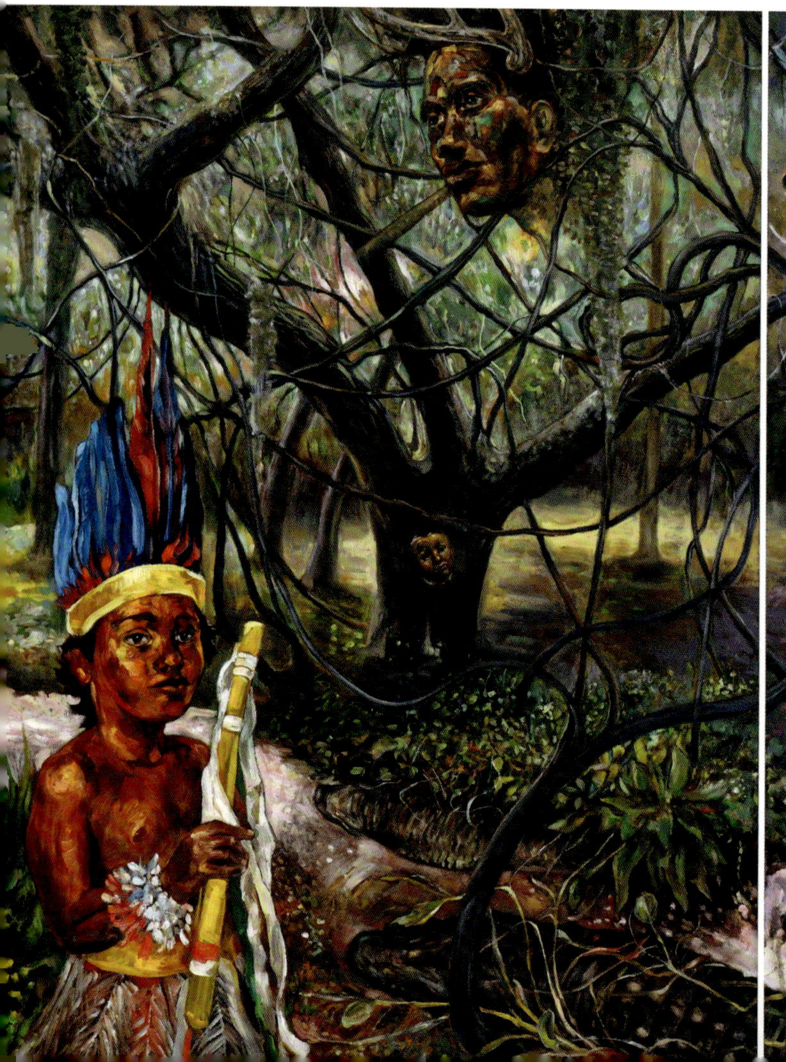

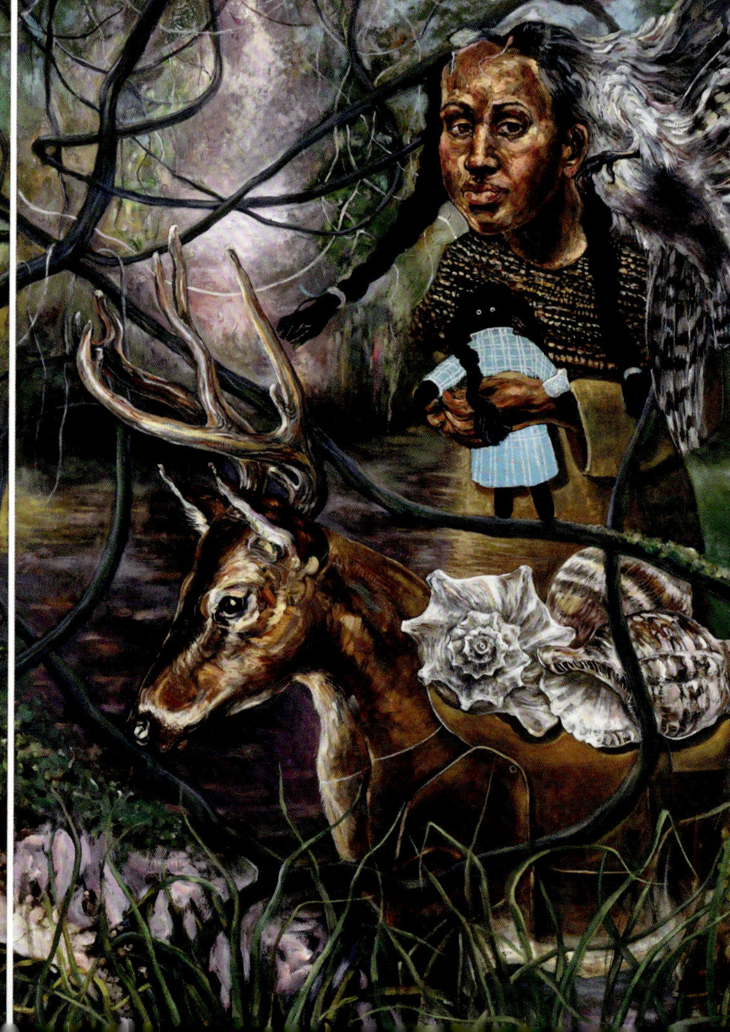

for other artworks, such as Emma Amos's *Sun Babe* (1987) and Margo Humphrey's *The Black Madonna* (2013). Dr. Lewis's compositions in the collection illuminate the influence she and Catlett had on Eric Key. Dr. Lewis is celebrated as a trailblazing art historian and artist who was dedicated to recovering, writing, and visualizing the broad history of Black labor and artistic production. In a 1992 oral history interview, Dr. Lewis remarked, "I see the artist as a visual kind of pathfinder, or forerunner or somebody who discovers something before historians even discover it, before a lot of people do..."[2] The collection reflects this sensibility of celebrating the distinct perspective of artists. Eric Key has balanced canonical masterworks with contemporary interventions to preserve the legacy of African American artists as pathfinders who create gateways to provocative new insights into the past, present, and future.

Also important to this collection is its visual documentation of recent American history in works created after 2015, a period defined by such events as the rise of the Black Lives Matter movement, a rapidly escalating environmental crisis, and the COVID-19 pandemic. Kyle Hackett's *New Negation 1* (2018) and Jamea Richmond-Edwards's *Easy Breezy Girl* (2020) represent the range of artistic responses, from the traditional marshaling of Black excellence through portraiture to the emergence of philosophies rooted in rest and reflection as resistance.[3] Paintings like Stefanie Jackson's *ZAPALA, Estuary of Regret* (2017) recall the incisive lessons of Key's collegiate interactions with art and artifacts created by North American indigenous communities in Hampton University's art collection. *ZAPALA* invites viewers to reconsider how we value nature and the resources that sustained generations of indigenous and African American communities. As a multifaceted capsule of the rich contours of Black culture and history, the Key Collection serves as a cultural monument to the dynamism of African American historical legacies and futures.

Melanee C. Harvey PhD
Associate Professor of Art History
Department of Art
Chadwick A. Boseman College of Fine Arts
Howard University

Stefanie Jackson, *ZAPALA, Estuary of Regret* (detail), 2017, Oil on canvas, 48" × 72" × 2", Courtesy of the Eric Key Collection, © Stefanie Jackson

ACKNOWLEDGMENTS

First and foremost, we thank Eric Key for sharing his passion and mission with all of us. His dedication to applying his resources as an arts administrator, curator, and collector to support African American artists professionally and personally has inspired many and has culminated in this exhibition of works that represent tangible contributions—*gateways*—for the ascent of African American artists. Visitors to *GATEWAYS: African American Art from the Key Collection* will gain a deeper understanding of how African American artists harnessed their collective identity against racial oppression and how collectors such as Eric Key have amplified their voices. We are pleased to aid in the promotion and storytelling of the important artists and artworks featured in this exhibition, and are proud to share this piece of history with communities across the United States and North America.

Although the Key Collection is personal in nature, it also serves as a historical record, allowing audiences to appreciate the rich history and evolution of African American art. This exhibition is derived from the remarkable broader Key Collection of over 500 pieces of art produced by African American artists and artists of African descent. These works offer insight into a multitude of cultural values such as family, community, respect, honor, integrity, generosity, and faith.

We join Eric Key in thanking IA&A Trustee Brenda Thompson and her husband Larry Thompson, who introduced us; as well as our founder David Furchgott, who was the first to visit Key's collection and who encouraged IA&A to pursue this project and to share it with a larger audience. We are immensely grateful to Melanee C. Harvey PhD, Halima Taha, and Adrienne L. Childs PhD for their insightful texts illuminating the significance of the collection, both as it relates to Eric Key and to the history of African American art.

Additionally, IA&A would like to provide a special thanks to photographers Greg Staley and John Woo for photographing this beautiful collection. We extend heartfelt appreciation to the individuals whose dedication made this exhibition possible. Anthony Stellaccio, IA&A's former Director of the Traveling Exhibitions Service, played a pivotal role in the initial selection of artworks. Dr. Sarah Klein, Senior Curator, provided invaluable curatorial insights and shaped the exhibition tour alongside Catherine Vasko. Amie Geremia, the current Director of the Traveling Exhibitions Service, provided guidance and support throughout the project.

We also express gratitude to our diligent copyeditor, David Walker, who meticulously reviewed all exhibition texts and essays, enhancing their quality. Our Registrars—Faith Herrington, Eileen Streeter, and Anna-Maria Royal—handled numerous logistical aspects with precision and efficiency, vital for realizing the exhibition.

Special recognition goes to our Exhibition Managers, Nora van Trotsenburg and Seth Dorcus, whose exceptional commitment, dedication, and tireless efforts were instrumental in organizing and overseeing the production of the catalogue, and ensuring the entire project remained on track. We are deeply grateful for their invaluable contributions.

Of course, Eric Key can never be thanked enough for sharing his journey with us and allowing his most precious possessions to be absent from his home for such a long time. International Arts & Artists, along with all who have had the privilege of experiencing these artworks in person, express our deepest gratitude to the collector for

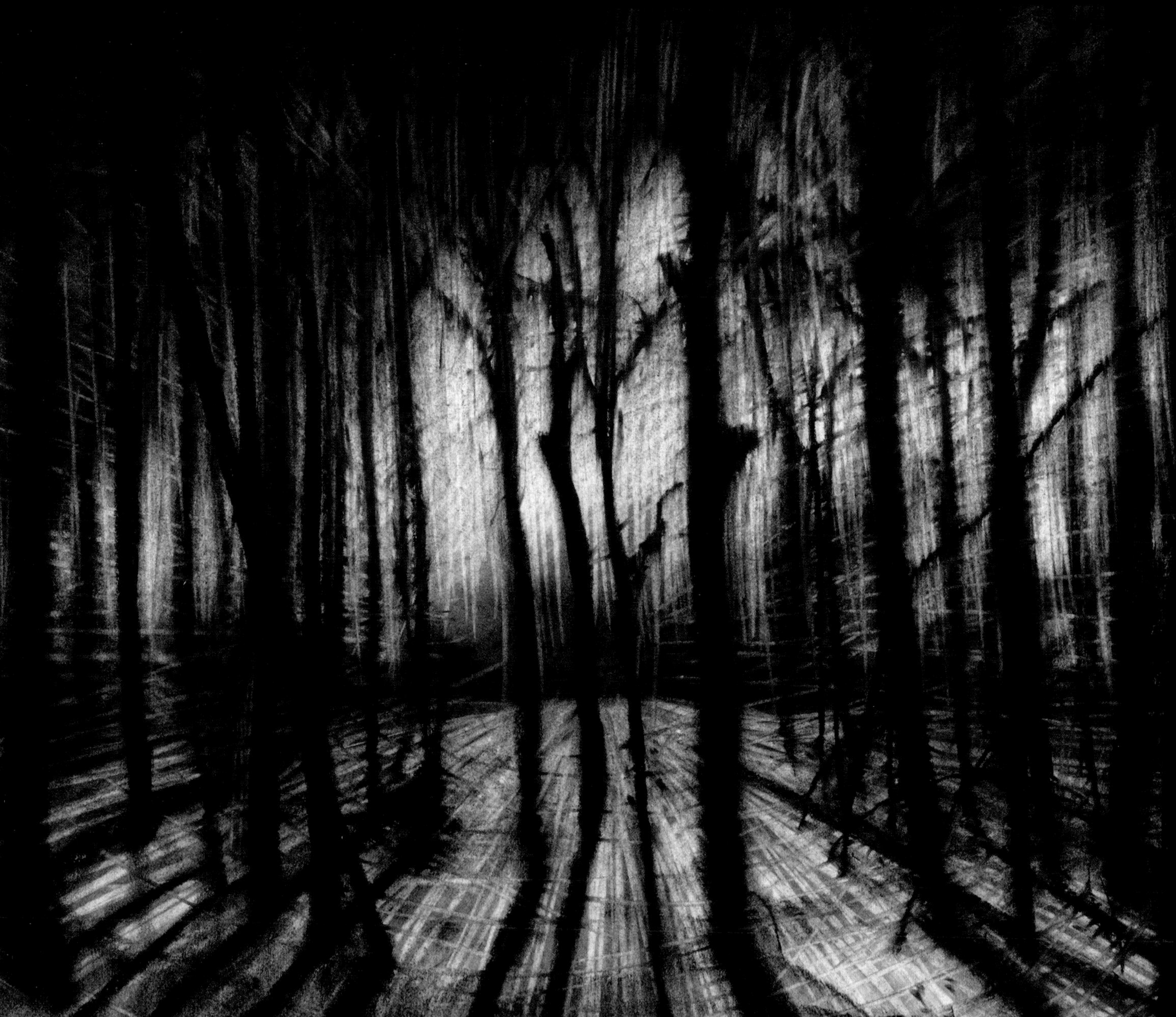

his generosity and vision in sharing this remarkable collection with the public. An exhibition of this magnitude involves many, and we extend special thanks to the numerous donors and supporters of IA&A, without whom our work—and ability to tell stories such as these—would not be possible. We are indebted to the artists for their diverse forms of personal and communal expression, which have educated and inspired us. Lastly, we are thankful to everyone who played a role, however small or grand, in mounting this exhibition.

For the Benefit of All,

Gregory D. Houston
President and Chief Executive Officer
International Arts & Artists

Ed Brown, *Untitled (sun through forest)* (detail), 2010, Charcoal on paper, 39½" × 50", Courtesy of the Eric Key Collection, © Edward Brown

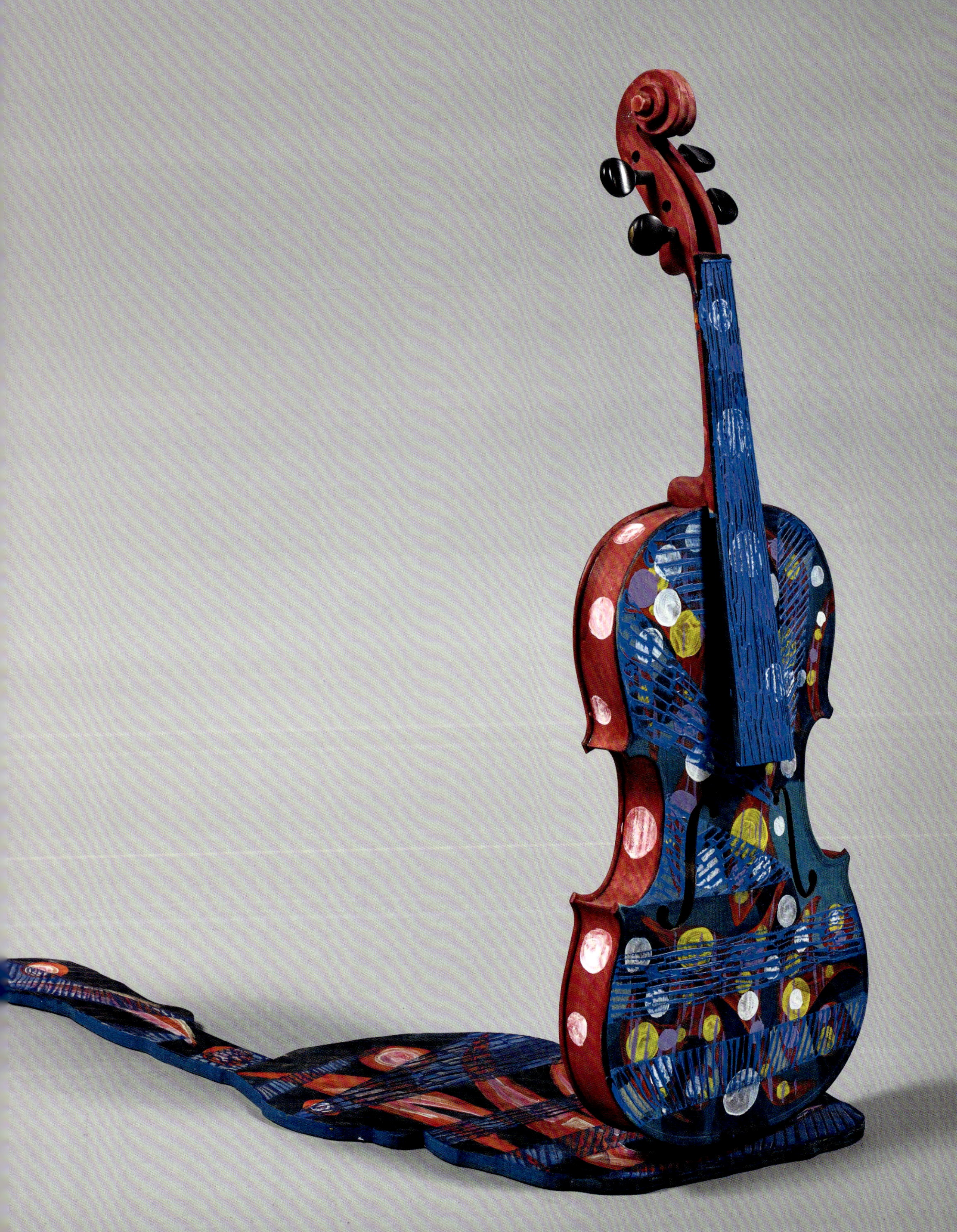

KEY TONAL RUMINATIONS

Halima Taha

In the vast realm of human existence, one eternal question has been central to all cultures, continents, and eras: "Who am I?" *GATEWAYS: African American Art from the Key Collection* unfolds an intricate tapestry that weaves together diverse perspectives, ancient beliefs, and cultural values about family, community, respect, honor, integrity, generosity, and faith. Eric Key's passion for collecting art by American artists of African descent began early in his career, stemming from his personal quest for identity and a desire to support and promote the work of these artists. His collection not only reflects his personal journey, but also serves as a broader American narrative of the Black experience, encompassing an extraordinary range of contexts and values.

Eric Key, a man of humble beginnings, has enriched the history of art collecting with his remarkable assemblage of more than 500 pieces of twentieth-century art produced by American artists of African descent. The exhibition, *GATEWAYS: African American Art from the Key Collection*, offers insight into his interdisciplinary sensibilities. It is a selection of 90 artworks, including works on paper, canvas, and sculpture, featuring artists from the Harlem Renaissance to the beginning of the twenty-first century.

Eric's collection provides a historical record, allowing audiences to appreciate African American art's rich and diverse history and its evolution. The Harlem Renaissance was a vibrant cultural and intellectual movement that emerged between 1919 and 1929, when Harlem, New York, became the hub for African American artists, writers, musicians, and intellectuals, who celebrated and asserted their cultural identity through the literary, performing, and visual arts. Philosopher and cultural arbiter Dr. Alain Locke, who published his seminal work *The New Negro* in 1925, played a significant role in the aesthetic and intellectual development of Black artists, emphasizing the importance of creating a post-colonial artistic voice to express the beauty and eloquence of themselves through

Eric Pryor
Shadow and Rhythm/Untitled (detail), 2002, Paint on wood, 22" × 10" × 22", Courtesy of the Eric Key Collection, © Eric Pryor

their work. This was a watershed moment for the African American art community, whose innovative work challenged racial stereotypes embedded by eighteenth- and nineteenth-century European scholars to justify slavery, colonization, and "racial" hierarchies. These scholars' "racial construct" perpetuated the notion that people of African descent were subhuman, unintelligent, and suitable only for labor and breeding. The idea that they could make fine art was considered laughable. The fallacy of this "racial construct" lost all credibility with the advent of twenty-first-century DNA testing.

From 1935, many Black artists participated and worked with other artists as part of the Works Progress Administration (WPA) until 1943. By the 1950s, Abstract Expressionism captivated the first generation of abstract artists, including Charles Alston (1907-1977), Romare Bearden (1911-1988), Beauford Delaney (1901-1979), and Norman Lewis (1909-1979). By the 1960s and 1970s, artists sought to promote Black cultural identity, empowerment, and liberation through the arts. The Black Arts Movement emerged as a cultural and political crusade emphasizing the creation of art that was explicitly political, socially conscious, and rooted in the Black American experience. In the 1980s and beyond, the art world became increasingly diverse and globalized. African American artists continued to make significant contributions to contemporary art. The artistic styles from the 1970s to the end of the twentieth century included Pop Art, Minimalism, Conceptual Art, Postmodernism, and Neo-Expressionism. During this period, artists explored new materials, techniques, and concepts, pushing at the boundaries of traditional forms and leading the art world to become increasingly interconnected and international, with artists from different cultures and backgrounds collaborating and influencing each other.

This collection mirrors Eric's experiences and dreams, opening an extraordinary gateway for inquiry, reflection, and exchange between culturally and intellectually diverse audiences. Each work of art tells a unique story through the artist's lens and Eric's interpretative connection. In this sense, it is analogous to the jazz tradition of "call and response." Specifically, a collector's response to an artwork is evident in both processes' interactive and dynamic nature. In jazz, call and response is a fundamental aspect of the music: it involves a musical dialogue between musicians, where one player presents a musical phrase (the "call"), and another player or the entire ensemble responds with a complementary phrase (the "response"). This back-and-forth creates the experience of improvisation, collaboration, and shared creativity during the performance. In the context of visual art, it highlights the dynamic interaction of ideas, emotions, and creative expressions between the artist and the viewer, an exchange that shapes and enriches the cultural traditions to which they belong.

Similarly, when collectors respond to an artwork, they create a dialogue with it. The artwork serves as the initial "call" that evokes a response from the collector. This response can take various forms, such as emotional reactions, intellectual interpretations, or the decision to acquire and collect the work. Collectors' diverse reactions to an artwork assimilate both processes' interactive and collaborative nature, serving as a gateway that bridges music and art.

The notion that art provides a gateway for self-discovery through a global lens is an understatement. A significant factor in the thirty-year evolution of Eric's collection is gleaned from his extensive world travel. As he encountered transformative ideas and art, he embarked upon his ceaseless quest for self-discovery, creating a collection of self-expression. For instance, the ancient Egyptians strove to understand the physical aspects of personal identity and the eternal essence that defines an individual as the "Ka" (soul). They immortalized their "Ka" through intricate tomb paintings and sculptures. Conversely, the Greeks contemplated the nature of the self through "ideal" forms they saw as the embodiment of perfection.

Similarly, Arab scholars explored self-identity through the Islamic sciences as the pathway to realizing one's true essence and achieving spiritual enlightenment. Through their poetry, calligraphy, and intricate geometric patterns, they expressed the interconnectedness of humanity and the harmonious unity that lies within the true self. Comparably, Taoist principles of embracing life's natural flow invite the collector to go beyond preconceived notions of beauty, materiality, and value. Many humans, bound by arrogance, value their own cultural perspectives as more significant than others. Eric, by contrast, embraces authenticity and spontaneity, encouraging us all to open ourselves fully to the experience of art and to its many connections which resonate within.

In contemplation of "Who am I?," the Buddhist teachings of impermanence and interconnectedness also emerge in the collection's diverse artworks, each capturing a distinct moment. Eric Key's quest shows the myriad influences of ancient thinkers, as he meticulously gathered pieces that embody the essence of human wisdom and self-knowledge. As Eric delved into developing a collection of self-expression, he embarked on a journey to safeguard and comprehend the complex mosaic of the human experience. His art collection serves as a visual journey for the viewer as well, inviting them to explore the depth of their own identities.

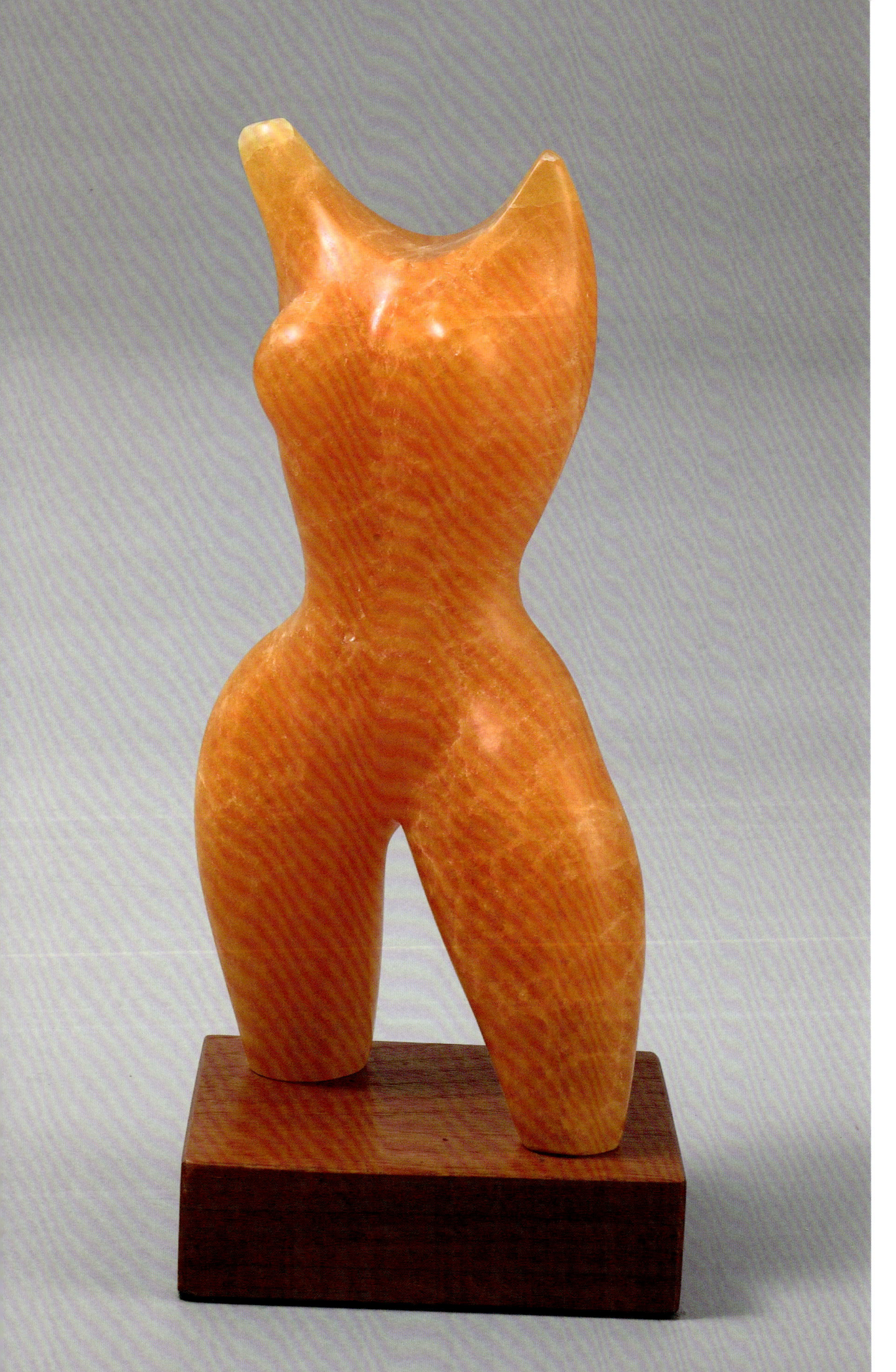

As we synthesize these diverse perspectives, we unveil the core of personal truth and reaffirm that collecting is more than a mere accumulation of objects. It reflects the innate desire to understand ourselves and the world around us. Through the preservation of art, ideas, and moments, we bridge the gaps between cultures and eras, fostering empathy, unity, and a shared sense of humanity. Eric Key's collection offers an in-depth look into African American visual culture, reflecting the artists' experiences, struggles, triumphs, and societal narratives. The sociological, geopolitical, cultural, and historical implications of art collecting are as layered as the materials artists use. Sociologically, art collections are a form of social expression that reflects an individual's or society's values, tastes, and preferences. For example, Eric Key's collection reflects his values of hard work, self-respect, mother wit, and family. It also mirrors his appreciation of African American people's undeniable perseverance and limitless creativity.

From a geopolitical perspective, fine art provides unique insight into a specific era's political atmosphere and values, helping future generations understand the global dynamics of political economies that impact art and other markets. Culturally, this body of work helps to preserve and propagate a specific heritage, narrating its rich arcs of social evolution and existential experience. Historically, art collections are tangible reflections of different eras, offering insights into the time's philosophical, cultural, and social paradigms. The Eric Key Collection preserves historic narratives of twentieth-century African American artistry, encapsulating the struggles, triumphs, and evolution of a vital African descendant landscape that has been sustained through American popular culture in the literary, performing, visual, and culinary arts. Its artistic excellence celebrates and serves as a testament to the resilience of Black culture and provides a shining beacon for future generations. It reaffirms art's ability to capture human experience, mirroring personal journeys, cultural heritage, and the broader societal landscape.

The African proverb "It takes a village to raise a child" asserts the importance of community in shaping individuals. It has resounding echoes in Eric's collection, which was built by the community that nurtured him. It was shaped by the relationships he cultivated with the artists and the shared experiences of fellow collectors and scholars. Together, they defined the collection's evocative, interconnected narratives about community, heritage, and personal history. For example, in Elizabeth Catlett's *Maternity* (1980) and *Torso* (1970) she celebrates Black womanhood with beauty, grace, and strength through women's multifaceted

Elizabeth Catlett
Torso, 1970, Orange onyx, 16" × 7¼" × 7¼", Courtesy of the Eric Key Collection, © 2023 Mora-Catlett Family / Licensed by VAGA at Artists Rights Society (ARS), NY

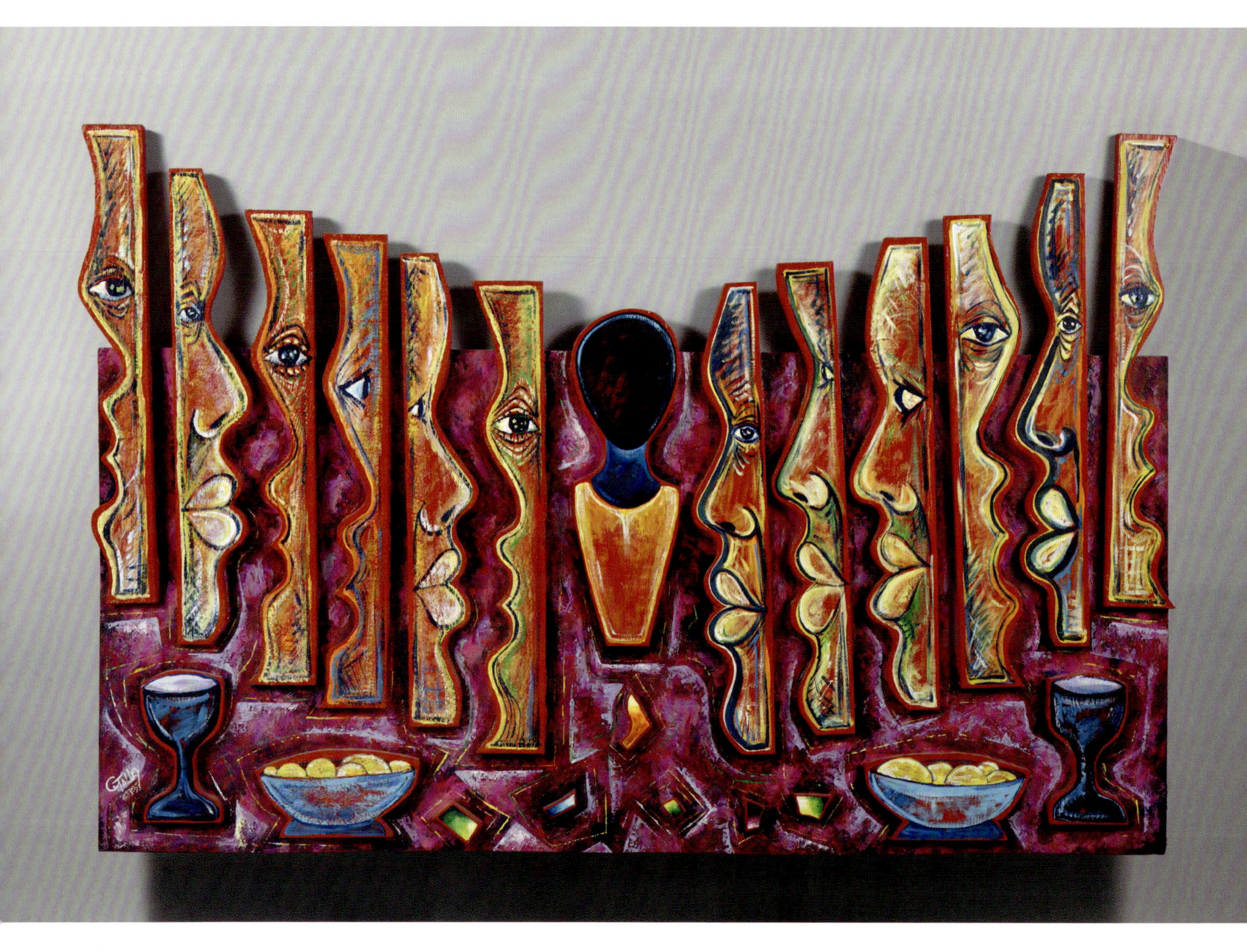

Clarence Talley
Last Supper, 1993, Paint, wood, 31¼" × 42" × 3", Courtesy of the Eric Key Collection, © Clarence Talley

Kyle Hackett
New Negation 1, 2018, Oil on aluminum, 7" × 5" × 1", Courtesy of the Eric Key Collection, © Kyle Hackett

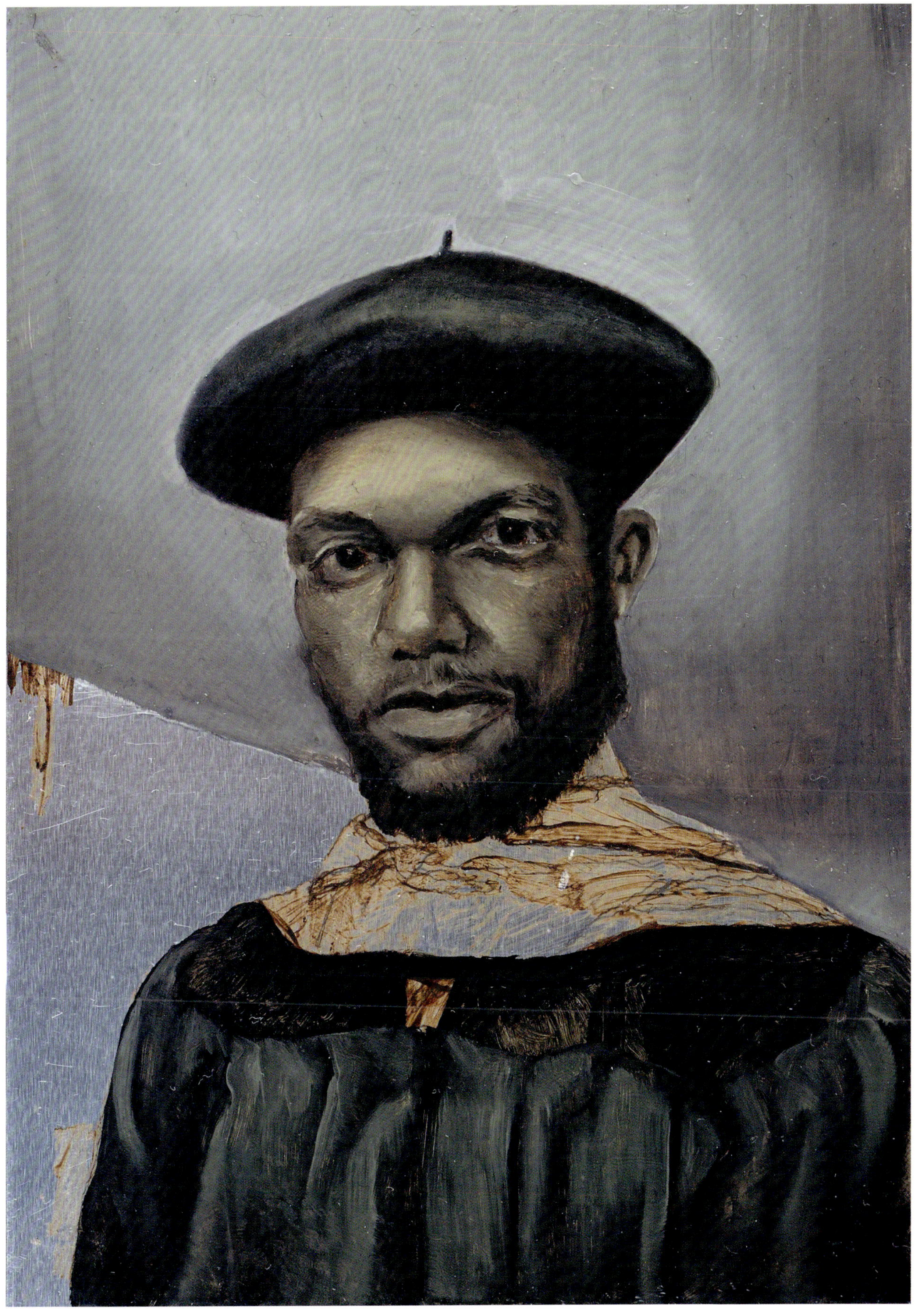

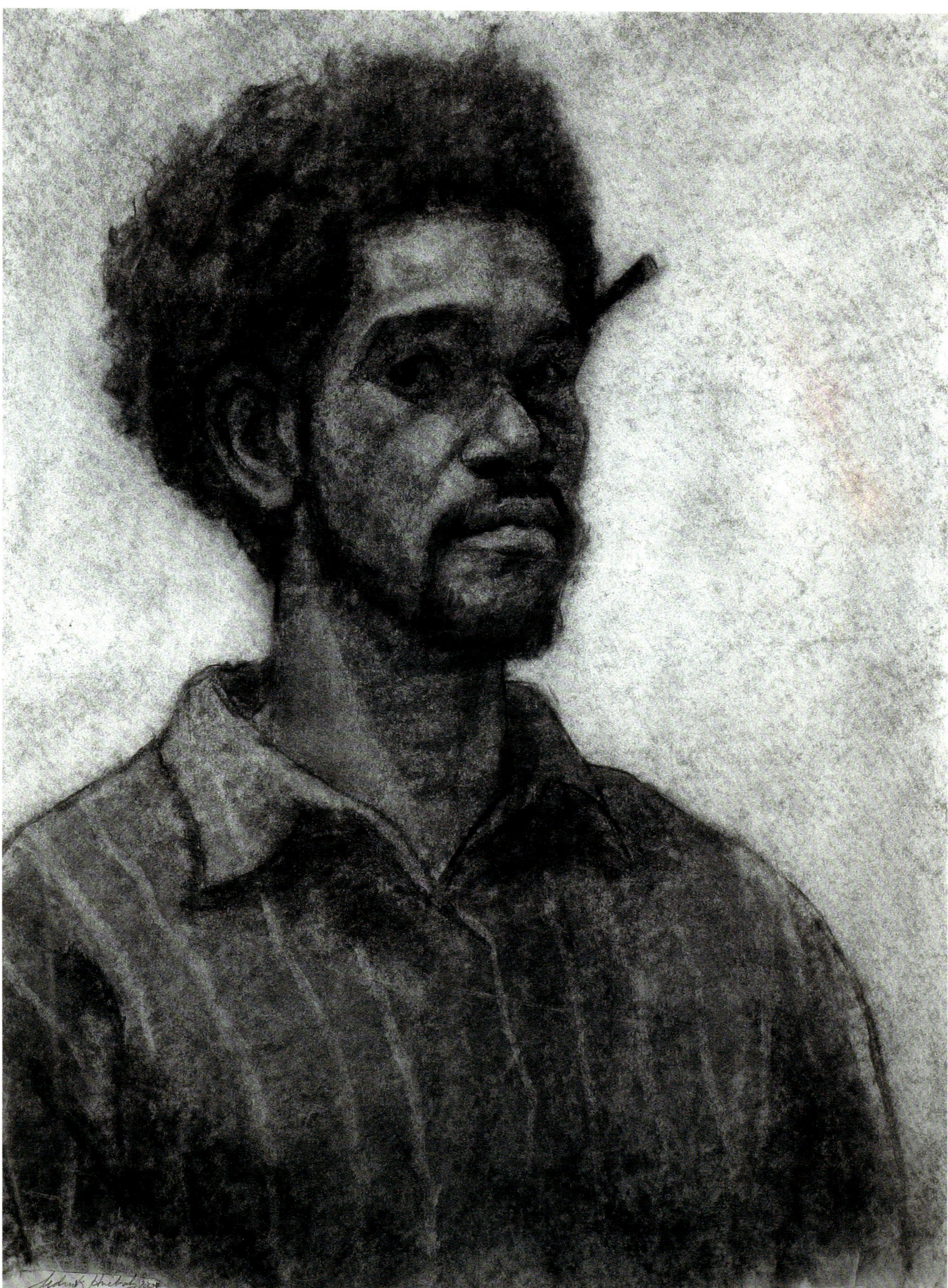

roles as daughters, sisters, aunties, mothers, friends, lovers, leaders, and homemakers. Likewise, Clarence Talley's *Last Supper* (1993), Kyle Hackett's *New Negation 1* (2018), and Sedrick Huckaby's *Self Portrait* (2001) all highlight Black men's strength, beauty, and accountability at home and within the community. Alfred Conteh's *Snap* (2019) creates a narrative of intergenerational hope, while Richmond Barthé's *Feral Benga* (1986) eloquently renders the strength and beauty of Black men without objectifying them, as enslaved Africans were often objectified as chattel and beasts of labor for public consumption. Within its historical and aesthetic richness, this collection is a unique and significant personal compilation, because it validates the sum of Eric's experiences and the collective journey of African American artists.

This collection resonates with James Baldwin's insightful words: "The purpose of art is to lay bare the questions which have been hidden by the answers." Each work in the collection raises questions about the artist's experience, African American history and culture, and the sociocultural and geopolitical context of the time. The art does not offer definitive answers but invites observers to engage in an ongoing dialogue, to seek understanding, and to appreciate the complex tapestry that is African American history and culture.

The African American cultural critic bell hooks emphasizes art's importance in shaping perception and narrative when she says, "There is power in looking."[1] Eric's collection embodies this power, gazing into various African American experiences and his own stories. It is not a passive collection but an active exploration of history, culture, and individuality. The collection mainly comprises figurative work, which evokes emotions, relationships, narratives, and social dynamics through a visual language that resonates with the viewer. It captures different communities, clothing, customs, and physical appearances. It provides insight into various civilizations' values, beliefs, and social structures. Each artist conveys a wide range of emotions through the human figure, from joy and love to sadness and despair. This emotional connection enhances the impact and relatability of each of the individual artworks. This is evidenced by the works of Eddie Moore, *Jesus Burial* (1995); Delita Martin, *Let Me Breathe* (2020); Margo Humphrey, *The Black Madonna* (2013); Kevin Cole, *Comfort and Pressure* (2014); Ben Jones, *Untitled (Fan)* (2001); Schroeder Cherry, *Color Test* (1995); Arthello Beck, *Vietnam* (n.d.); and Richard Mayhew, *Spring Mood Series #4* (2018). Moreover, the collection resonates with Nigerian author Ben Okri's statement, "The most authentic thing about us is our capacity to create, overcome, endure, transform, love, and be greater than our suffering."

Sedrick Huckaby
Self Portrait, 2001, Charcoal on paper, 30½" × 24¾" × 2", Courtesy of the Eric Key Collection, © Sedrick Huckaby

Figurative art has played a pivotal role in exploring and representing individual and collective identities, including diverse "racial," ethnic, gender, and cultural identities, challenging stereotypes and promoting inclusivity and intellectual diversity. This genre of art has maintained a sense of continuity and connection with art history and traditions. It has been a constant presence throughout various art movements and periods, adapting to ever-changing styles and aesthetics while retaining its fundamental focus on the human form. Even amid abstract and conceptual art movements, figurative art has remained relevant and continues to evolve. Contemporary figurative artists often incorporate new techniques, reinterpret traditional approaches, and explore the intersections between representation and abstraction. The art pieces in Eric's collection are testaments to this enduring spirit of creativity and resilience, portraying the triumphs and personal struggles of African American artists and reflecting Eric's journey and experiences.

At the end of the twentieth century, the market for Black visual culture advanced to the international stage. Recently, many collectors have become more interested in acquiring big names substantiated by high auction sales prices, Instagram influencers, or the top-ten headline-makers. This collection represents a stark contrast to these trends. Eric focuses squarely on artists' backgrounds, motivations, challenges, and triumphs. He has not merely collected their work but has developed relationships with them, gleaning deep insights into their lives and personas. Each piece in the collection mirrors Eric's collecting journey, personal experiences, and humanity. His respect for the artists and their work is evident, as is his commitment to discovering and supporting lesser-known artists who follow a linear historic pedigree with the more than four hundred documented years of African Americans producing meritorious artistic expression. This commitment illuminates the path for these artists to gain recognition and allows their work to be seen and appreciated.

Art attracts a range of personalities, backgrounds, and sensibilities but, at its best, embodies a refreshing blend of humility and humanity. In this case, Eric's purposeful sincerity reflects fundamental virtues that significantly influence the depth and breadth of his collection. Modesty, as a collector's garment, exemplifies the collector's recognition that art is a vast field and one's collection is just a tiny hectare. It means understanding that each piece of art carries a depth of meaning and history that may never be fully comprehended. Eric's humility shows itself in his sensitive approach to his collection. He acknowledges the diverse experiences and narratives encapsulated in each art piece, appreciating their inherent

Richmond Barthé
Feral Benga, 1986, Bronze, 19" × 4½" × 4½", Courtesy of the Eric Key Collection, © Richmond Barthé

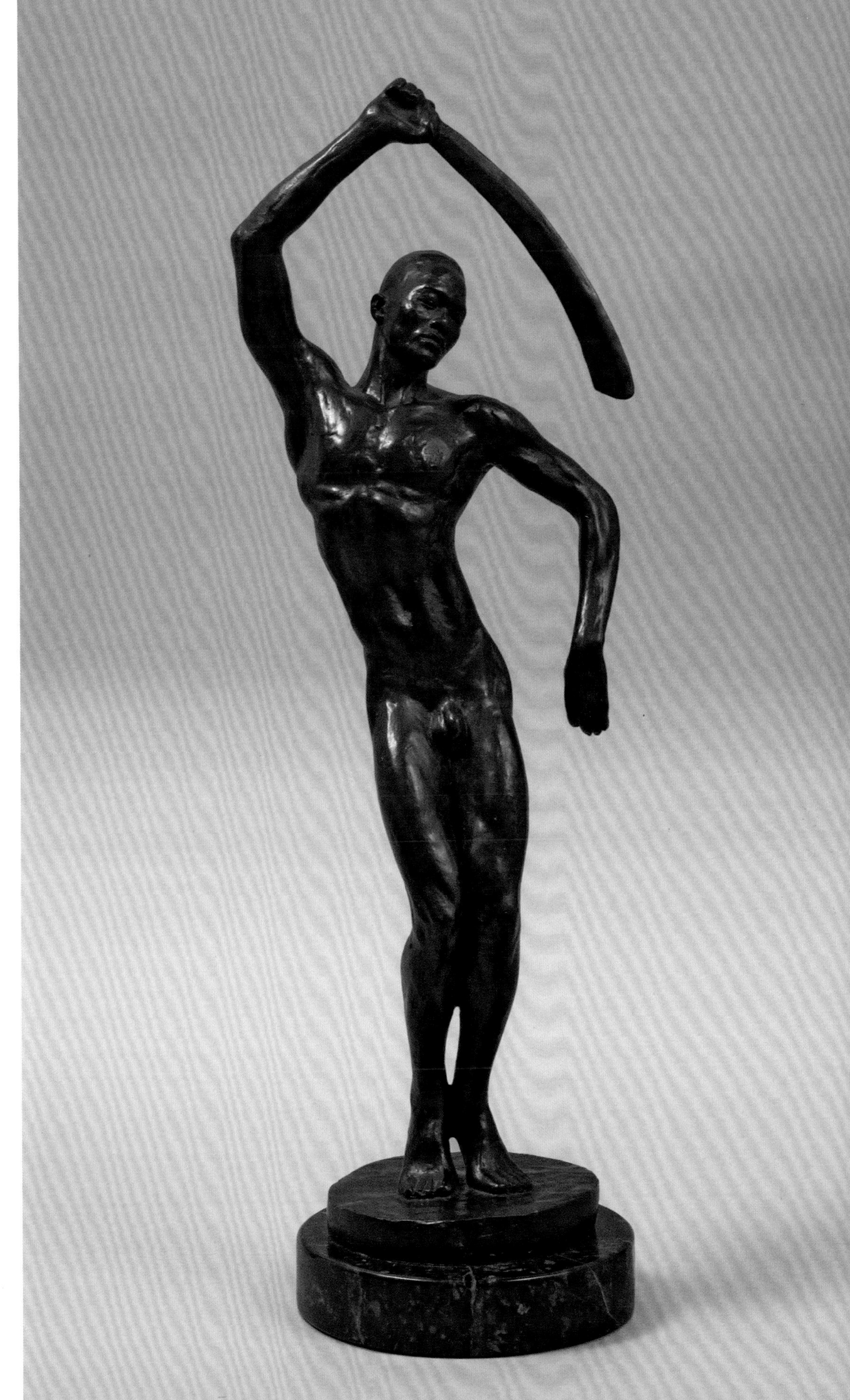

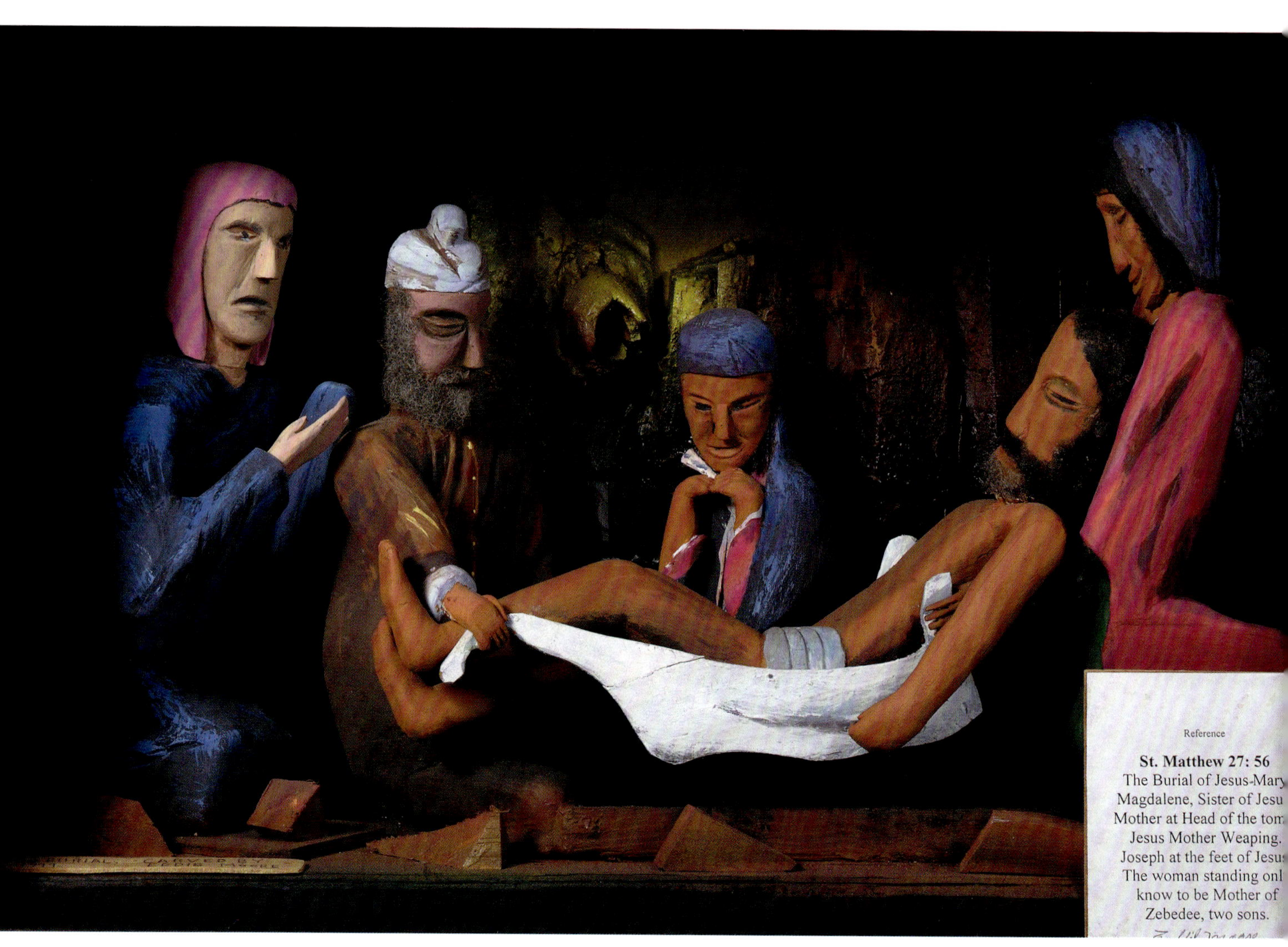

Eddie Moore
Jesus Burial, 1995,
Painted wood,
21"× 20"× 12", Courtesy of the Eric Key Collection, © Eddie Moore

value rather than merely their monetary cost or the artist's fame. This humility allows him to see beneath the surface, explore lesser-known artists, and appreciate the richness of the broader African American art scene, thereby adding depth to his collection.

Humanity, on the other hand, reflects the collector's ability to connect with the artists and their journey on a human level. Eric's collection demonstrates his humanity; he did not merely acquire art pieces, he built relationships with the artists and sought to understand their motivations, struggles, triumphs, and backgrounds. This human connection adds a unique layer of depth to his collection, as each art piece is not just an object but an embodiment of an individual's journey and experiences. Moreover, Eric's humanity is evident in his commitment to supporting lesser-known artists. This commitment goes beyond expanding his collection; it is about recognizing and appreciating these artists' talents and their contributions to the rich mosaic of African American art. This dimension has helped broaden the breadth of his collection, making it more diverse and inclusive.

Sincerity, meanwhile, is about the authenticity of the collector's interest and passion for art. Eric's sincerity as a person shines through in this collection, as he celebrates the historical, cultural, and aesthetic value of each piece. This approach adds depth to his collection as a true reflection of his personal experiences and values, reiterating how fine art can serve as a portal to global understanding by transcending geographical and cultural boundaries. The Eric Key Collection invites audiences to challenge preconceived notions, broaden their horizons, and foster empathy and compassion for diverse perspectives. Ultimately, it elicits a deeper appreciation of cultural and intellectual diversity, encouraging dialogue and fostering global interconnectedness. The collection exemplifies art's ability to illuminate social, political, and economic issues important to artists and their communities, providing a platform for raising awareness and promoting discussions that transcend borders.

In conclusion, Eric Key's collection is a profound distillation of his character and values, and a testament to the richness and diversity of twentieth-century African American visual culture. Its aesthetic arc exemplifies this, evoking emotional responses of awe, joy, melancholy, and intrigue. The impact of art demonstrates its timelessness in the way it evokes emotions, spurs introspection, and encourages self-reflection, all of which are essential components of the eternal, infinite inquiry, "Who am I?"

The emotional resonance of the artworks inspires solace, inspiration, and a sense of connection, all due to Eric's personal experiences and the

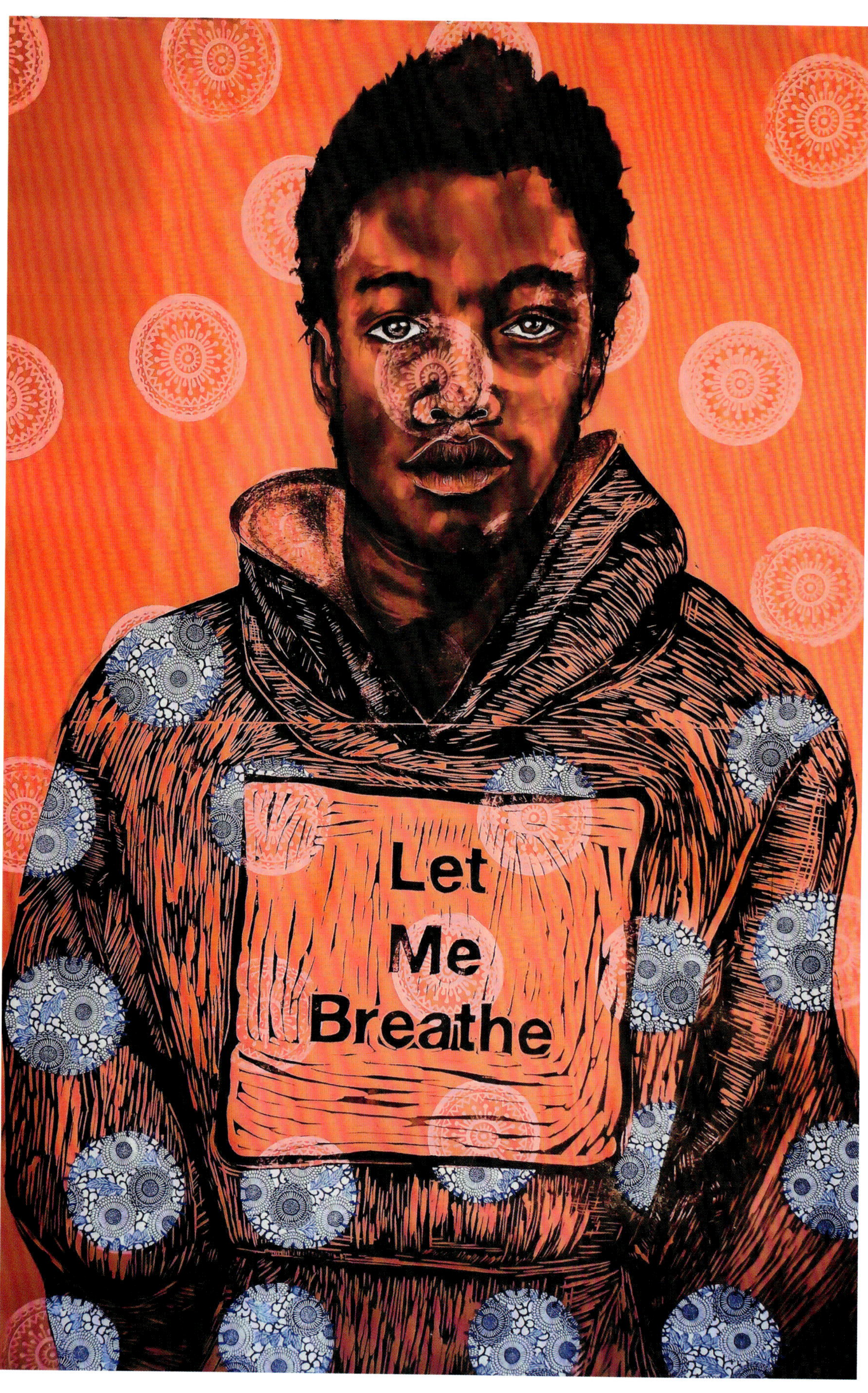
Let
Me
Breathe

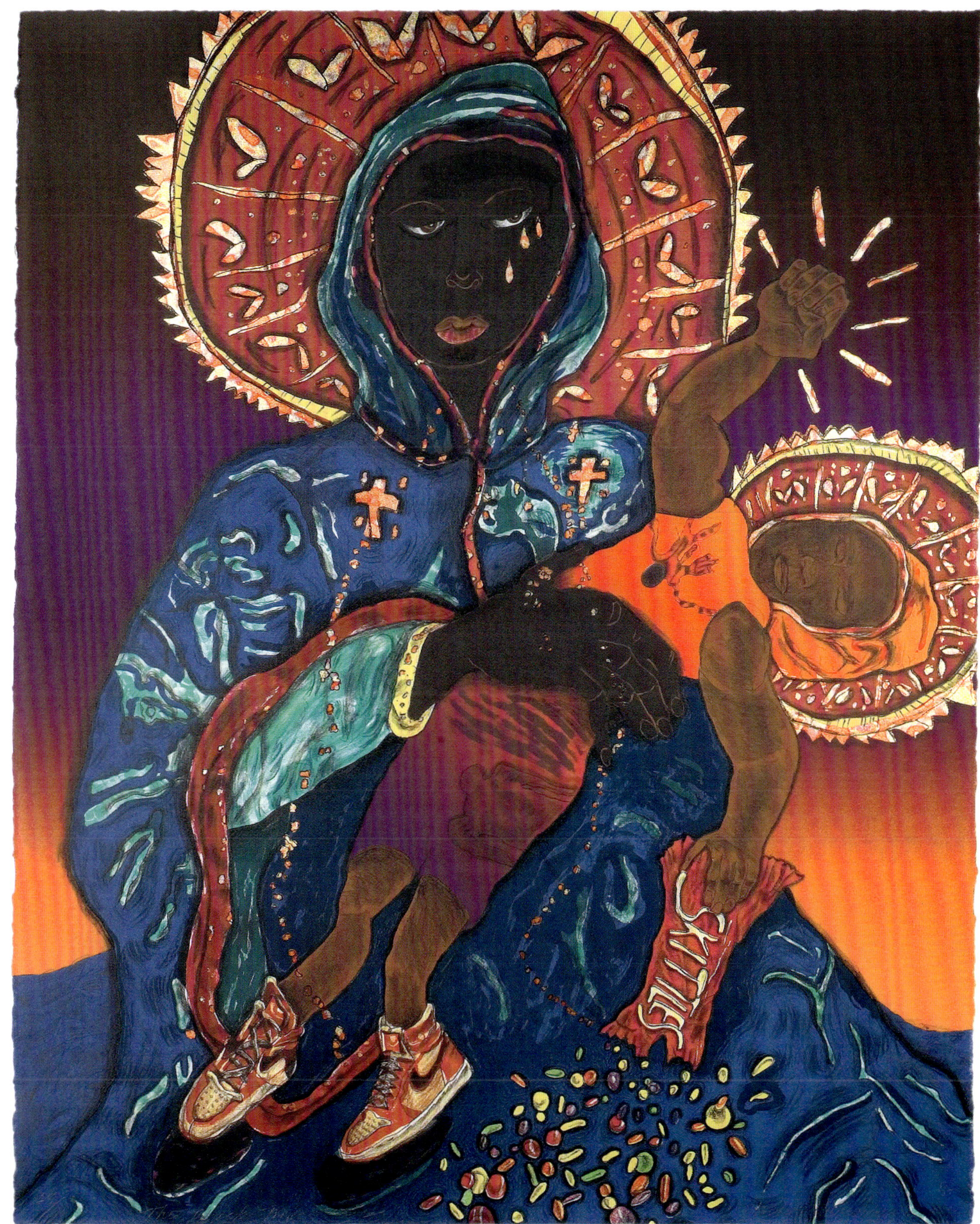

Delita Martin
Let Me Breathe, 2020,
Relief print on paper,
36" × 24", Courtesy of
the Eric Key Collection,
© Delita Martin

Margo Humphrey
The Black Madonna (26/30),
2013, Color lithograph
with gold leaf on paper,
27" × 22", Courtesy of
the Eric Key Collection,
© Margo Humphrey

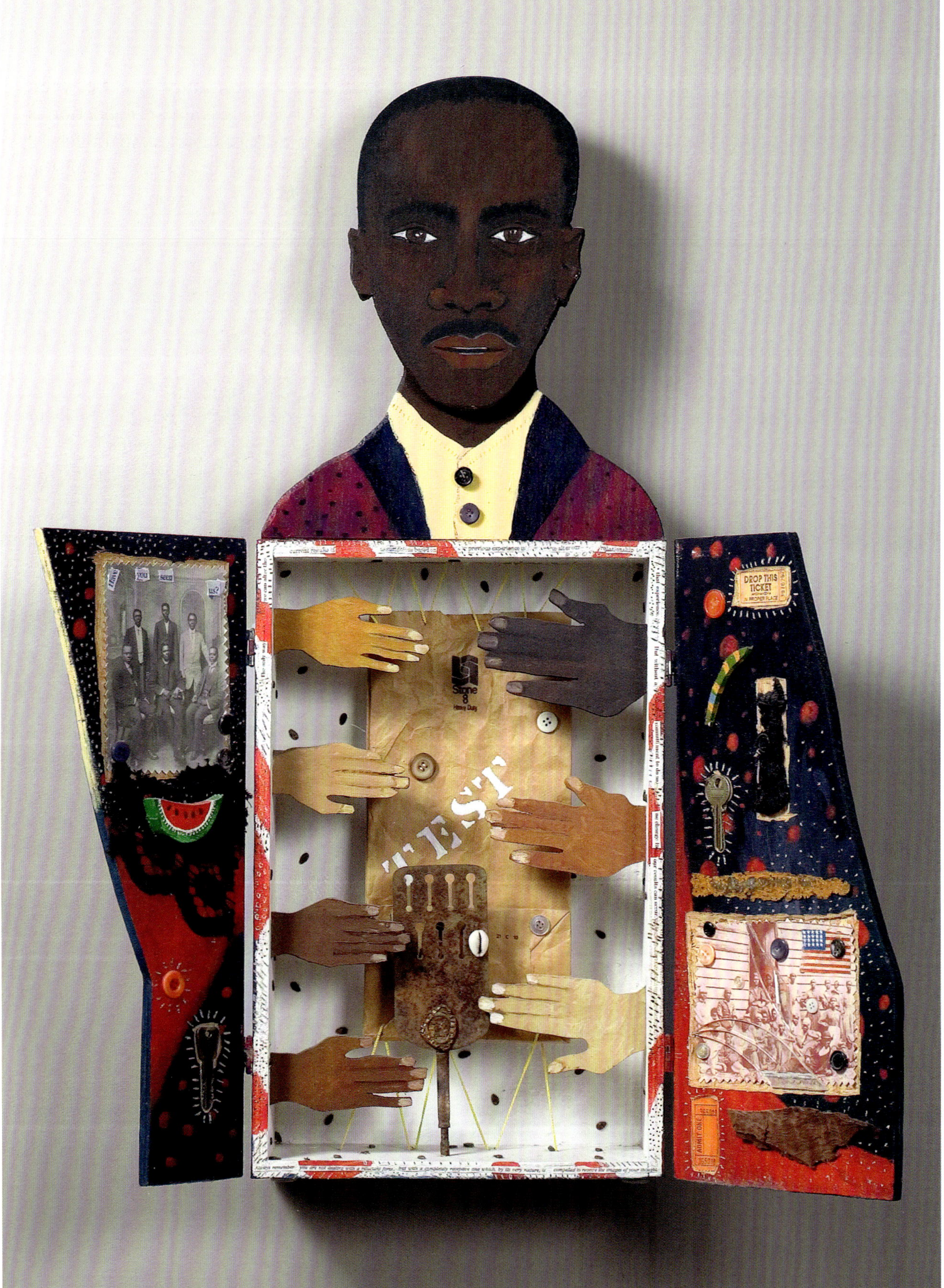
DROP THIS TICKET
Stone
8
TEST

shared human understanding that created a profound bond between himself, the artist, and the work of art. Sharing a private art collection is about displaying art and sharing stories, experiences, and perspectives, all contributing to the collective cultural and historical narrative. Overall, the interest, time, and passion reflected in Eric Key's collection of fine art by Americans of African descent are instrumental in expressing the human condition, documenting history, fostering emotional connections, and exploring identity through the centuries. Its enduring significance lies in its ability to reflect and engage with humanity's shared experiences and stories.

GATEWAYS: African American Art from the Key Collection is steeped in the rich history of Black visual culture. It is a testament to the power of art as a vehicle for personal expression, cultural preservation, and societal commentary. It embodies the community spirit, the power of looking, and the authentic human capacity to create and endure. This collection is a beacon for future collectors, artists, and art enthusiasts, demonstrating how art can weave together the threads of individual experience, cultural heritage, and broader societal narratives. Eric's upbringing and clarity of purpose have dramatically shaped the lens by which he sees the world as it is and how he wants it to be, and his indelible impressions of women, men, siblings, and the church accentuate his love and appreciation for family, faith, and community. These sensibilities have shaped his personal and professional life with a deep sense of accountability to all the communities of which he is a member, making this collection as unique as his fingerprint.

Schroeder Cherry
Color Test, 1995, Mixed-media assemblage, 33" × 29" × 5", Courtesy of the Eric Key Collection, © Schroeder Cherry

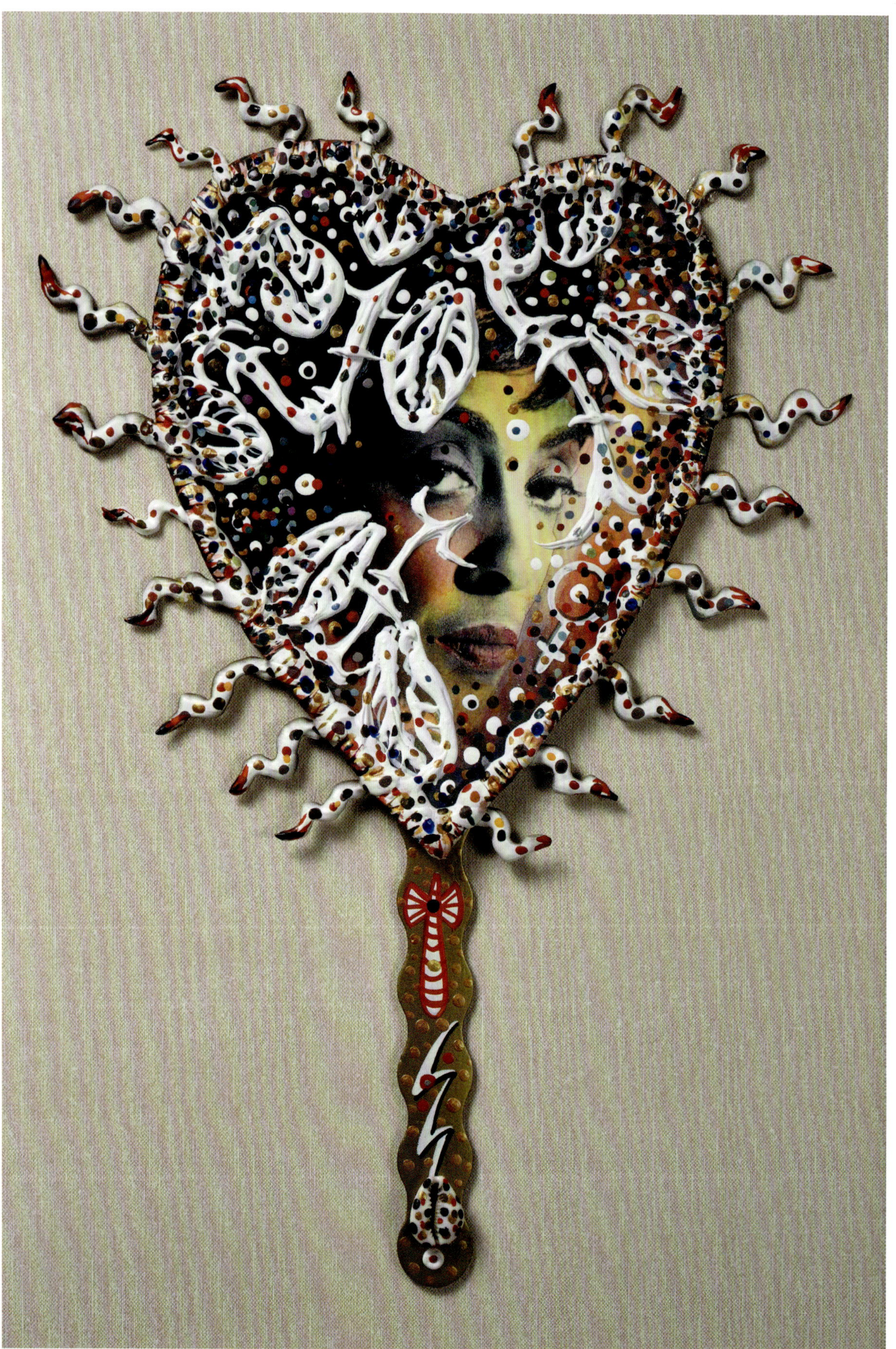

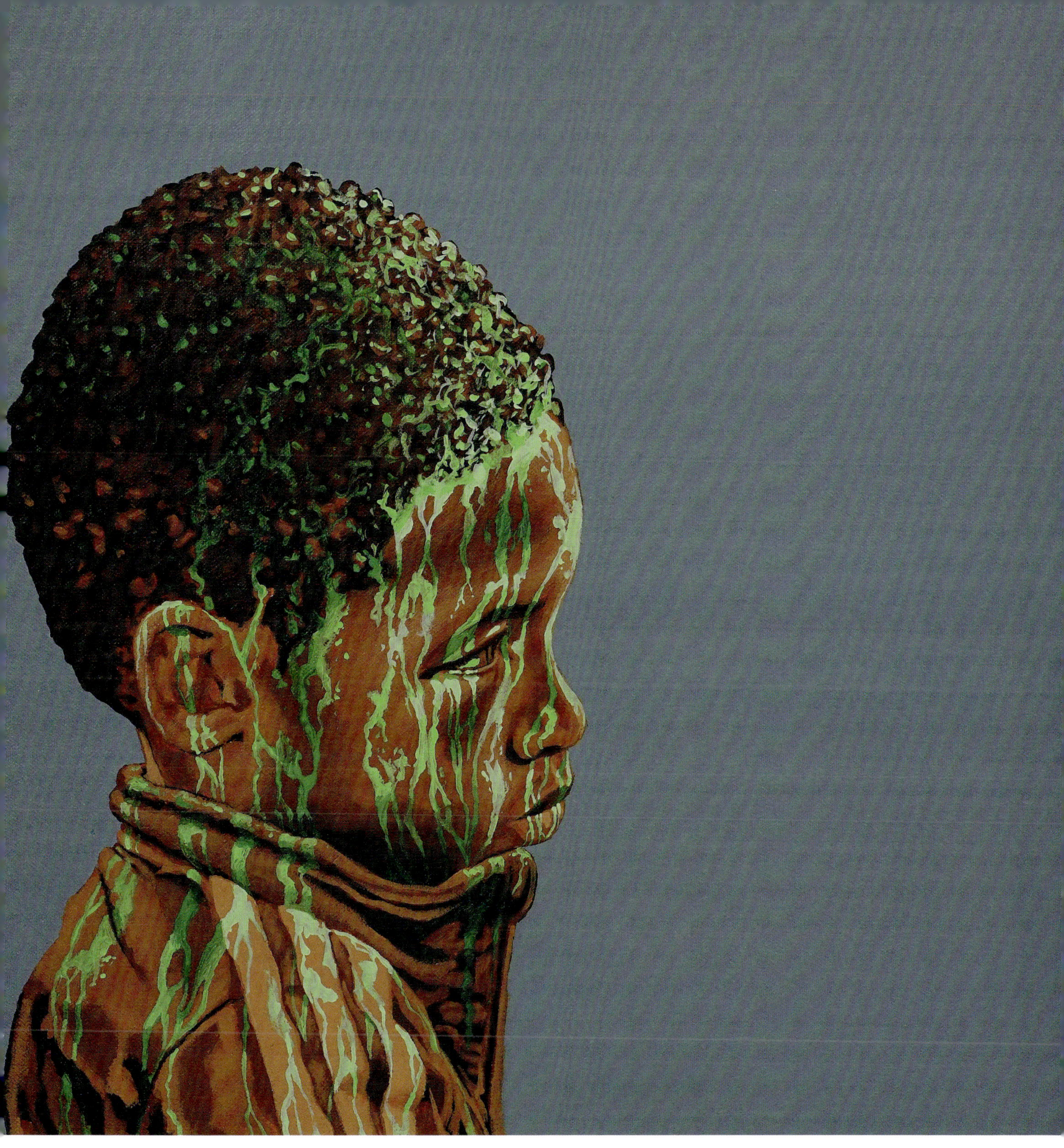

Ben Jones
Untitled (Fan), 2001, Mixed media, 22¼" × 15¼" × 3", Courtesy of the Eric Key Collection, © Ben Jones

Alfred Conteh
Snap, 2019, Acrylic on canvas, 14" × 14" × 3", Courtesy of the Eric Key Collection, Photographed by Alfred Conteh, © Alfred Conteh

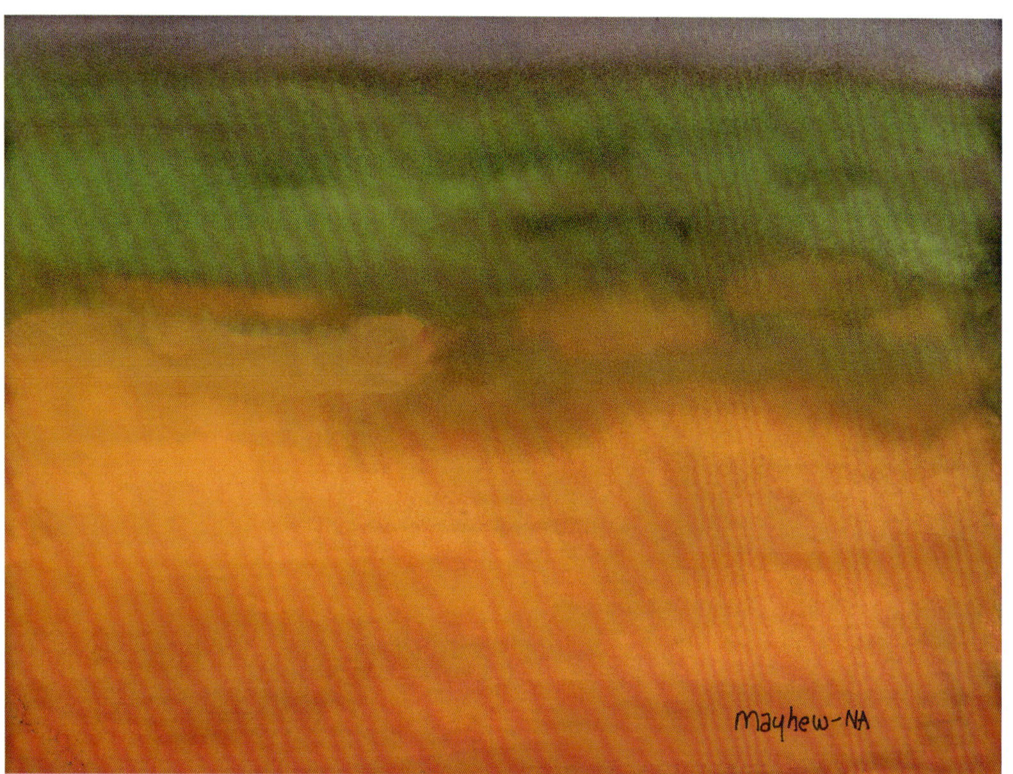

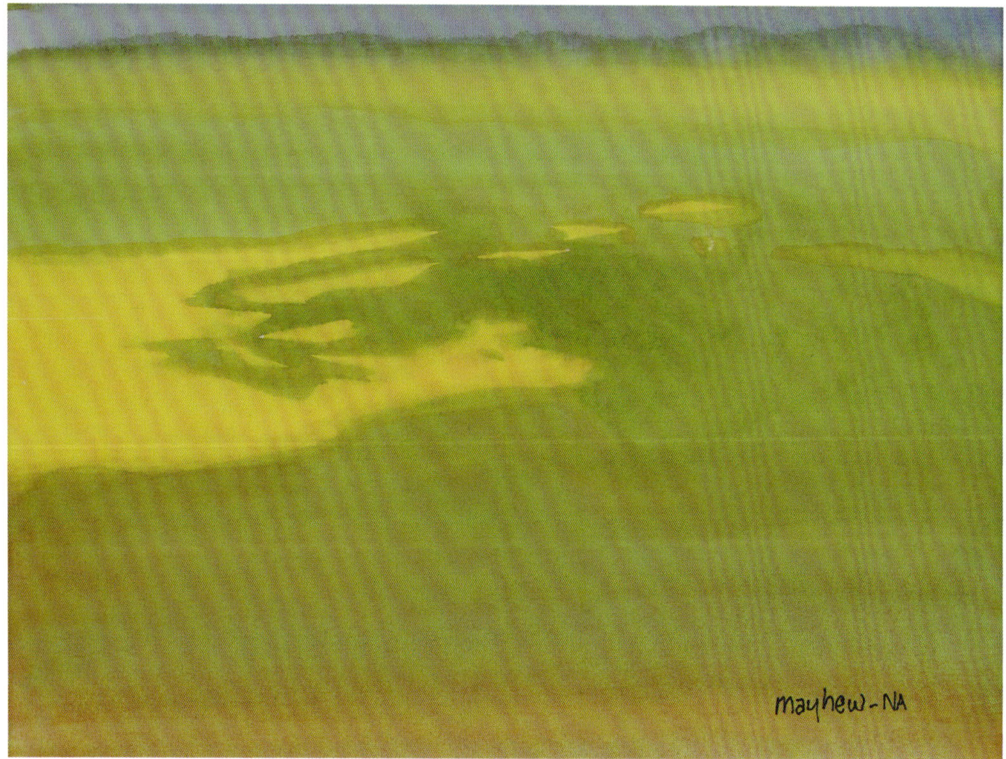

Richard Mayhew
Spring Mood Series #4 (Rust Green Landscape), 2018, Watercolor, 9" × 12" × 2", Courtesy of the Eric Key Collection, © Richard Mayhew

Richard Mayhew
Spring Mood Series #6 (Yellow Green Landscape), 2018, Watercolor, 9" × 12" × 2", Courtesy of the Eric Key Collection, © Richard Mayhew

EXHIBITION HIGHLIGHTS

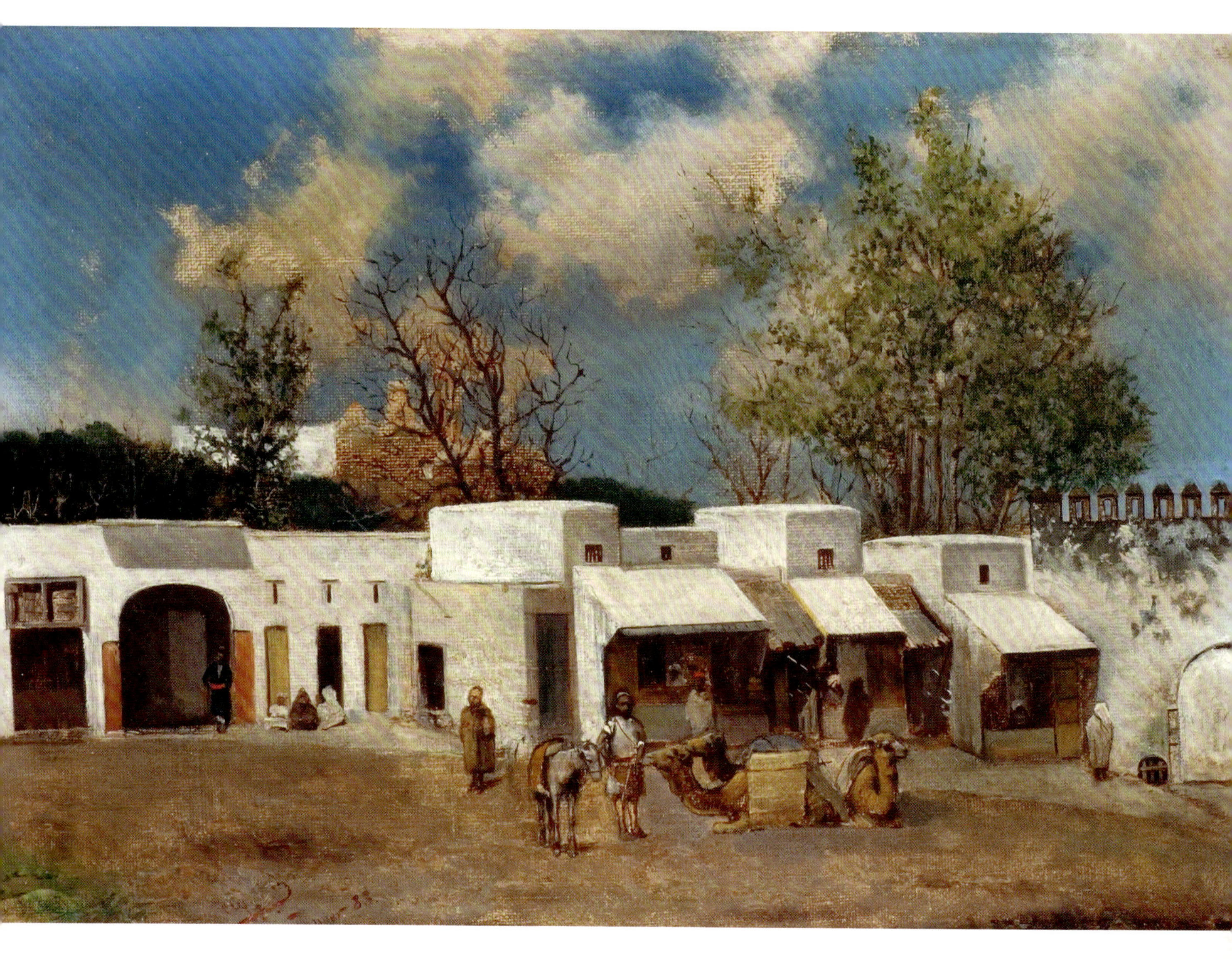

Henry Tanner
Tangier, 1888, Oil on canvas, $12\frac{1}{2}$" × $16\frac{1}{2}$", Courtesy of the Eric Key Collection, © Henry Tanner

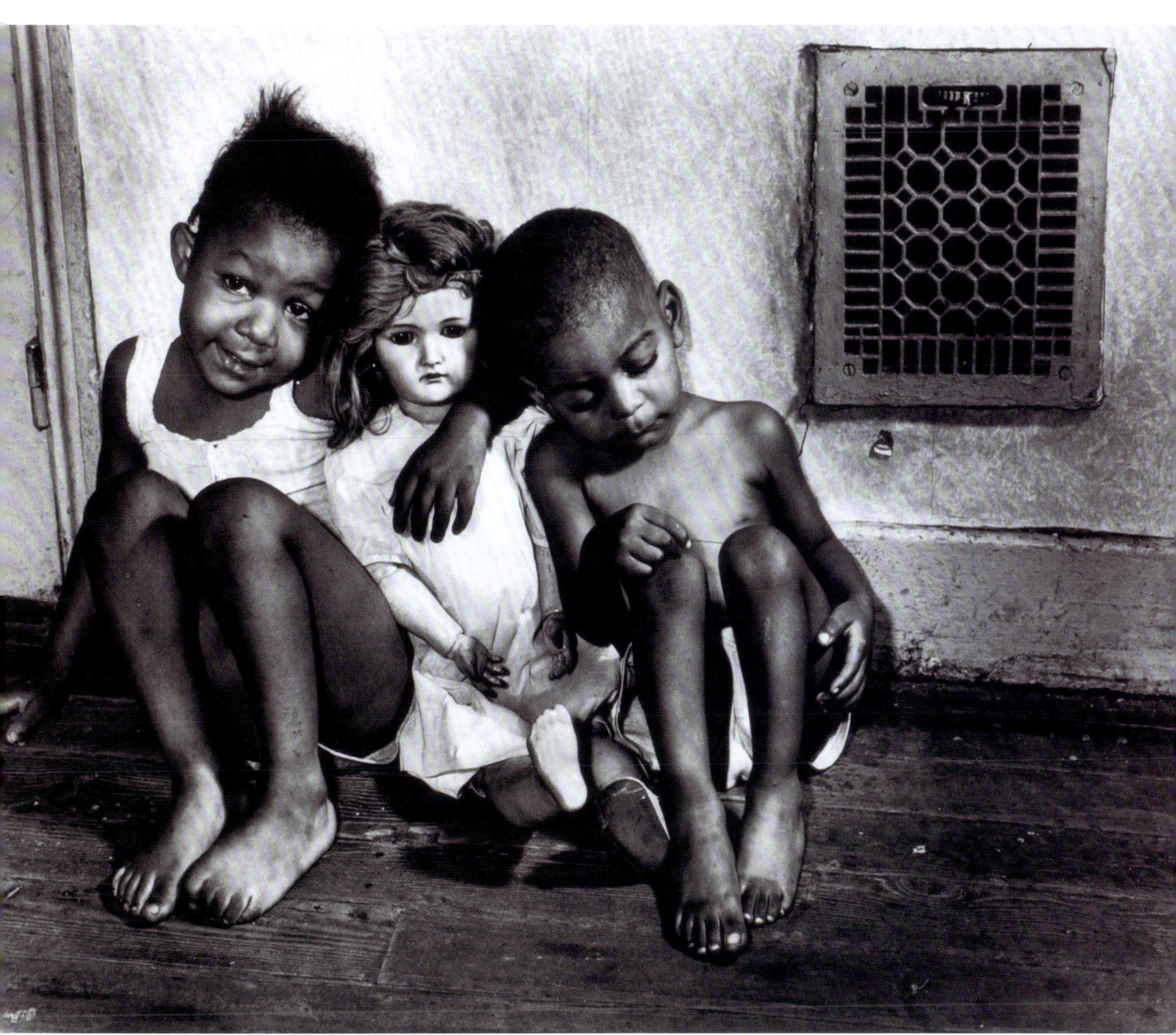

Gordon Parks
Children with Doll, *Washington D.C.,* 1942, Photograph, 22" × 25", Courtesy of the Eric Key Collection and of The Gordon Parks Foundation, © Copyright The Gordon Parks Foundation

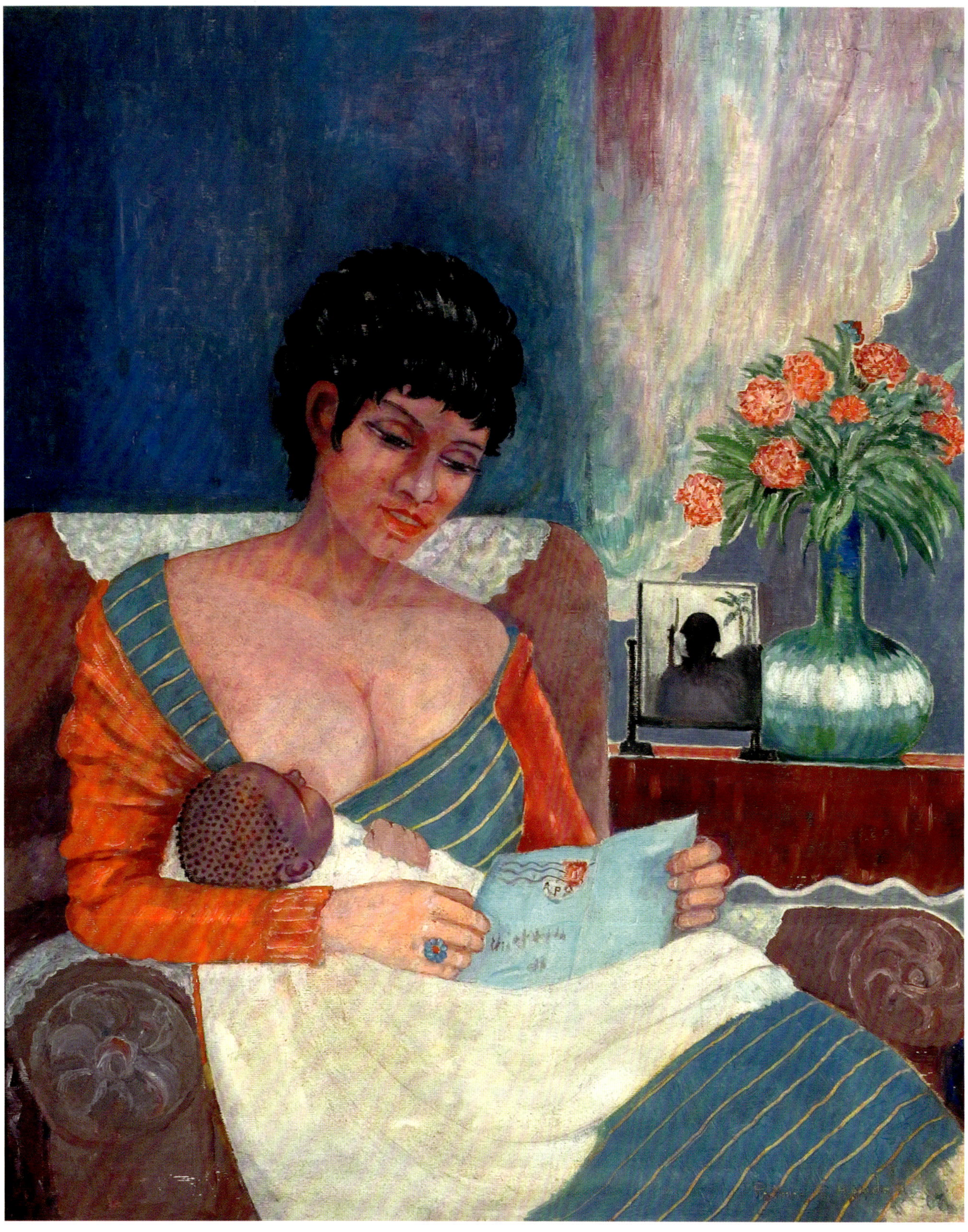

Palmer Hayden
G.I. Bride, 1967, Oil on canvas, 33" × 28" × 2", Courtesy Hayden Family Revocable Art Trust and the Eric Key Collection, © Lisa L. Crane, Trustee, Hayden Family Revocable Art Trust

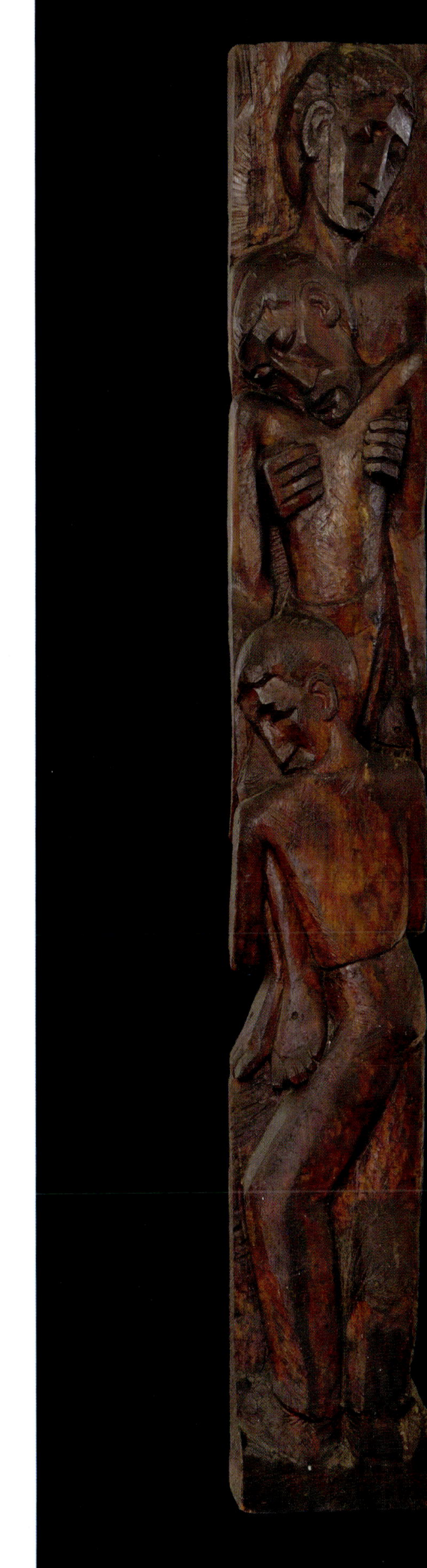

William "Bill" Taylor
Christ, 1961, Wood, 68" × 10" × 3½", Courtesy of the Eric Key Collection, © William "Bill" Taylor

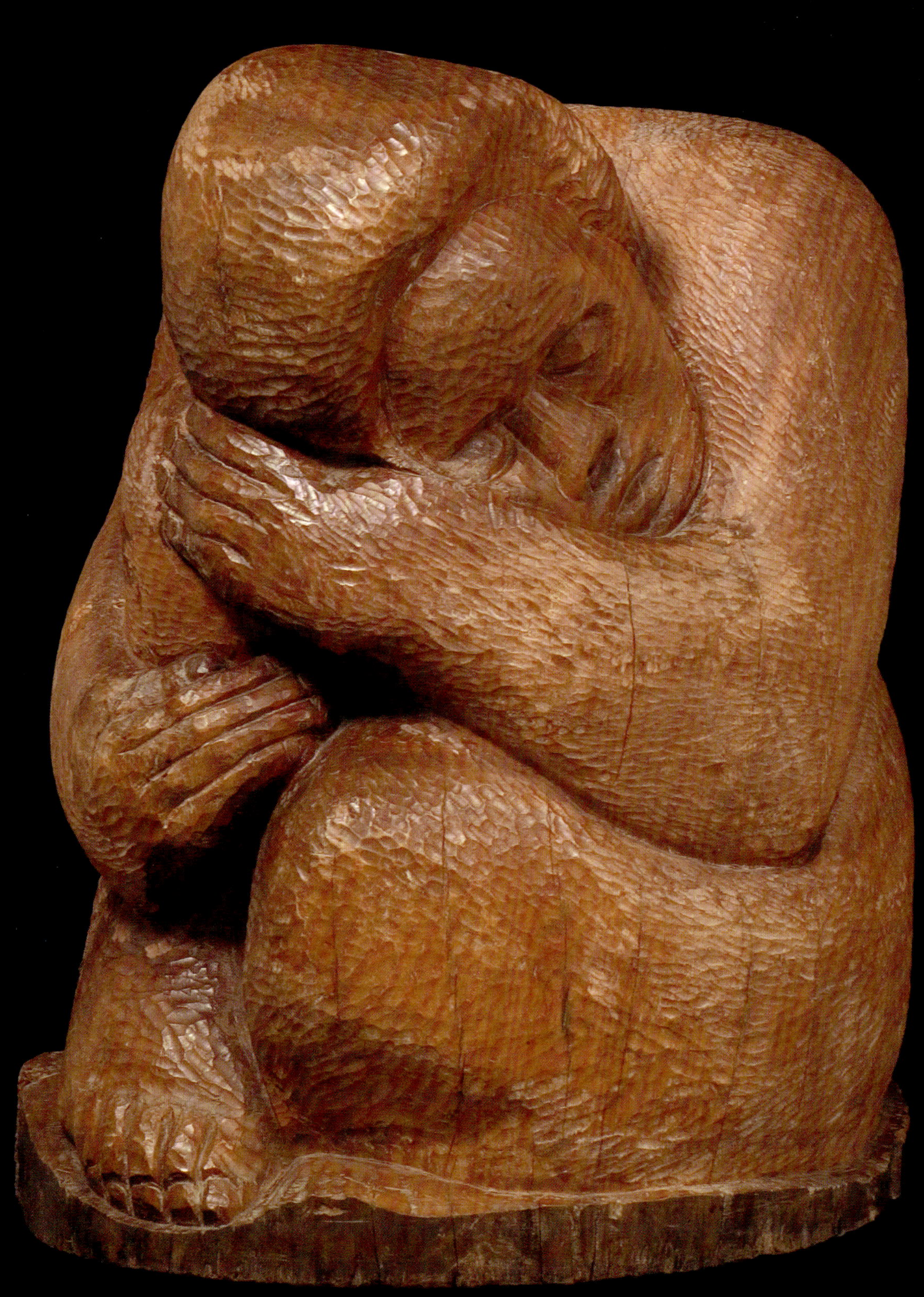

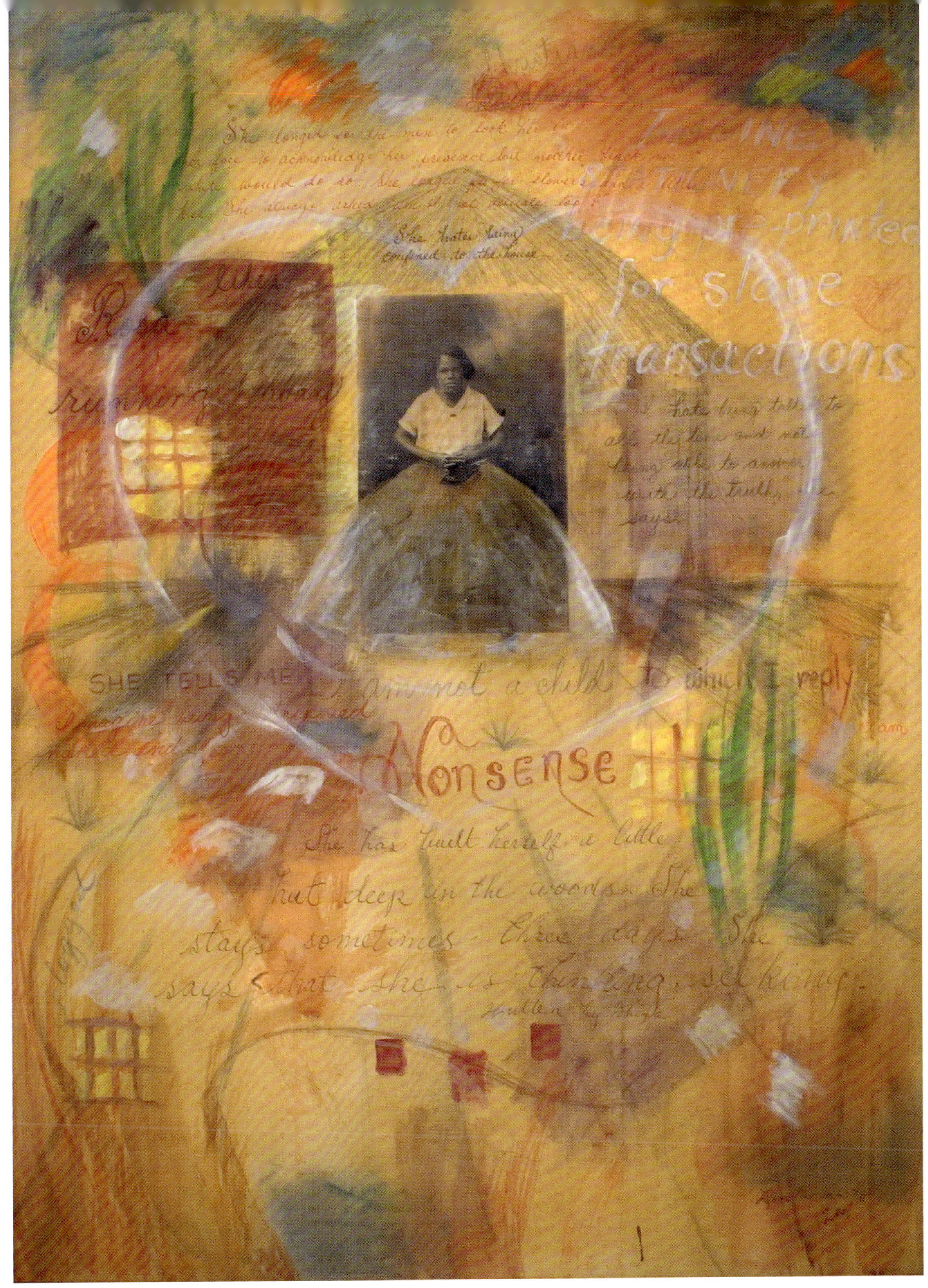

William Anderson
Untitled (Female wood carving), 1970s, Wood, 36" × 25" × 25", Courtesy of the Eric Key Collection, © William Anderson

Lynn Marshall Linnemeier
Nonsense, 2001, Watercolor and pencil on paper, 77" × 56¼" × 1½", Courtesy of the Eric Key Collection, © Lynn Marshall Linnemeier

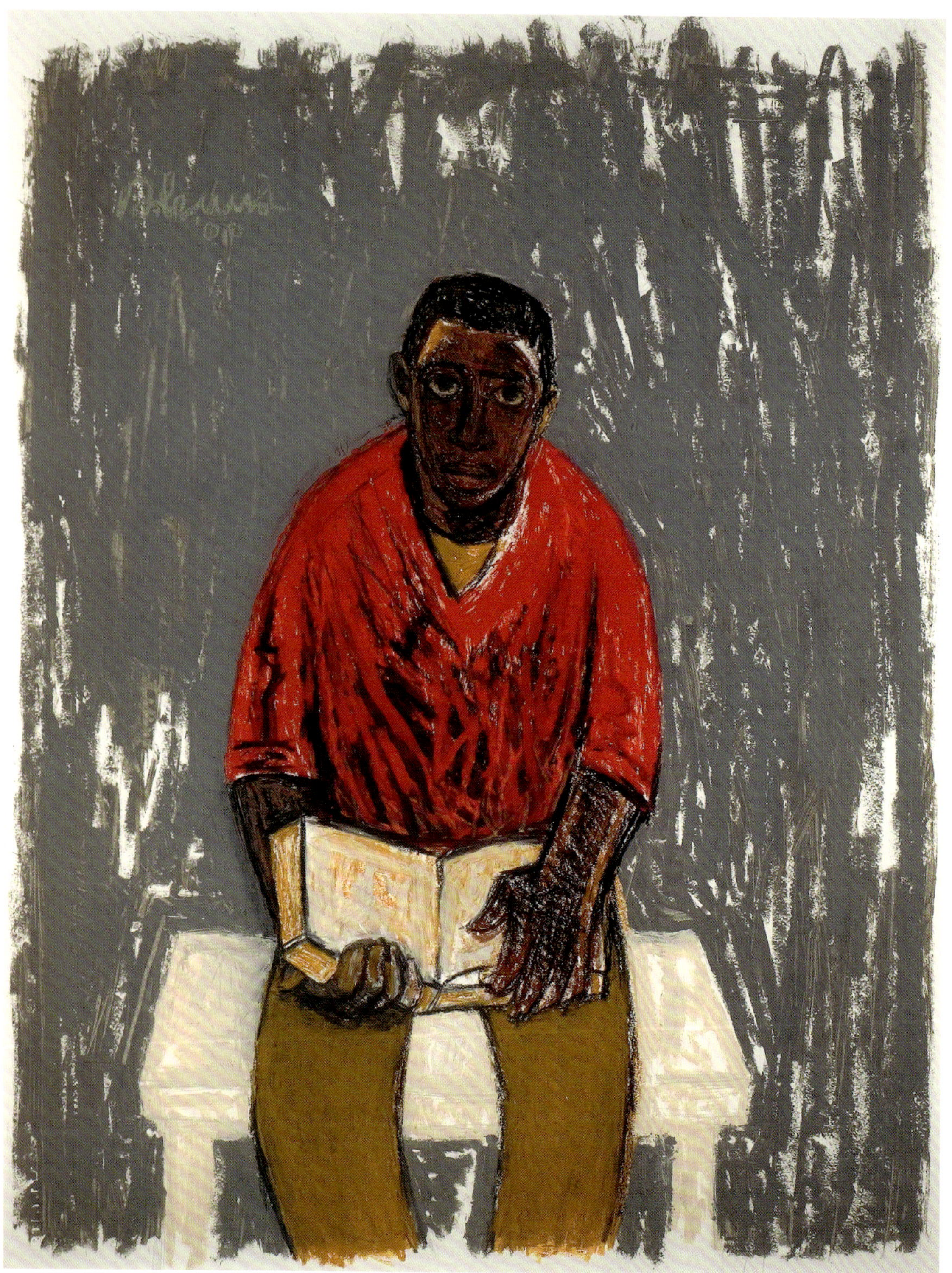

Samella Lewis
We've Always Wanted to Know How to Read and Write, 2000, Oil stick on paper, 36" × 29" × 2", Courtesy of the Eric Key Collection, © 2023 Samella Lewis / Licensed by VAGA at Artists Rights Society (ARS), NY

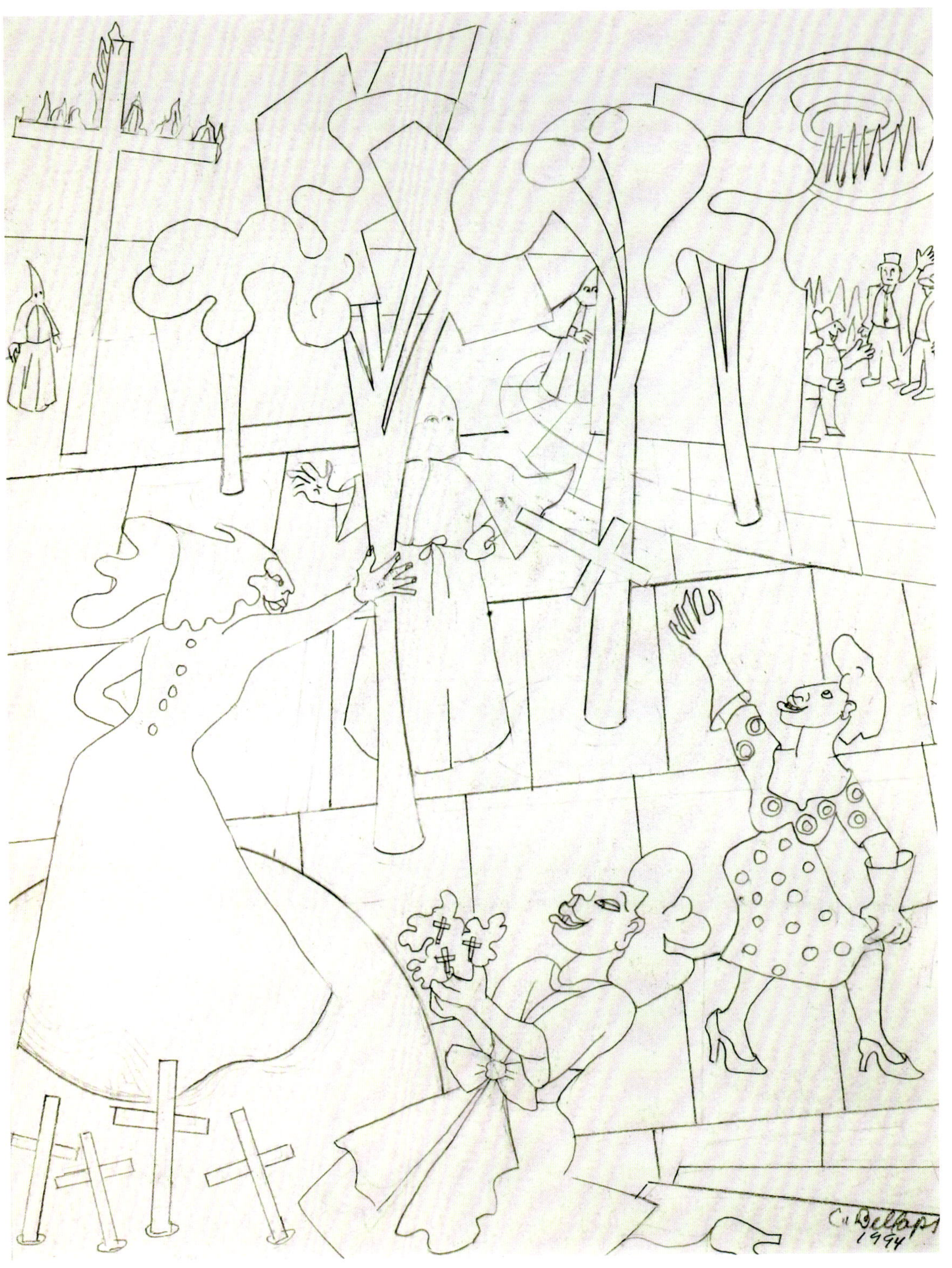

Camille Billops
Untitled (The KKK Boutique), 1994, Pencil on paper, 19" × 17" × 2", Courtesy of the Eric Key Collection, the estate of the artist, and Ryan Lee Gallery, NY, © Camille Billops

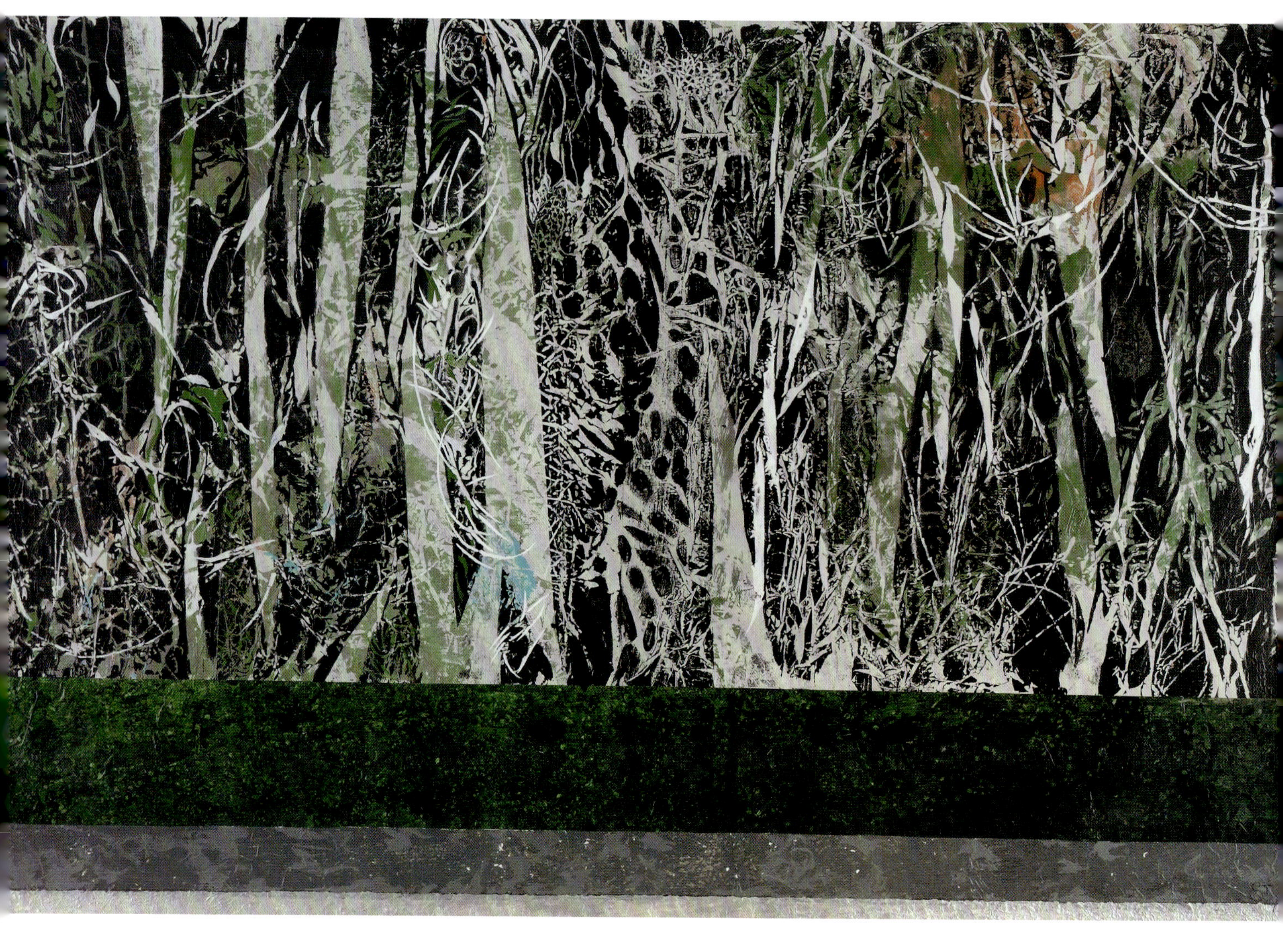

Freddie Styles
New Collage Series: Winter, 2017, Acrylic on gessoed paper, 33½" × 47¼" × 2⅜", Courtesy of the Eric Key Collection, © Freddie Styles

Martha Jackson Jarvis
Ideograph #3, 2018, Mixed media, 65½" × 45½" × 2", Courtesy of the Eric Key Collection, © Martha Jackson Jarvis

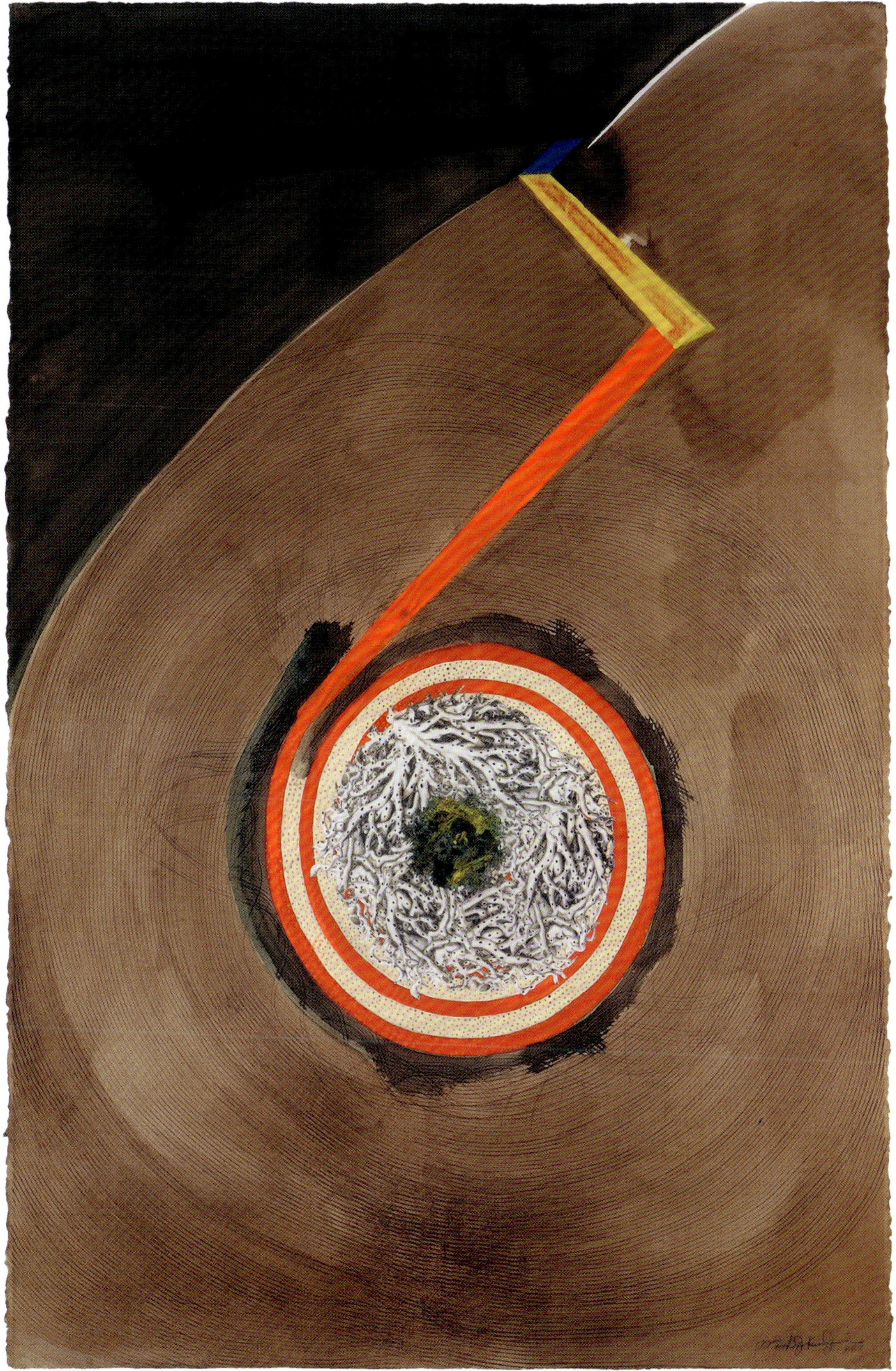

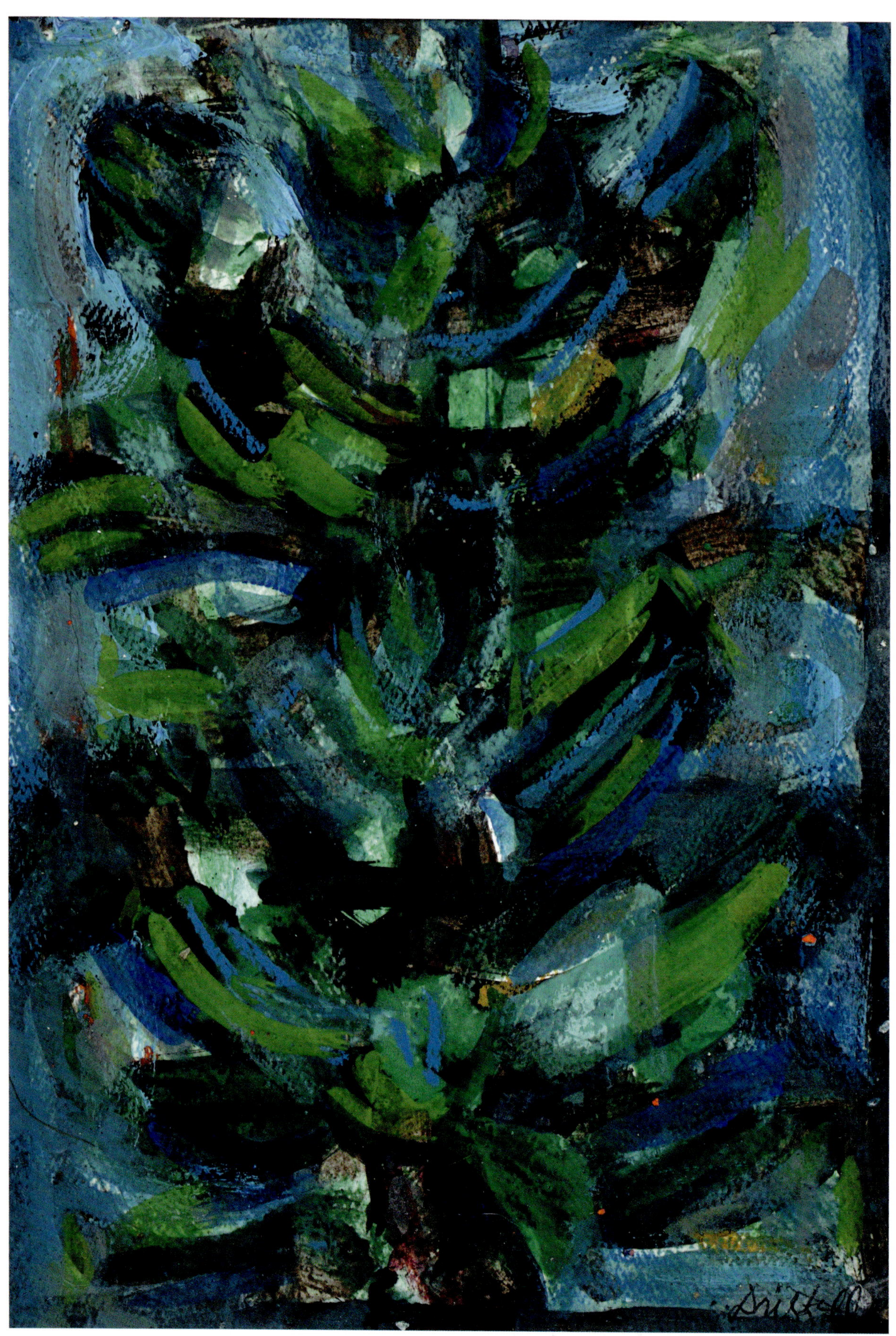

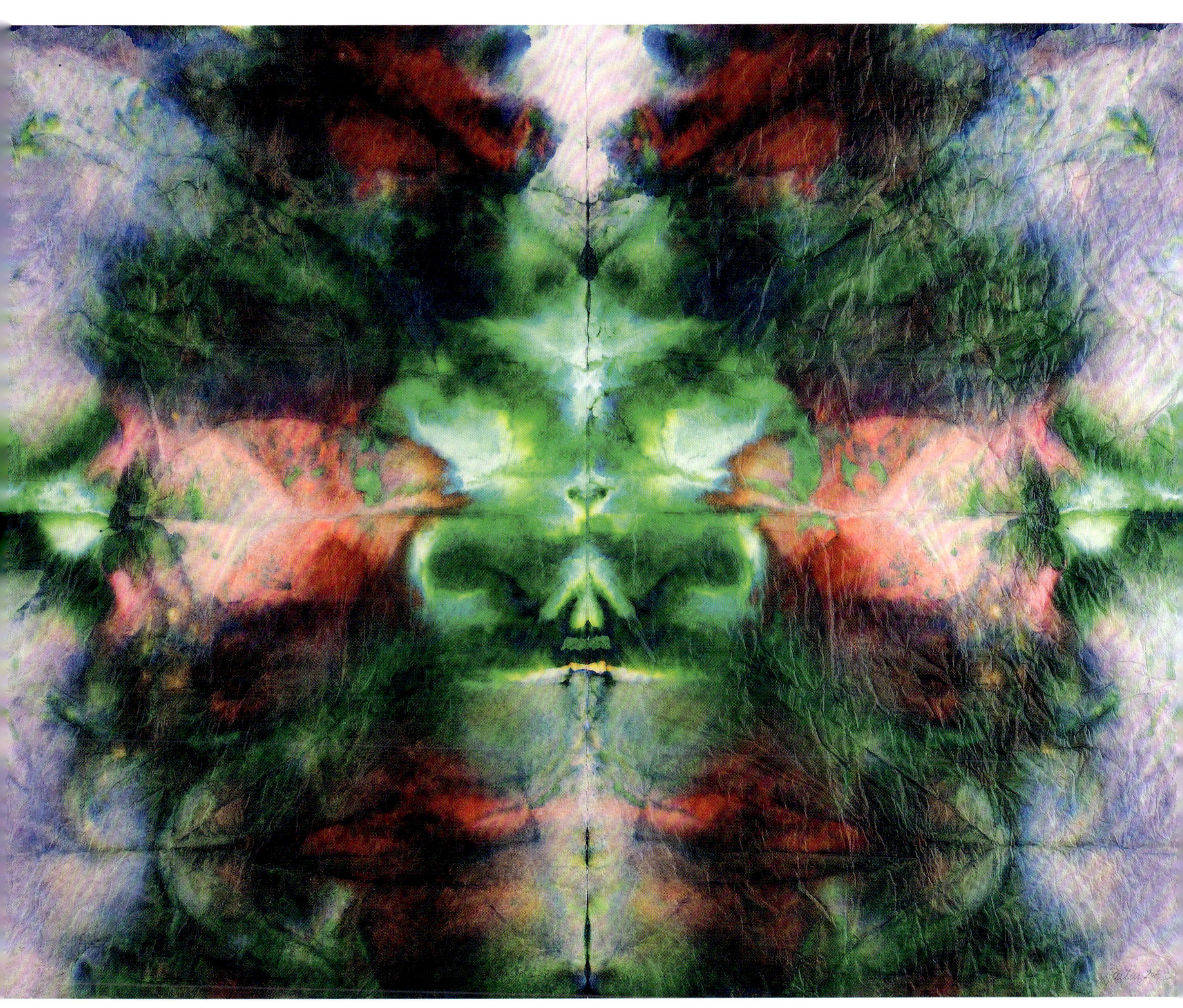

David Driskell
Pine, 1971, Acrylic on paper, 20¼" × 16¼" × 2", Courtesy of the Eric Key Collection, © David Driskelll

Maya Freelon
Balance, 2017, Watercolor on paper, 37½" × 46" × 2⅓", Courtesy of the Eric Key Collection, © Maya Freelon

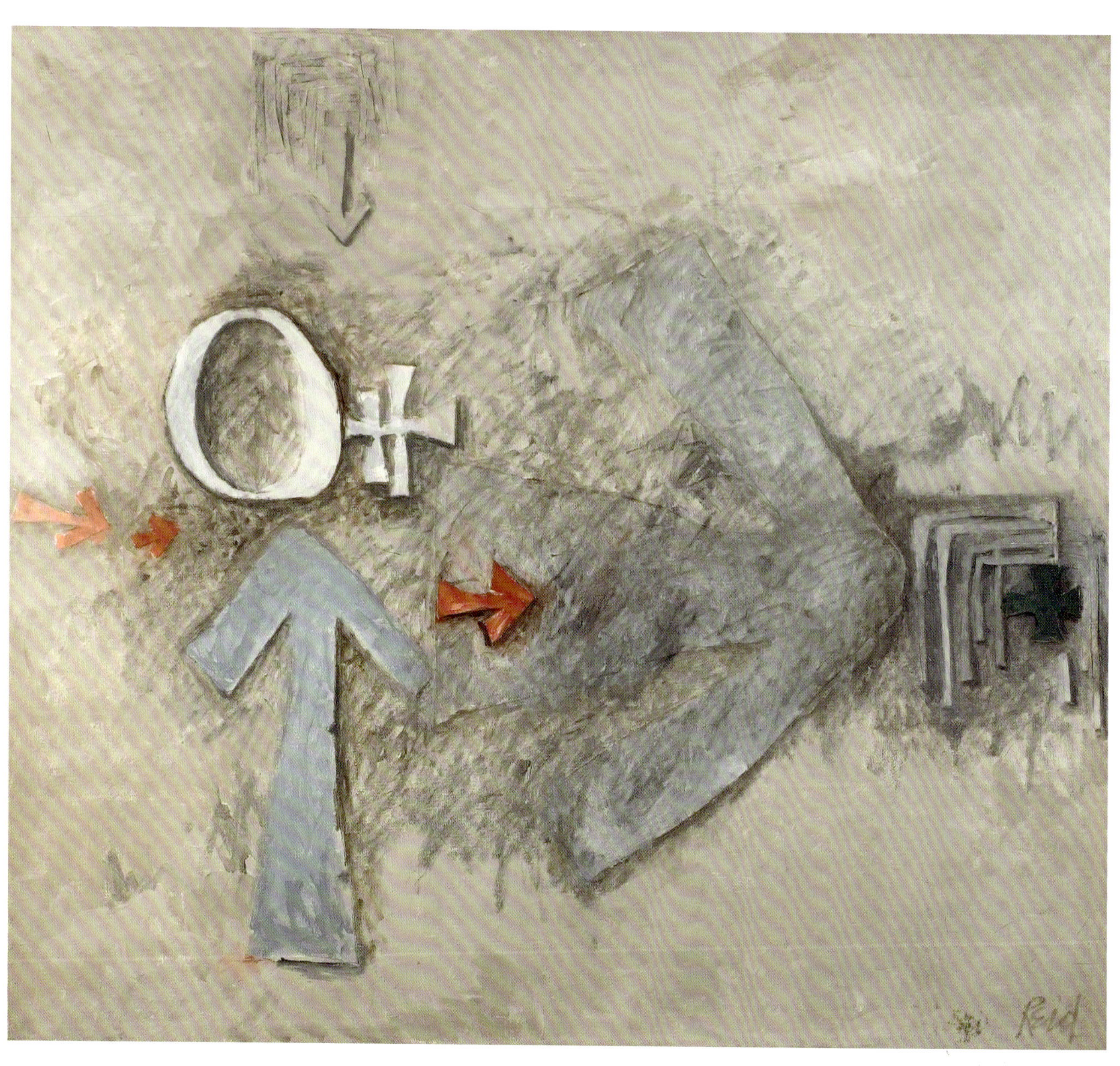

Robert Reid
Follow the Leader, no date,
Oil and collage on linen,
37½" × 41 ¼" × 1¾", Courtesy of the
Eric Key Collection, © Robert Reid

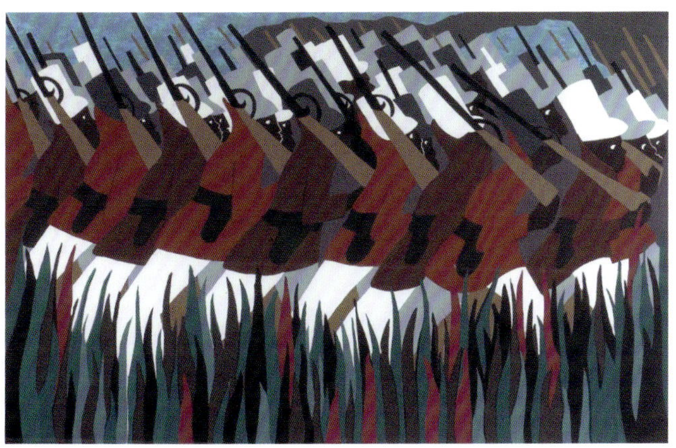

Jacob Lawrence
The March, 1995, Silkscreen on paper (99/120), 18" × 28" × 2", Courtesy of the Eric Key Collection, © 2023 The Jacob and Gwendolyn Knight Lawrence Foundation, Seattle / Artists Rights Society (ARS), NY

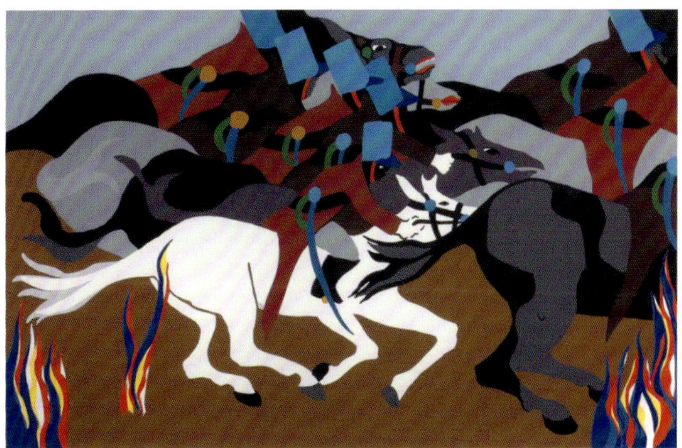

Jacob Lawrence
Toussaint at Ennery, 1989, Silkscreen on paper, 18" × 29" × 2", Courtesy of the Eric Key Collection, © 2023 The Jacob and Gwendolyn Knight Lawrence Foundation, Seattle / Artists Rights Society (ARS), NY

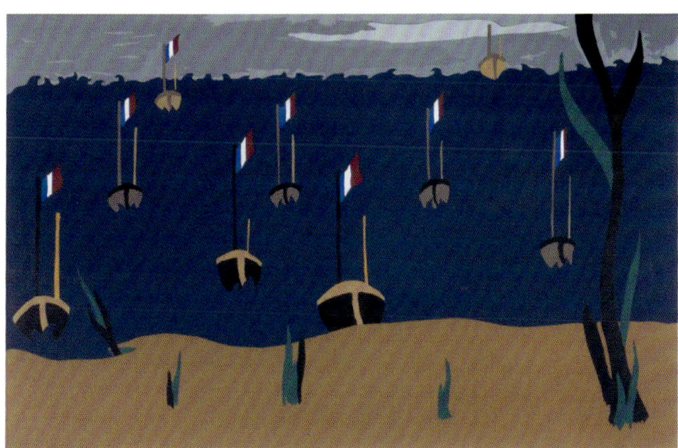

Jacob Lawrence
Flotilla, 1996, Silkscreen on paper (92/120), 18" × 28" × 2", Courtesy of the Eric Key Collection, © 2023 The Jacob and Gwendolyn Knight Lawrence Foundation, Seattle / Artists Rights Society (ARS), NY

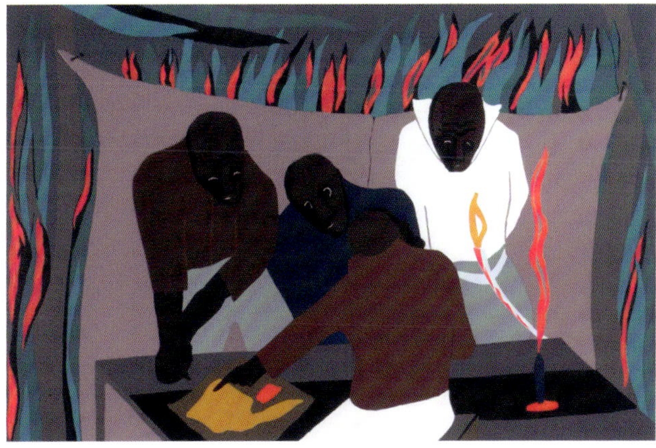

Jacob Lawrence
Strategy, 1999, Silkscreen on paper (12/120), 18" × 28" × 2", Courtesy of the Eric Key Collection, © 2023 The Jacob and Gwendolyn Knight Lawrence Foundation, Seattle / Artists Rights Society (ARS), NY

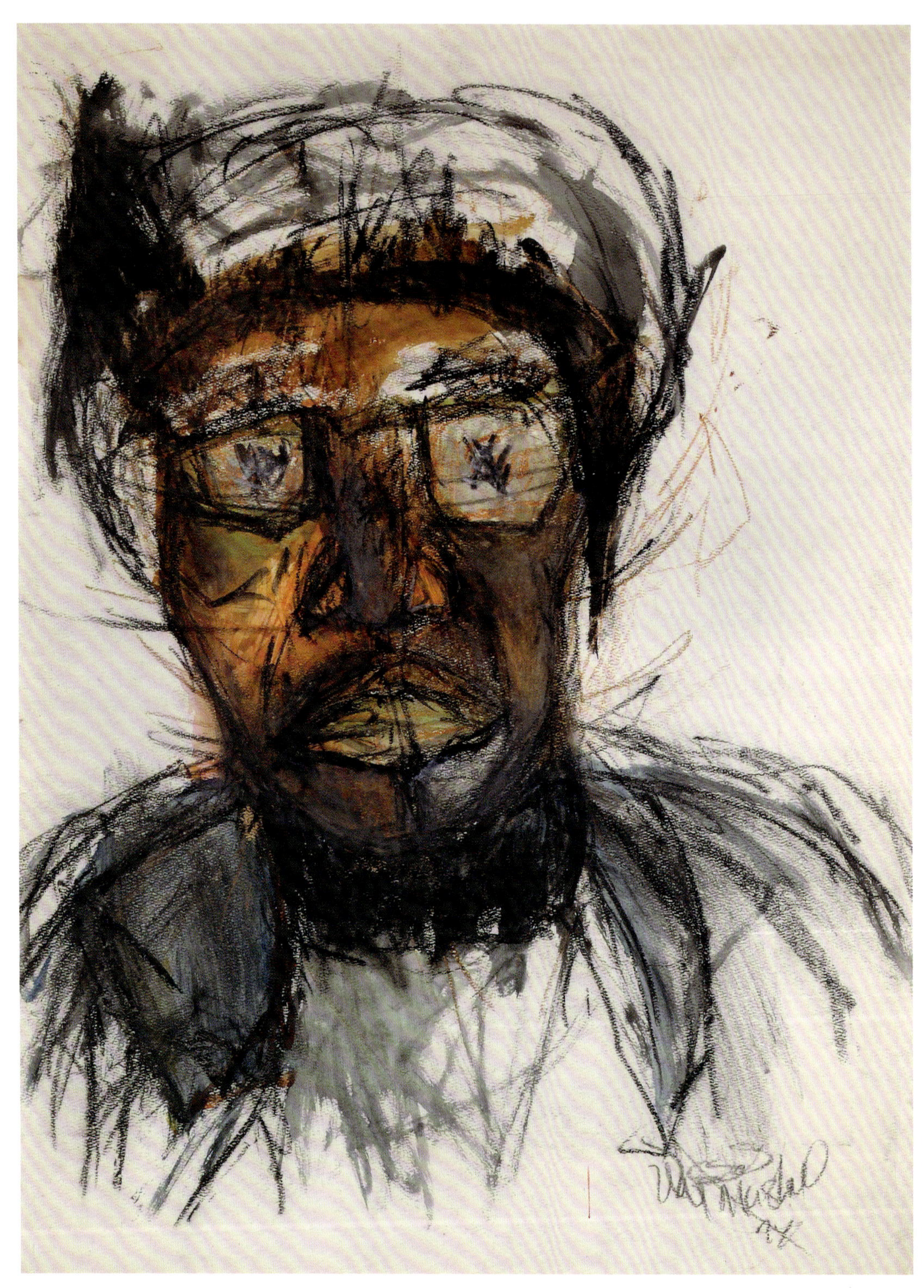

Ulysses Marshall
Man Child, 1974, Acrylic on paper, 39" × 33⅜" × 1¼", Courtesy of the Eric Key Collection, © Ulysses Marshall

Jamea Richmond-Edwards
Easy Breezy Girl, 2020, Mixed media, 72" × 48" × 2", Courtesy of the Eric Key Collection, © Jamea Richmond-Edwards

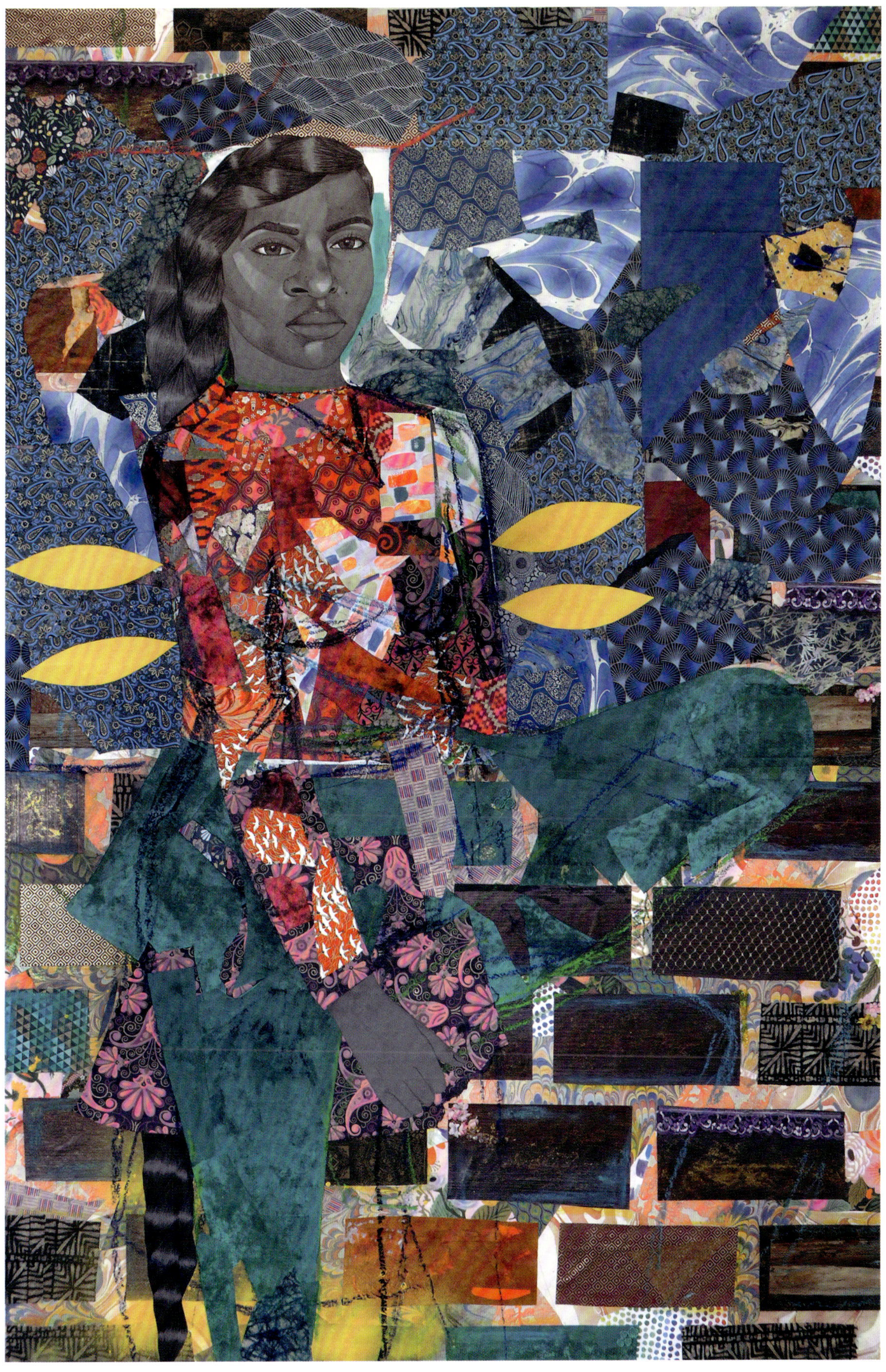

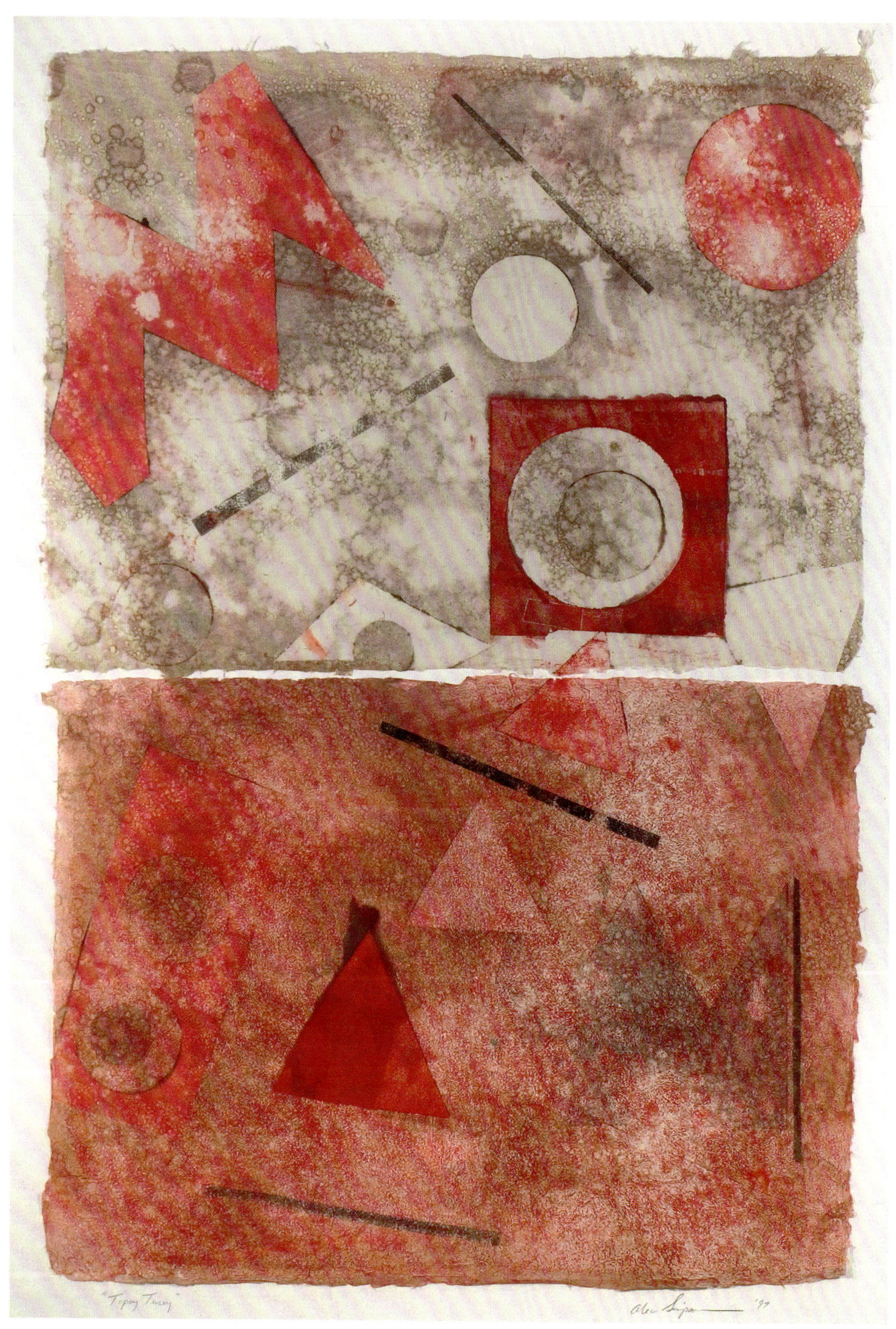

Alec Simpson
Topsy Turvy, 1997,
Monotype on paper,
46”× 33”× 2”, Courtesy of the Eric Key Collection, © Alec Simpson

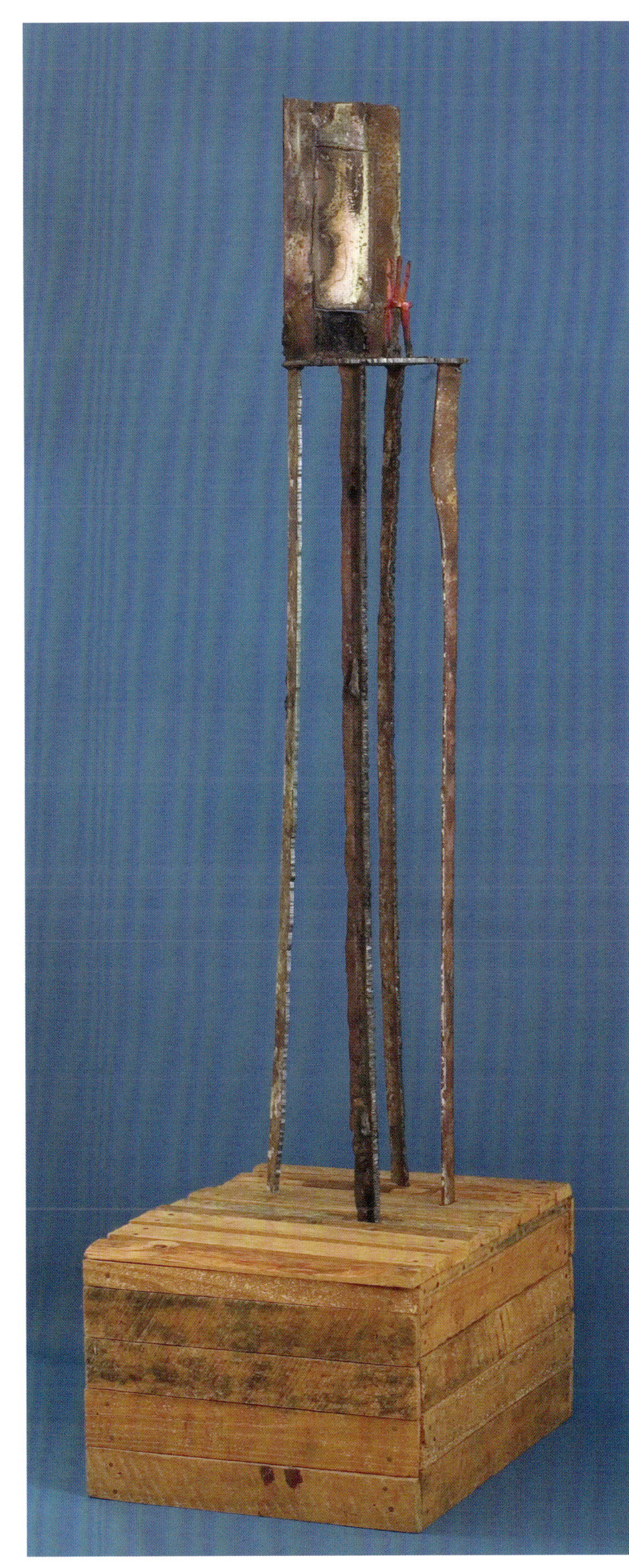

Faheem Majeed
Grandma Chair, 2009, Paint, metal, wood, 75¼" × 19⅝" × 26⅝", Courtesy of the Eric Key Collection, © Faheem Majeed

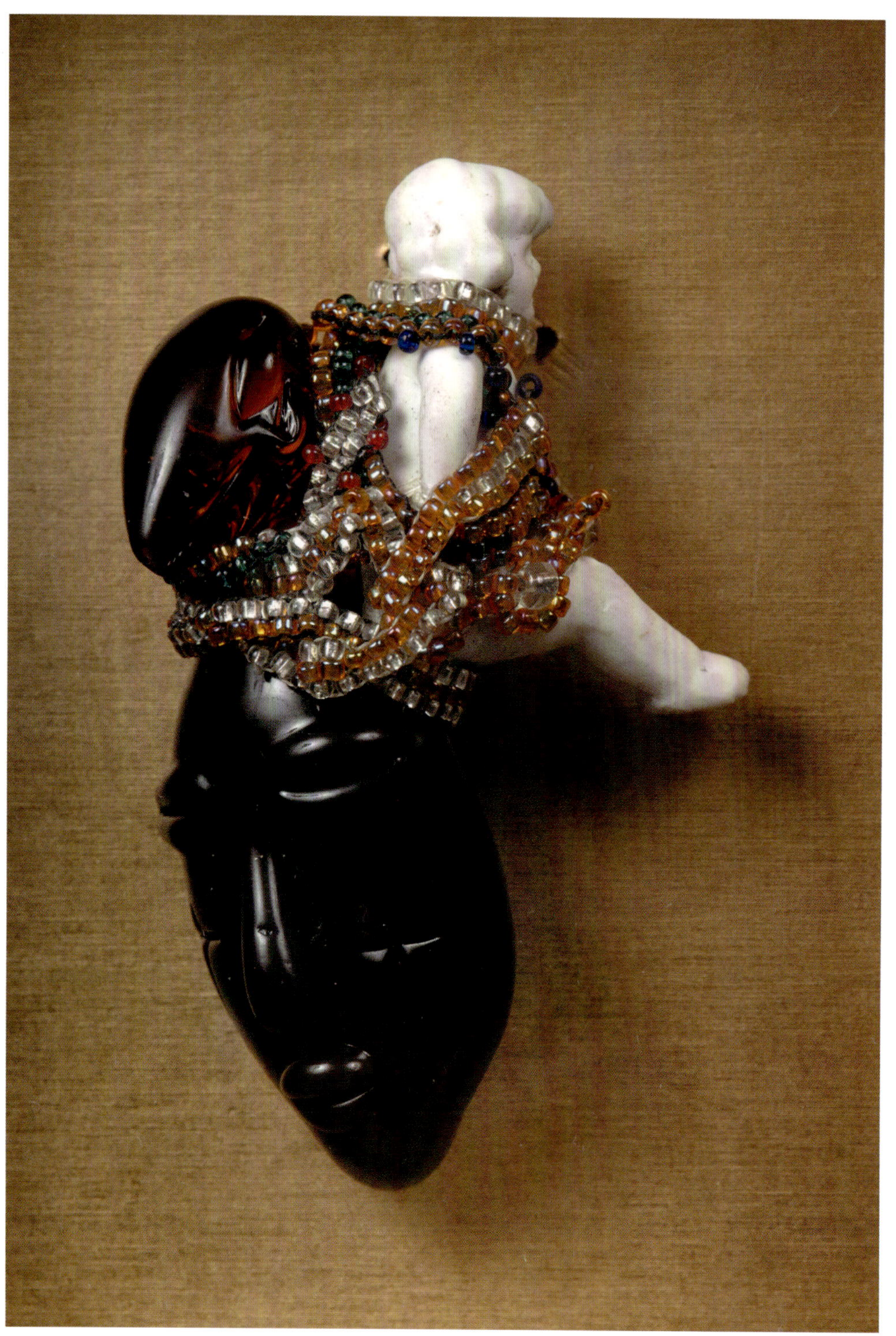

Joyce Scott
Untitled, 2014, Porcelain, blown fused glass, beads, 10" × 8" × 3", Courtesy of the Eric Key Collection, © Courtesy of Goya Contemporary Gallery for Joyce Scott

Prentice H. Polk
Henry Baker, 1984, Photograph, 22½" × 16½", Courtesy of the Eric Key Collection, © Prentice H. Polk

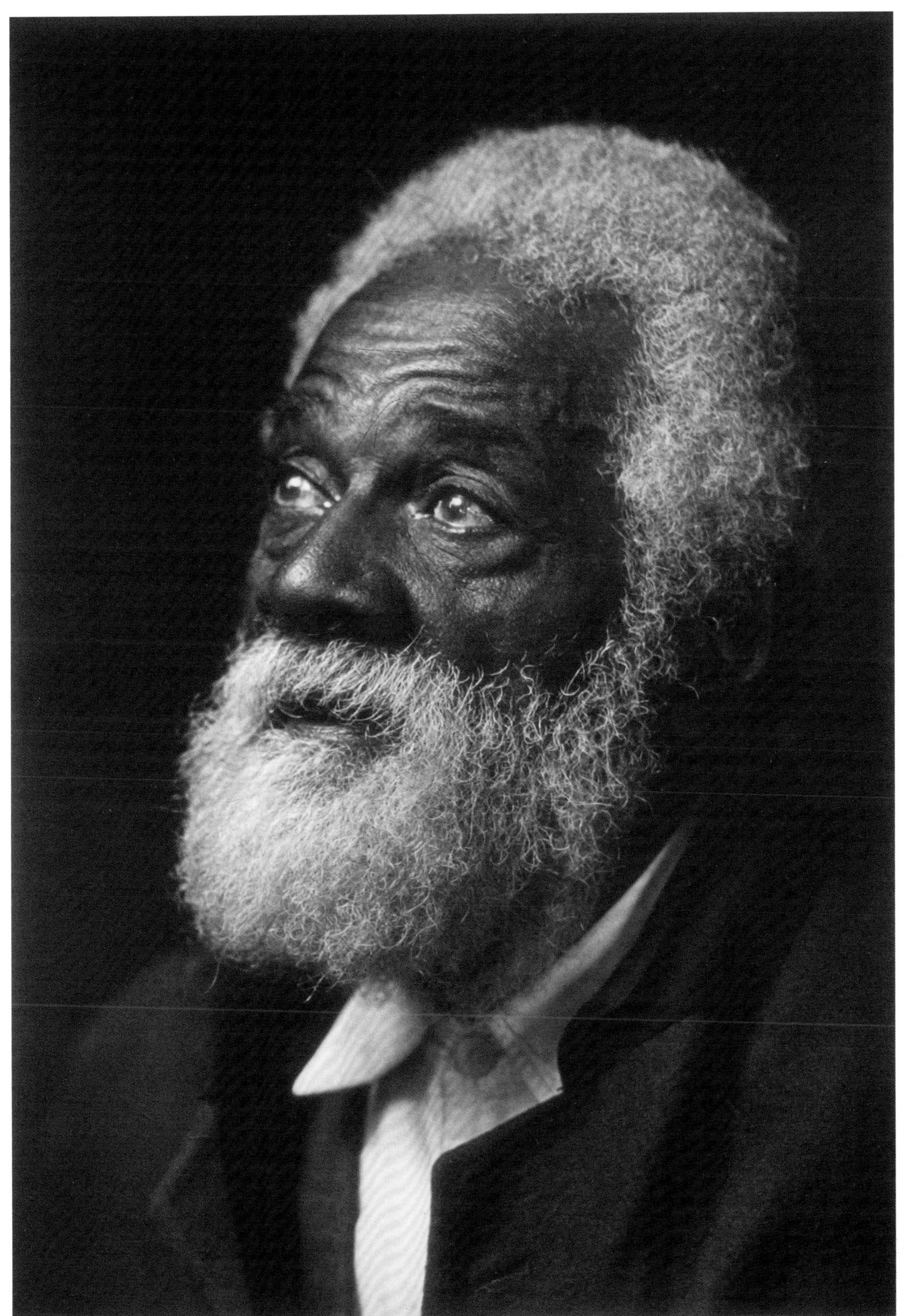

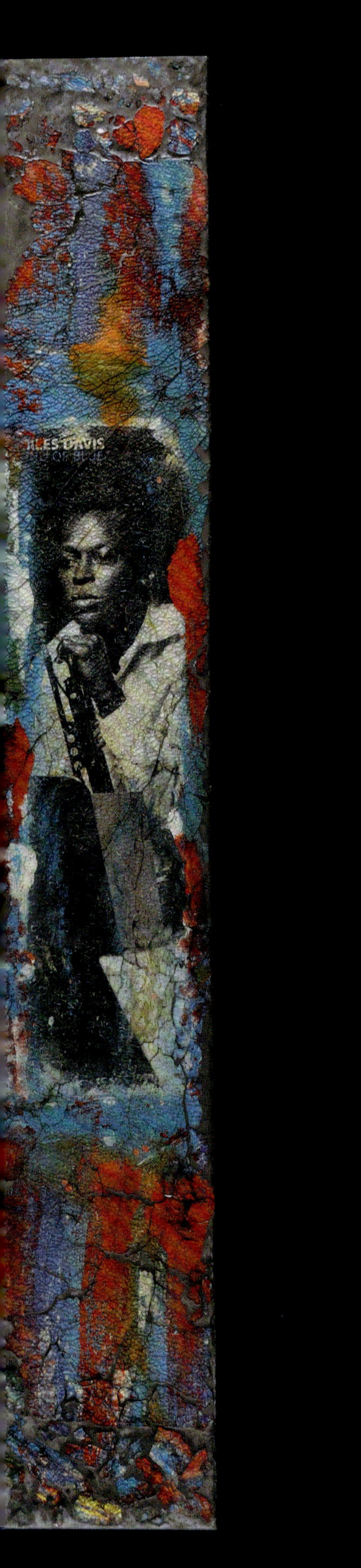

Loring Cornish
Contemplation, 2015,
Mosaic glass, paint,
79" × 12" × 1", Courtesy of
the Eric Key Collection,
© Loring Cornish

Floyd Coleman
Colonial Wars and Things,
1970–1971, Acrylic on canvas,
61" × 61" × 2", Courtesy of
the Eric Key Collection,
© Floyd Coleman

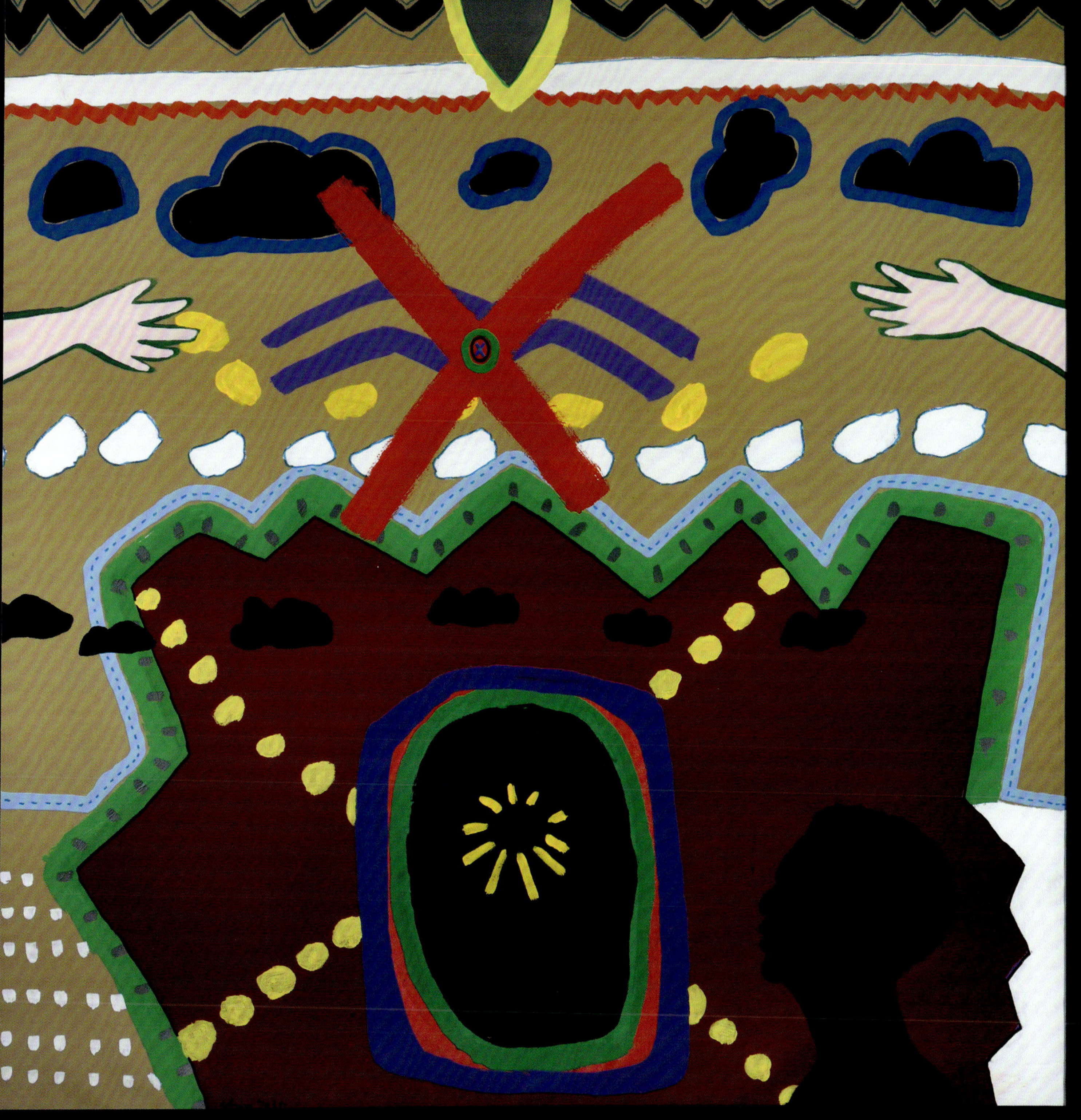

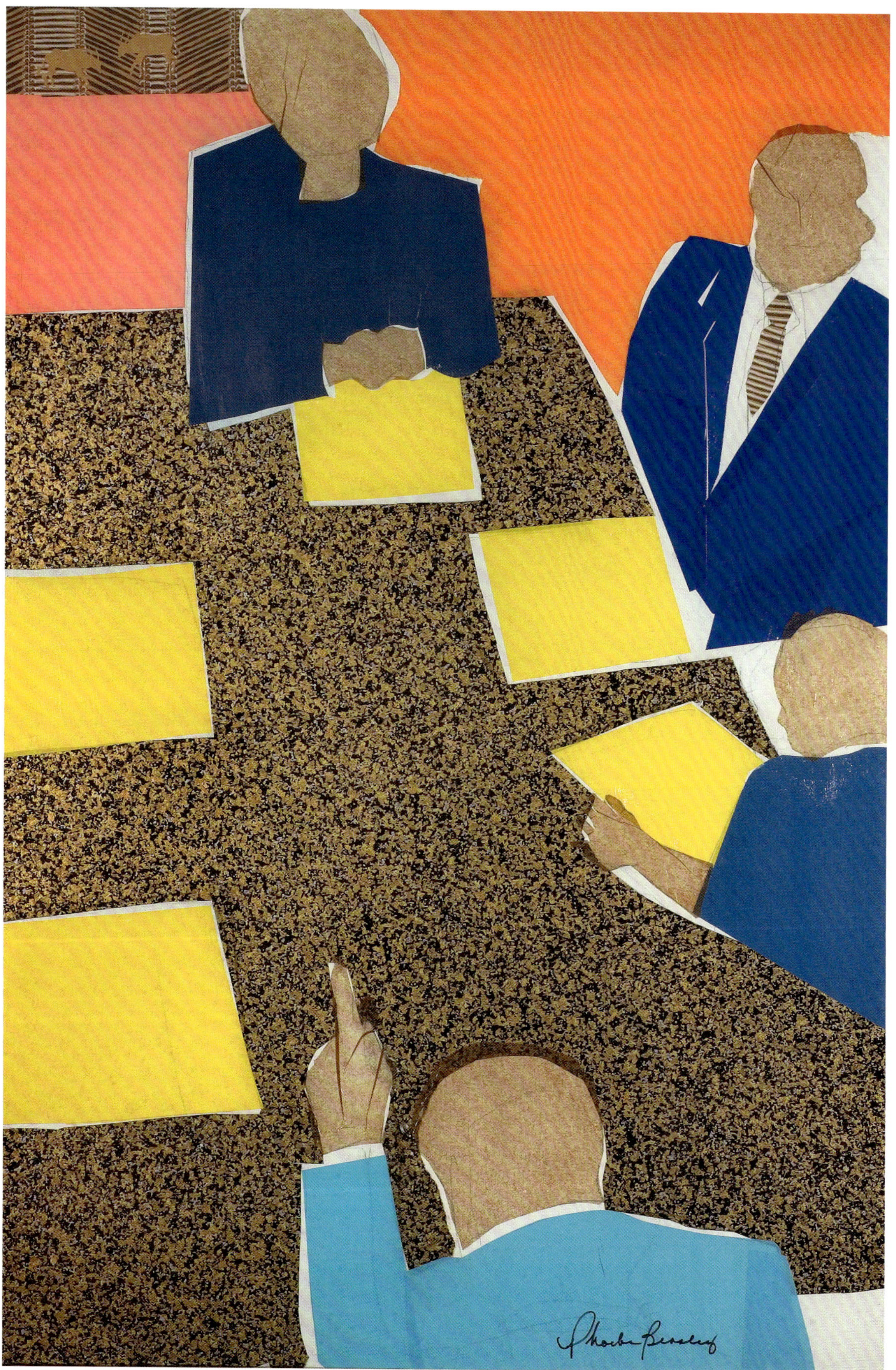

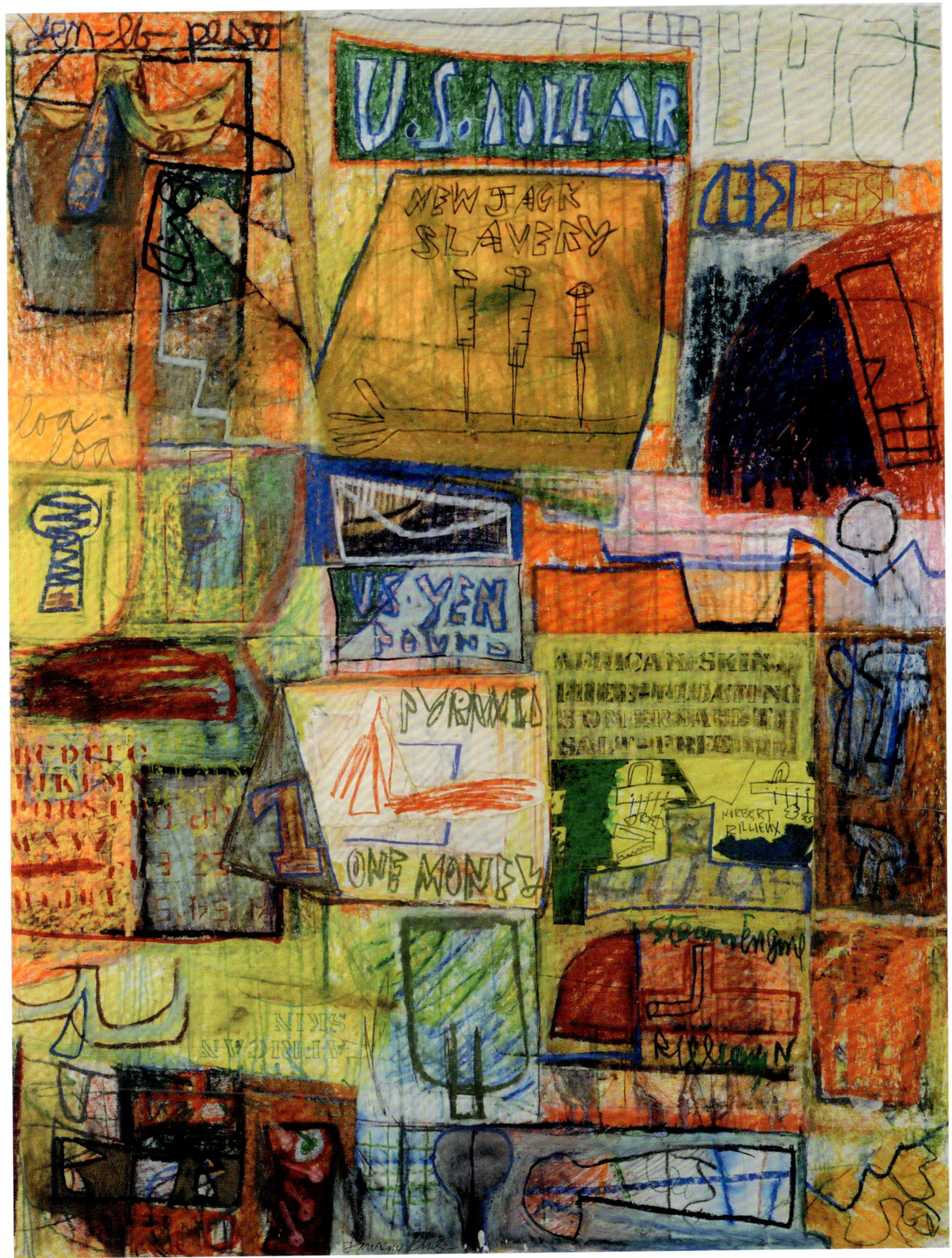

Phoebe Beasley
Yellow Legal Pad #3, 1999, Collage on paper, 36" × 24" × 2", Courtesy of the Eric Key Collection, © Phoebe Beasley

Lawrence Philp
US Dollar, 1999–2000, Mixed media, 62" × 48" × 2", Courtesy of the Eric Key Collection, © Lawrence Philp

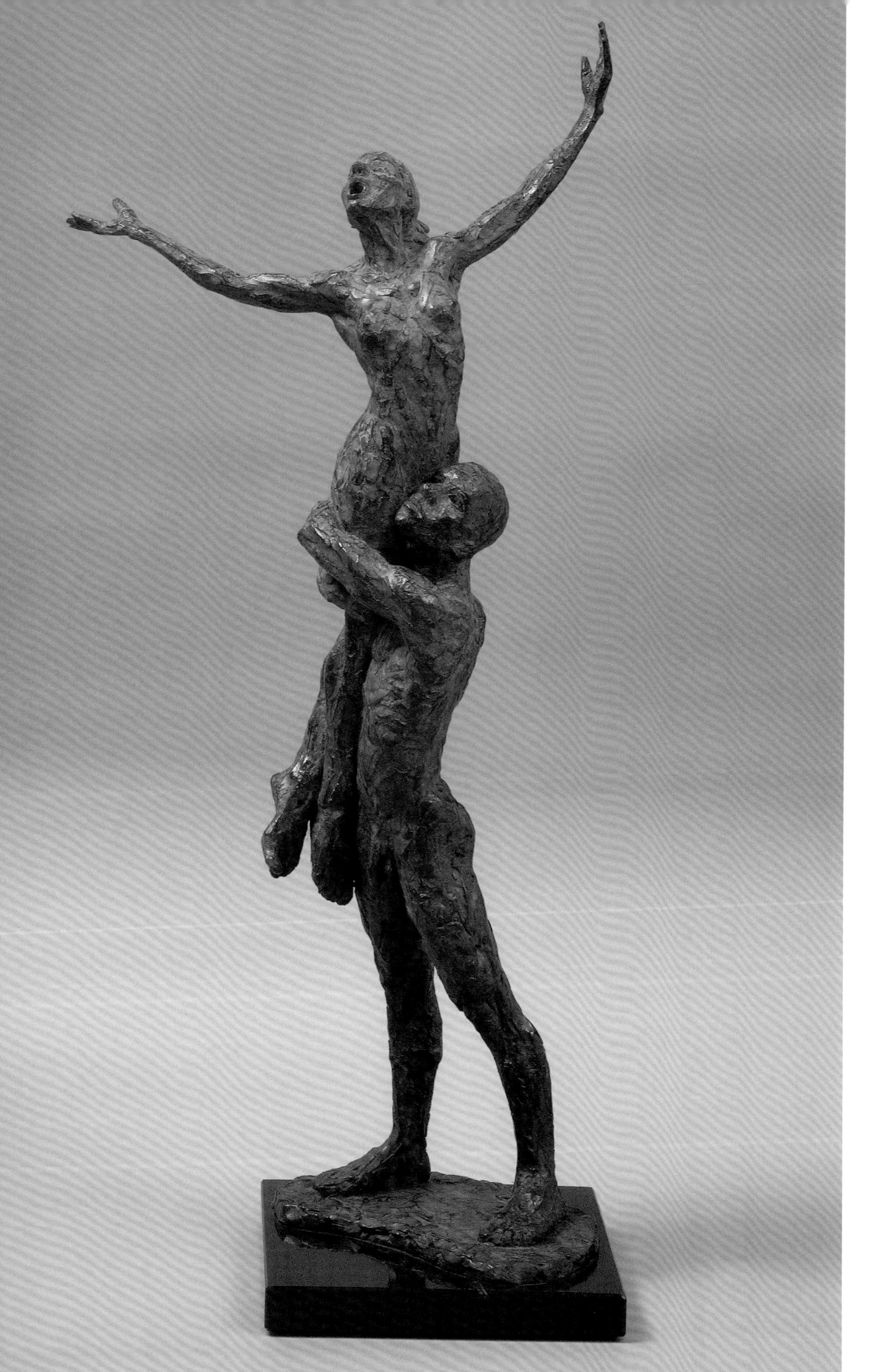

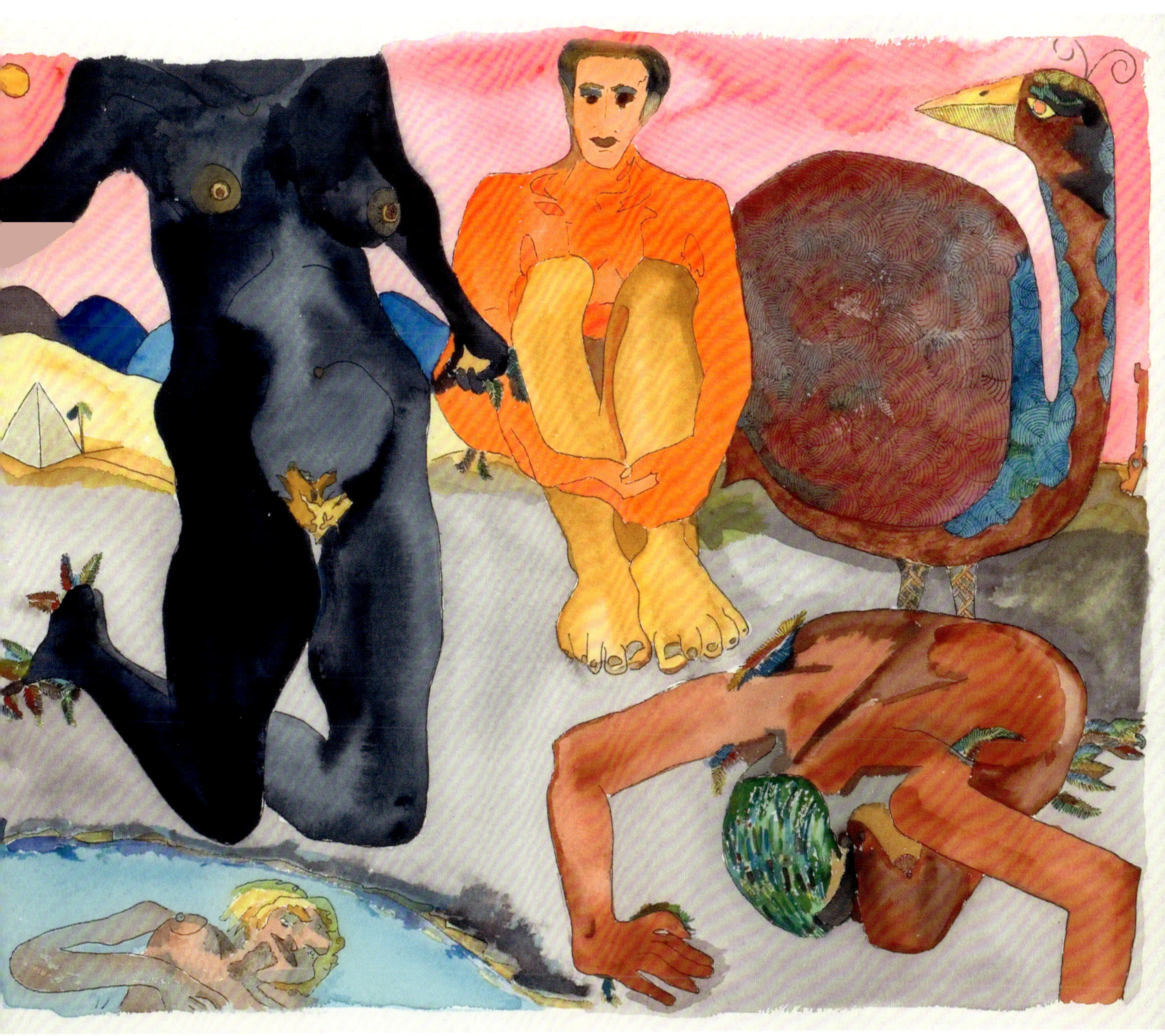

Basil Watson
Dancers, 1995,
Bronze, green patina,
28" × 13" × 8", Courtesy of the Eric Key Collection, © Basil Watson

Percy Martin
Three Bushwomen, no date, Watercolor on paper,
30" × 33" × 2", Courtesy of the Eric Key Collection, © Percy Martin

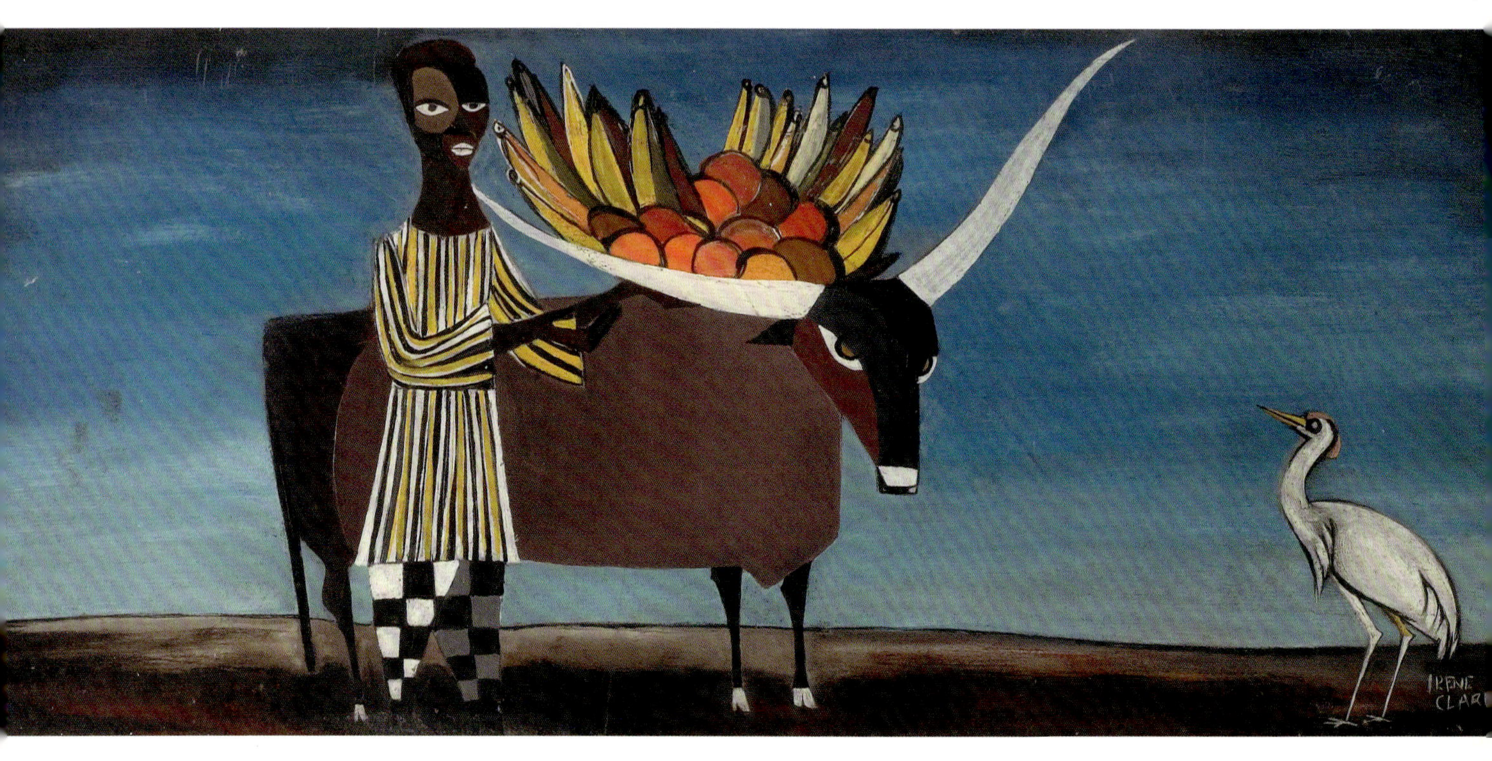

Irene Clark
Man with Bull with Horn,
1970s, Acrylic on board,
9" × 19½", Courtesy of the Eric
Key Collection, © Irene Clark

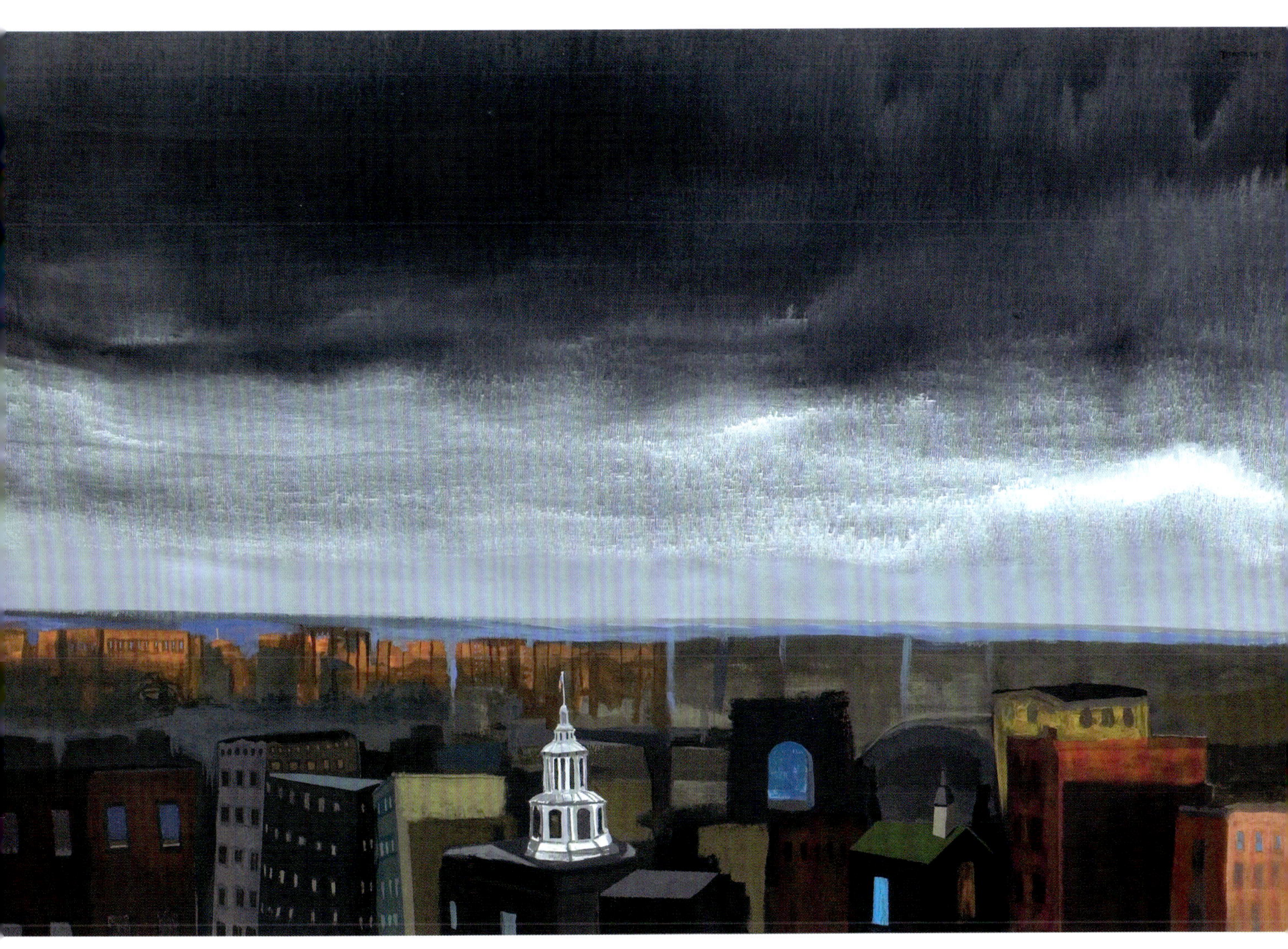

James Brantley
Balance of Power on the Street Where You Live, no date, Acrylic on board, 33" × 47" × 2", Courtesy of the Eric Key Collection, © James Brantley

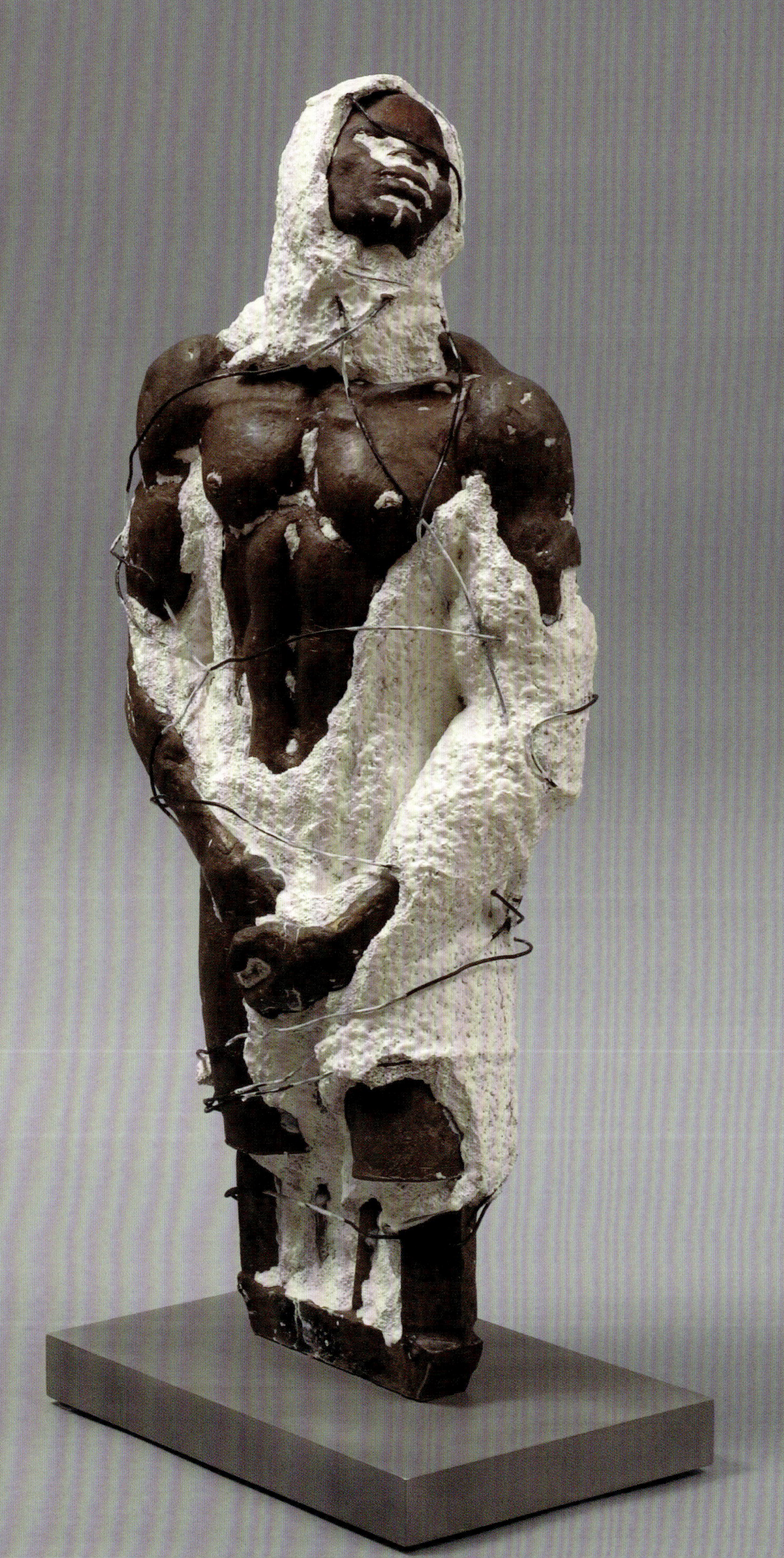

A MATTER OF REPRESENTATION

FIGURING "AFRICAN AMERICAN ART" IN THE KEY COLLECTION

Adrienne L. Childs PhD

In 1973, Chicago artist Charles Wilbert White, the consummate painter, draftsman, and printmaker, produced an etching of a young Frederick Douglass. White, one of the most important African American artists of the twentieth century, was keenly aware of the role that image-making plays in Black social and cultural activism, and dedicated his career to interpreting Black life in America. His image of Douglass, the foremost Black abolitionist in American history, not only memorializes an important historical figure, but also furthers Douglass's decades-long deployment of his own likeness in the service of racial justice. White's etching combines elements from several of the numerous original photographs that Douglass sat for beginning in the early 1840s until his death in 1895. Referred to as the most photographed American of the nineteenth century, Douglass carefully constructed his image. Douglass's 168 photographs not only humanized him but also aided him in his quest for the abolition of slavery and the recognition of the humanity of the "negro" race.[1] Douglass's utilization of the image of the Black body—his Black body—was a powerful and progressive tool in the shaping of African American identity in the nineteenth century, and initiated a representational strategy in African American visual culture that continues to drive the field to this day.

Douglass's intrepid personal quest helped to sow the seeds for the early twentieth-century call to a collective Black consciousness that coalesced into the New Negro Movement, and later the Harlem Renaissance. This radical shift in Black activism emphasized that representation and creative expression could be vehicles for defining the modern "negro," and that art could serve as an essential arm in this multi-pronged project of social and cultural uplift. The concept of the New Negro—a form of Blackness steeped

Artis Lane
Emerging into Spirit,
1993, Bronze, wire, resin,
21" × 9¼" × 6¼", Courtesy of the
Eric Key Collection, © Artis Lane

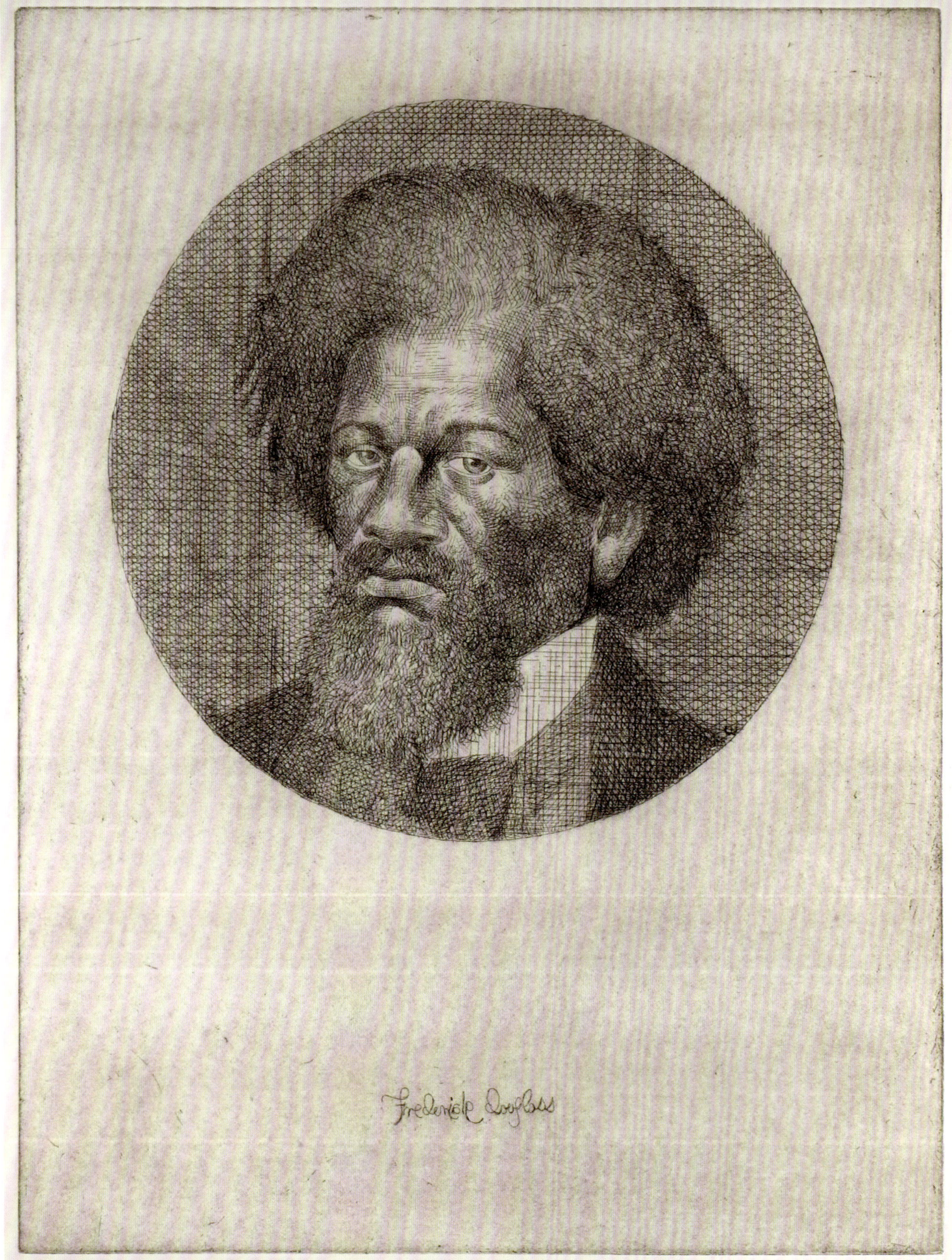

A.P.

CHARLES WHITE

in modernity and progressive politics—was in large part a repudiation of the stereotype of the "Old Negro." There was a shared understanding that the preponderance of damaging images, such as the elderly banjo player in Thomas Hovenden's 1885 etching *Dem was good ole days* (fig. 1), were not only born of a nostalgia for the plantation culture of the Old South, but were also vehicles for the continued oppression of Black people in the guise of art. In reaction to these tactics, a growing cadre of professionally trained New Negro artists, illustrators, and photographers explored ways in which their artistry could resist and refute the stereotype, create an authentic representation of Blackness, and serve the race writ large. The depth and breadth of this movement was captured by Alain Locke in his 1925 anthology *The New Negro,* which included essays, poems, music, images, photographs, and more, that embodied this flowering of cultural energy.[2] The book was a major catalyst for Black artists who chose to answer the call to fashion a new spirit of Black identity in their artistry. A good example of this modern spirit is William H. Johnson's *Woman in Red Dress on Yellow Chair* (fig. 2). Johnson offers a radically contemporary Black persona rendered with modernist aesthetics and a sense of style and presence. Even though Black identity has always been fluid, unstable, and complex, certain representational virtues such as respectability, status, and sartorial modernity were widely used in portraiture to counter vicious stereotyping. Portraiture was a generative creative force that served racial progress, a collective identity construction, and the repudiation of racial oppression.

Although the Key Collection exhibited in *GATEWAYS* largely features artists from later in the twentieth century, it is evidence of the image of the Black body's defining role in Black creative practice. Richmond Barthé and William E. Artis are two sculptors represented in the collection who were associated with the Harlem Renaissance and whose works take up the Black male—a perpetually contested terrain—albeit toward differing ends. Artis's bronze bust *Michael,* a sculpture of a Black male youth, is a traditional portrait bust given a pared-down modernist approach. Since antiquity, cultures in Africa and Europe have produced bronze sculpture to enshrine the image of important individuals. Here, Artis takes on this exalted medium to represent a young Black male with elegance and sensitivity. Simply called *Michael,* the portrait is both intimate and universal. With similar elegance, Barthé sculpted a bronze figure of Féral Benga, the Senegalese dancer, whom he encountered on a trip to Paris in 1934.[3] Benga was an exotic sensation and the male counterpart to Josephine Baker, both complex figures who performed as "primitives" in Jazz Age

Charles Wilbert White
Frederick Douglass,
1973, Etching on paper,
33" × 27" × 1", Courtesy of The Eric Key Collection, © Courtesy of The Charles White Archives

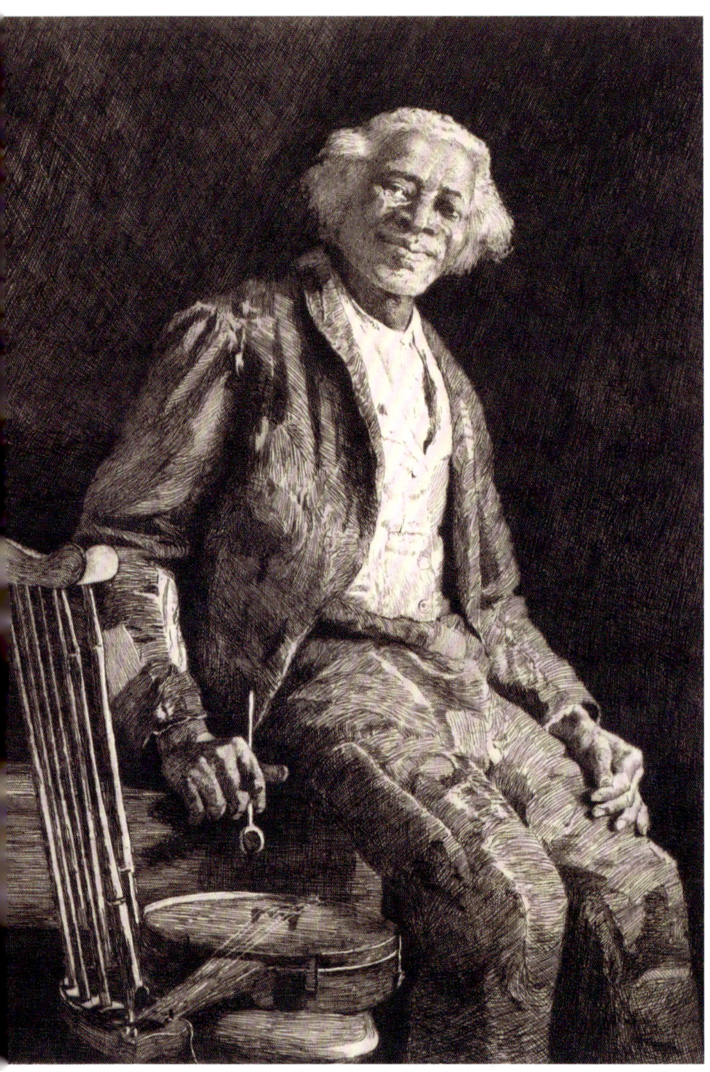

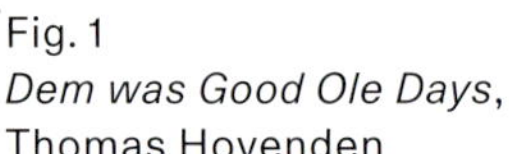

Fig. 1
Dem was Good Ole Days,
Thomas Hovenden

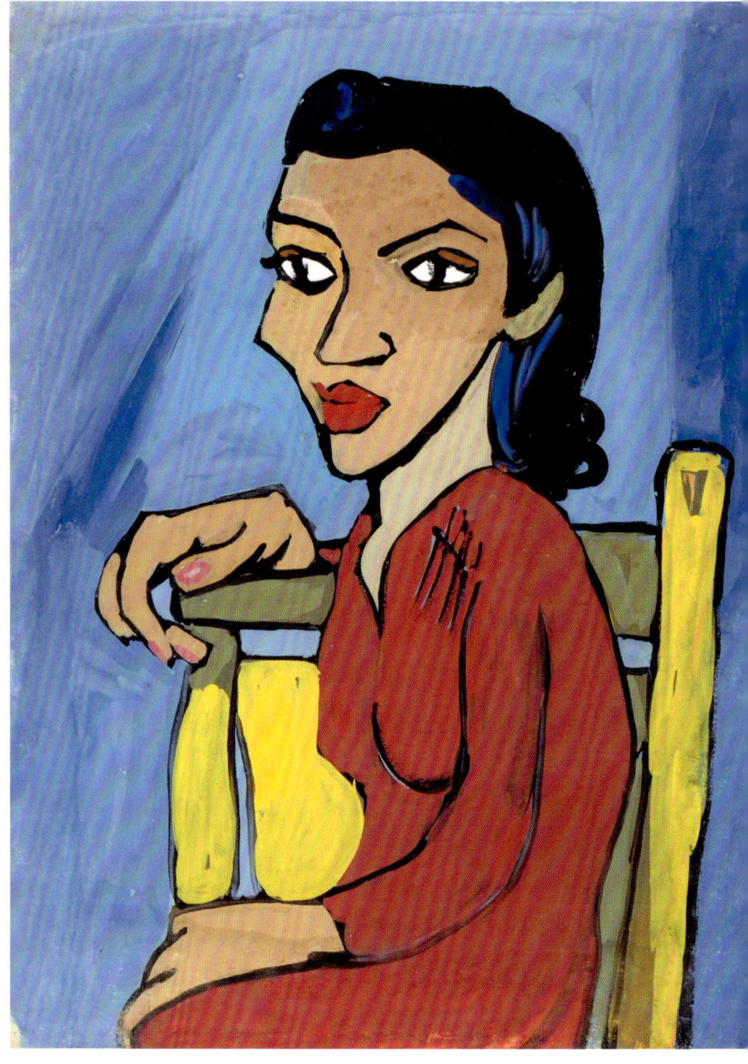

Fig. 2
Woman in Red Dress on Yellow Chair, William H. Johnson

Europe. Barthé depicts Benga nude while performing his famous saber dance. Barthé's sculpture was crafted with his signature combination of classicism laced with homoerotic undertones.[4] *Feral Benga* introduces the importance of Black diasporic creative identities and practices in the formation of an international modernist culture that spanned from Senegal to Paris to New York.

Artis's sensitive treatment of the young *Michael* in 1950 is echoed 67 years later in Charles Edward Williams's *Untitled (Boy with Skull Cap with Yellow Band)*, both extending honorific gestures to Black boyhood. Barthé's focus on the muscular body resonates in the work of Artis Lane and James McMillan. In the wake of their New Negro activist predecessors, Preston Sampson and Al Burts continue to celebrate the beauty and dignity of the Black male well into the twenty-first century. Kyle Hackett channels Douglass's serial use of the self-portrait; however, his focus is both inward and outward. In his painting *New Negation 1,* he depicts himself in academic regalia—the embodiment of educational achievement. Indeed, Hackett is a first-generation college student. Yet Hackett's aim is not simply to tout Black advancement, but also to interrogate and complicate it, as he reflects on his interior psychological experiences versus the external image of social progress.[5]

The Key Collection includes works that illustrate the expansive creative approaches of many African American artists who have chosen to depict facets of Black womanhood—a subject also deeply invested in the figurative tradition. Elizabeth Catlett, an artist who was nurtured by the energies of the Harlem Renaissance, combines her interest in African art, pre-Columbian art, and European modernism in her dedication to the Black female. Her elegant sculptural work celebrates the universal qualities of Black motherhood in *Maternity* and *Family*. Nelson Stevens, on the other hand, engages the sensuous nature of the Black female in *Untitled (nude female)* from 1980. His figures' nudity, frontal poses, large stature, and stoic attitudes are reminiscent of Picasso's landmark *Les Demoiselles d'Avignon* of 1907. Picasso's painting of a group of prostitutes demonstrates his appropriation of African art—and is often considered to mark the birth of modern art. Stevens retrieves Picasso's use of "African-ness" and applies expressive brushwork and a color palette that are wholly his own. A member of the Black Arts Movement collective AfriCobra (African Commune of Bad Relevant Artists), Stevens was an activist artist whose work aimed to demonstrate pride, power, beauty, and the tangibility of Blackness.

Unfortunately, the voices of Black female artists were often marginalized in the male-dominated Black Arts Movement. Feminist artists such as Catlett and Emma Amos established *themselves* as arbiters of the Black female body—taking the power to represent Black womanhood back from both Black and white male artists. In *Sun Babe,* Amos presents a self-defined and self-contained sensuous Black woman sunbathing. She is indeed sexualized, but on her own terms. Renée Stout's female-centric work

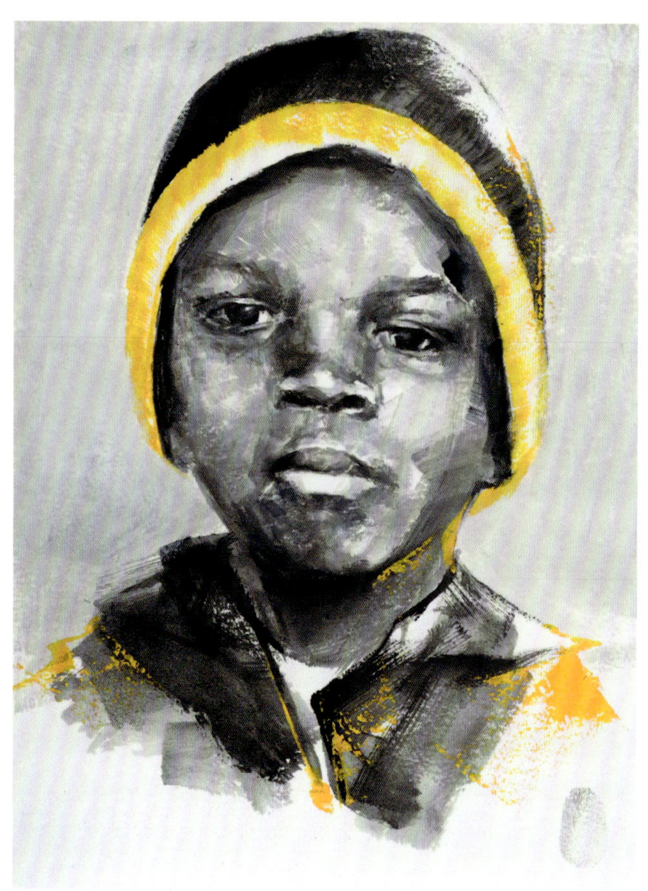

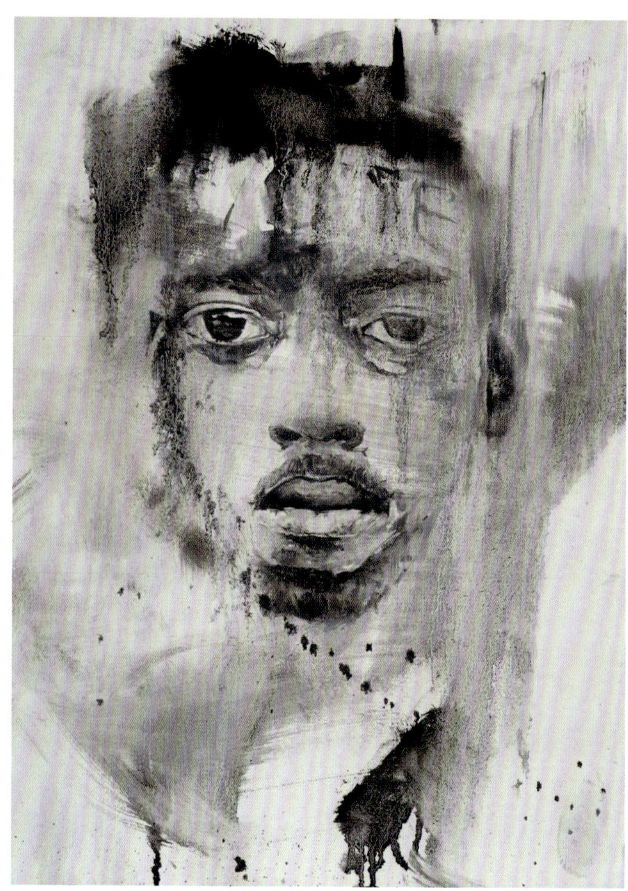

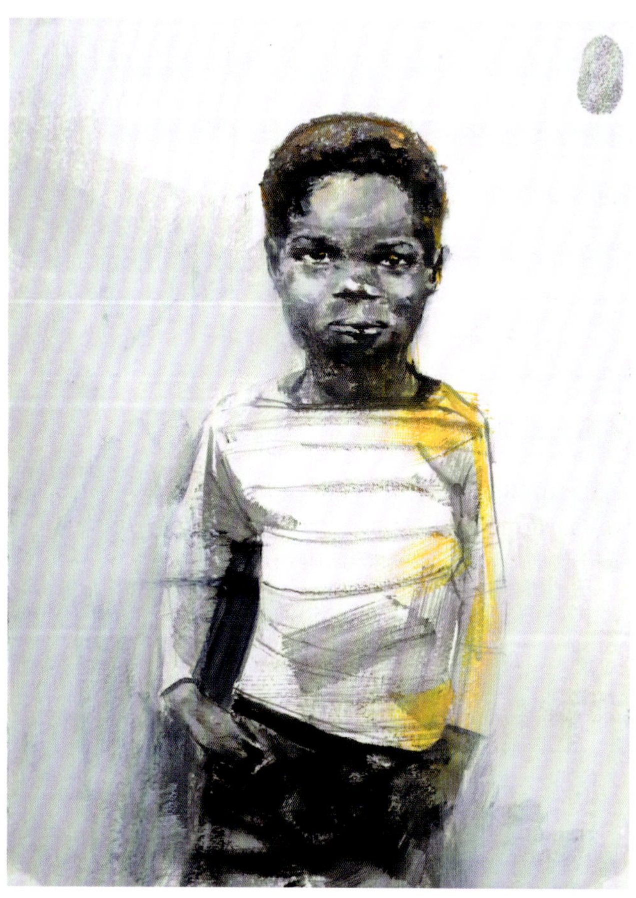

Charles Edward Williams
Untitled (Boy with Skull Cap with Yellow Band), 2017, Oil on watercolor paper, 12" × 9" × 2", Courtesy of the Eric Key Collection, © Charles Edward Williams

Charles Edward Williams
Hope, 2016, Oil on watercolor paper, 12" × 9" × 2", Courtesy of the Eric Key Collection, © Charles Edward Williams

Charles Edward Williams
Untitled (Boy in Shirt), 2017, Oil on watercolor paper, 12" × 9" × 2", Courtesy of the Eric Key Collection, © Charles Edward Williams

often engages the spiritual powers of Black women. In fact, Black women's spiritual praxis has recently been theorized as "Conjure Feminism," a field of inquiry that charts the art of conjure and mysticism in Africana women as a feminist tool that protects, sustains, and empowers.[6] Stout's 2009 lithographic interpretation of *Marie Laveau*, the renowned nineteenth-century Voodoo practitioner from New Orleans, draws upon histories of Black female spiritualism and the power that Black women wielded through the metaphysical. With a similar nod toward the mystical, Stefanie Jackson's 2017 painting *ZAPALA, Estuary of Regret* is a surrealistic rumination on the history of Sapelo Island off the coast of Georgia. Once named Zapala during the Spanish colonial era, Sapelo was a native American island colonized by Spanish missionaries and later home to enslaved Africans whose descendants inhabit the island today. Jackson's canvas weaves the harsh histories and fragmented memories of colonization into the tangled landscape, where past and present meet in a dreamscape.

In addition to centering the figure in the visual discourse of American Blackness, African American artists have seized on the power of art to absorb, interpret, and represent history—their history—through narrative figuration. We find that issues of enslavement and freedom are an enduring leitmotif in the art of African Americans. The importance of lighting the past is another legacy of the Harlem Renaissance's emphasis on Black artists telling Black stories. Artists such as Aaron Douglas and others answered Locke's call to look toward their ancestral legacy of African art to develop a visual language that would authentically represent Blackness. He charged them to use this language to recount histories lost, buried, or neglected. Douglas's untitled gouache from 1934 reflects his absorption of Cubism and African art (to which the Cubist movement was indebted) as he imagines the fraught trajectory of Africans in America. Douglas's scene is set in an imaginary foliate landscape with Egyptian pyramids, a large church, and several Black figures. With broken chains on their wrists, Douglas's silhouetted figures look toward the sky in a hopeful gesture, charting their journey from Africa, through enslavement to freedom. Here, in one stroke, Douglas encapsulates the arc of African American history from Africa through emancipation. Douglas's signature aesthetic has become emblematic of Harlem Renaissance visual culture. Similarly, Jacob Lawrence focuses many of his modernist-inflected narrative works on the dialectic between slavery and emancipation, between North and South, between oppression and freedom. Lawrence was known for his serialized paintings and prints that, scene by scene, narrated important events in Black history. Four silkscreen prints based on Lawrence's 1938

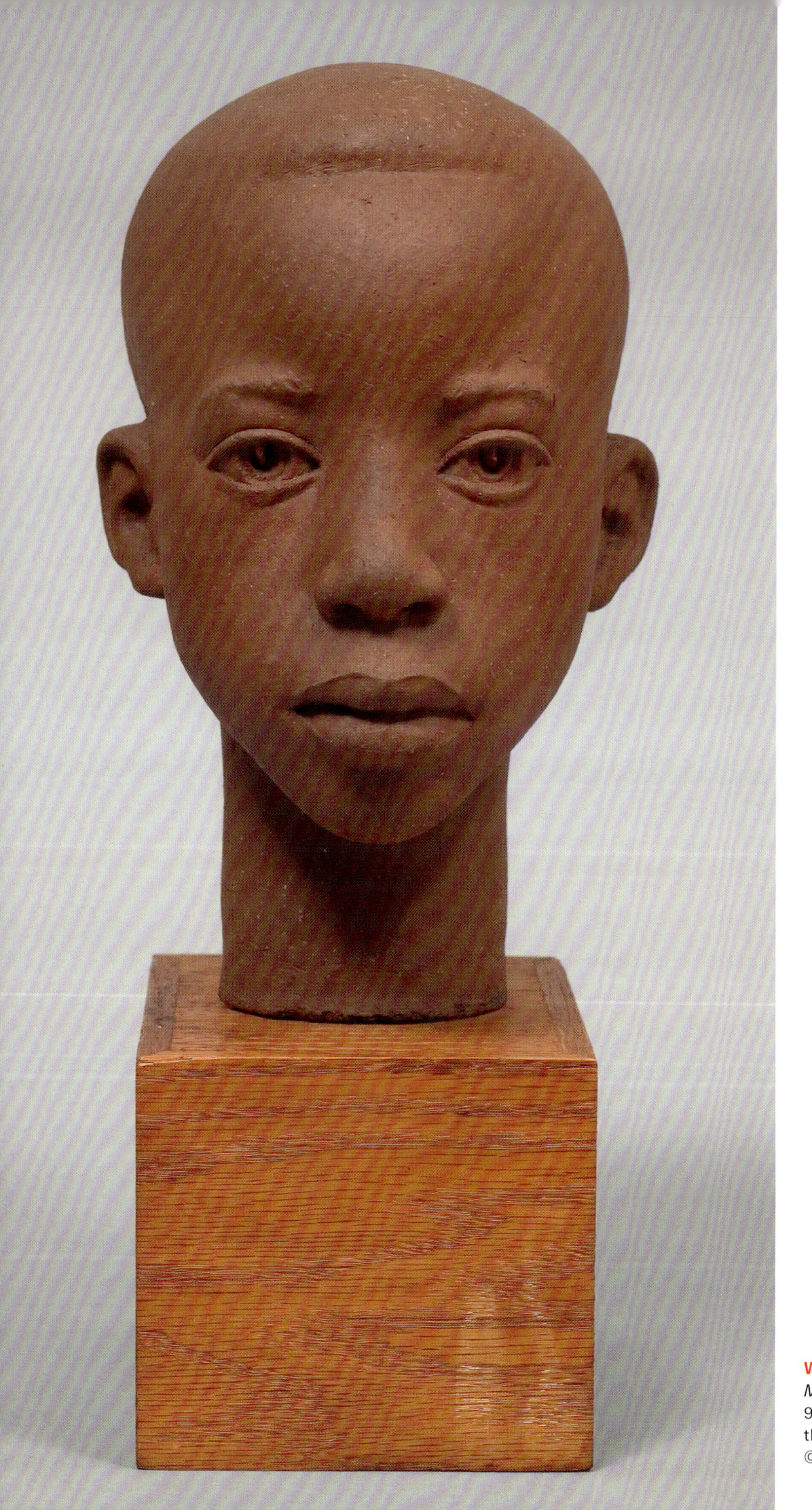

William E. Artis
Michael, 1950, Terra cotta, 9” × 6” × 7”, Courtesy of the Eric Key Collection, © William E. Artis

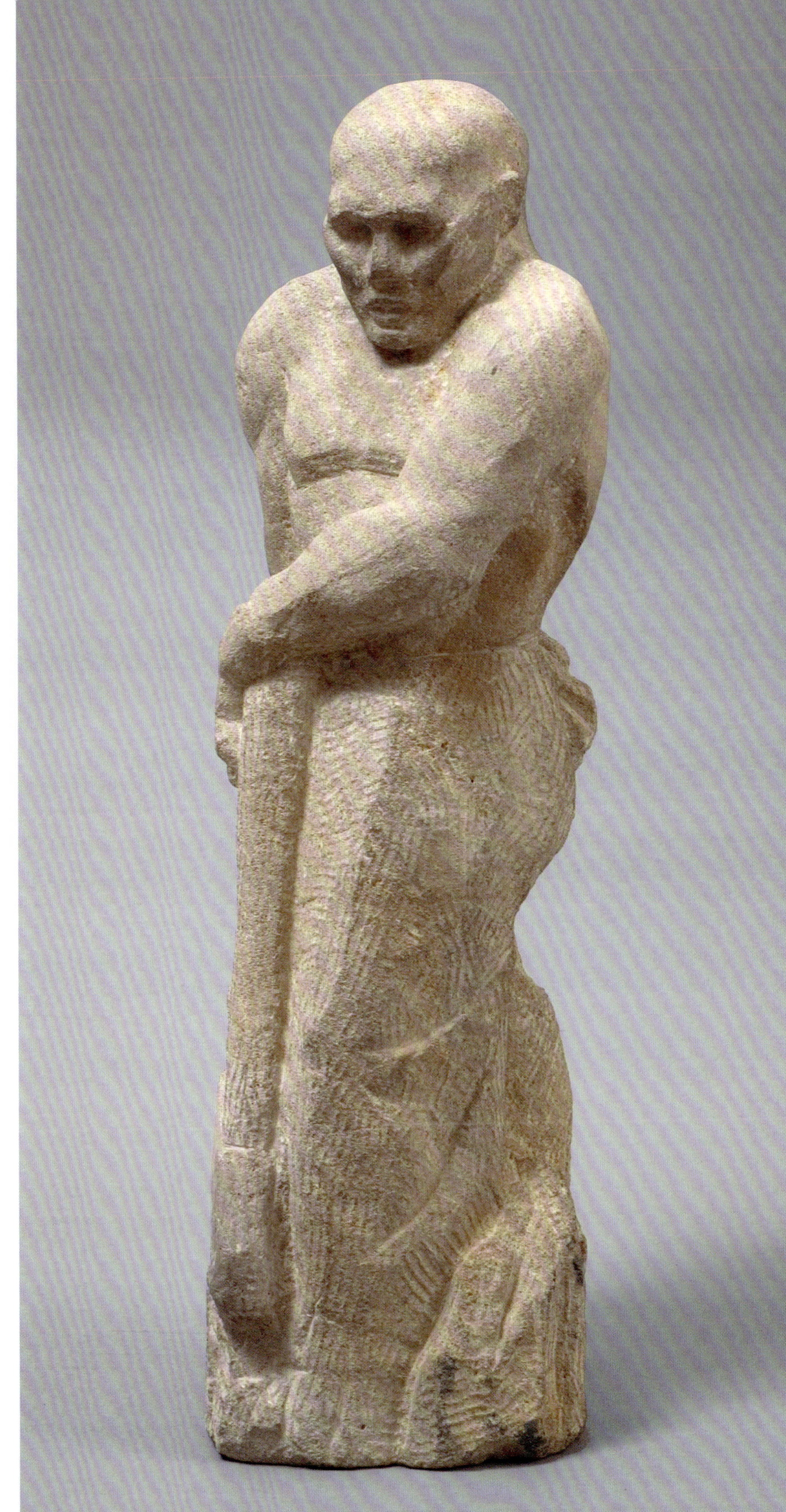

James McMillan
Untitled, 1952, Stone,
17" × 5½" × 6¾", Courtesy
of the Eric Key Collection,

series *The Life of Toussaint L'Ouverture* are part of a biographical history of the Haitian revolutionary Toussaint L'Ouverture and chronicle events that led to the first successful slave revolt in the Americas.

As the twentieth century progresses into the twenty-first, Black artists become immersed in the Civil Rights, Black Power, and eventually Black Lives Matter movements, and provide important reflections on the social struggles that have shaped a collective Black experience in America. Reginald Gammon's powerful painting *A Triptych for the Black Church (MLK and Mothers)* represents both Martin Luther King and Malcolm X, two assassinated Black leaders. The central panel depicts an image of Jim Jones, the Peoples Temple cult leader who orchestrated the mass murder-suicide of nearly a thousand church members with a largely Black population. These unexpected juxtapositions between assassinated leaders and murdered everyday people speak to the devastating consequences of racism in the United States. Kevin Cole takes a conceptual approach to issues of racial justice in his 2014 mixed-media work *Comfort and Pressure*, in which his signature motif—the necktie—symbolizes the struggles and triumphs of Black American men. The tie can be an instrument of lynching as well as a symbol of empowerment. The bold colors and patterns refer to dynamics of music as a Black cultural expression. Here, Cole synthesizes history and memory into lyrical abstractions. Schroeder Cherry takes on the social politics of colorism in his mixed-media assemblage *Color Test*. In it, Cherry references the notorious paper bag test—a term that refers to the discriminatory practice within the Black community whereby an individual whose skin was darker than a paper bag would not gain admission to certain groups or obtain privileges within the community. This speaks to the notion that the lighter-skinned Black person was seen as having more value and beauty. This is a deeply painful dynamic within the Black community that has both historical and contemporary ramifications. These works exemplify how Black artists have used the creative and compelling nature of art to mine and interpret important inflection points in the complex experiences of Black people.

While the figurative tradition in the service of social aims—documenting, affirming, and celebrating the multivalent concept of Blackness—has been a driving force in the history of art by African Americans since the New Negro Movement, it is by no means an all-encompassing ethos. In fact, it can be a point of contention. Black artists have always had individual conceptions of what art should be, and have aspired toward developing singular aesthetic modalities. The way in which the Black figurative tradition ties art to the politics of racial identity has been an

Preston Sampson
Portrait, 2000, Watercolor with collage paper, 18" × 12", Courtesy of the Eric Key Collection, © Preston Sampson

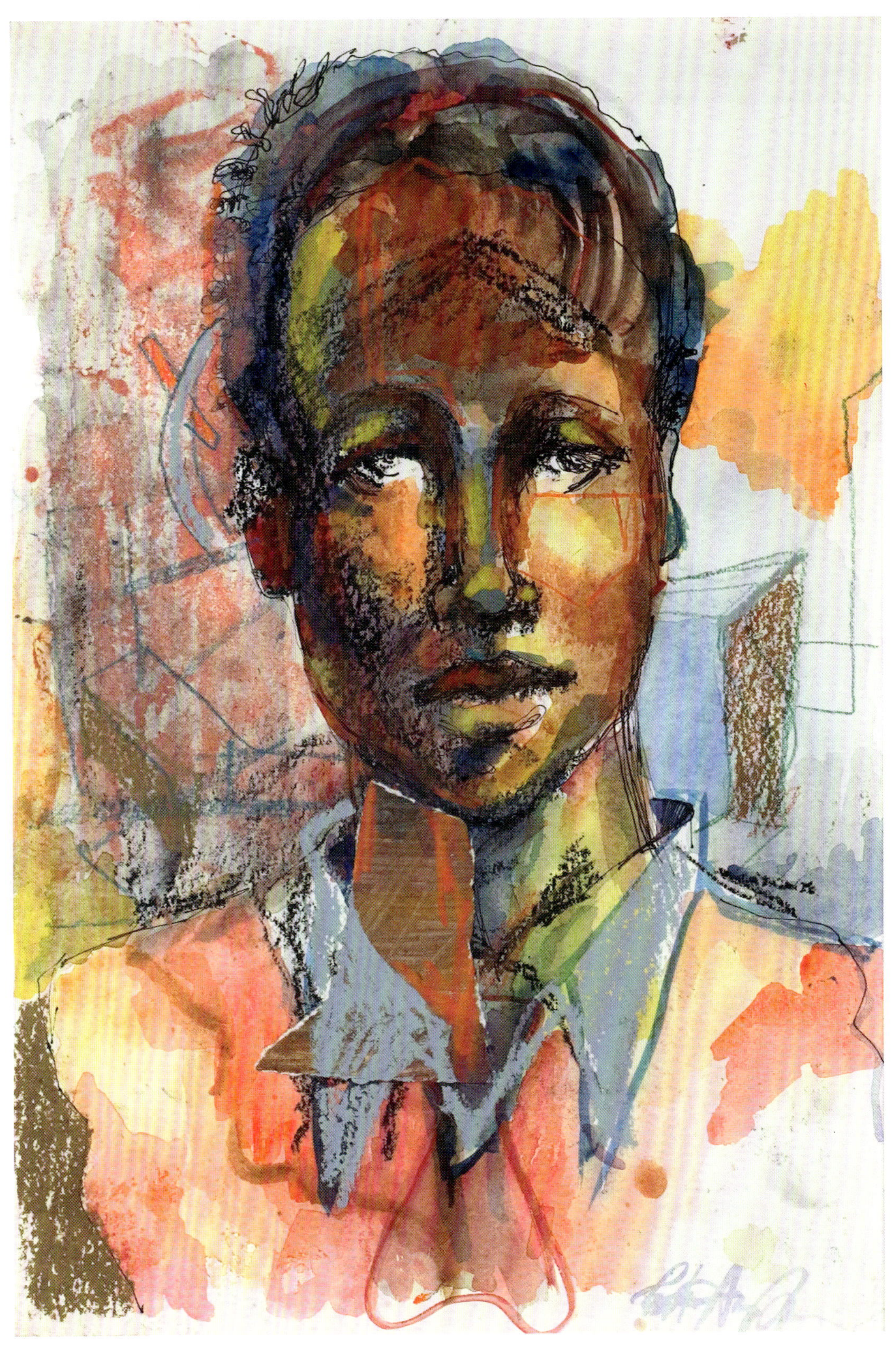

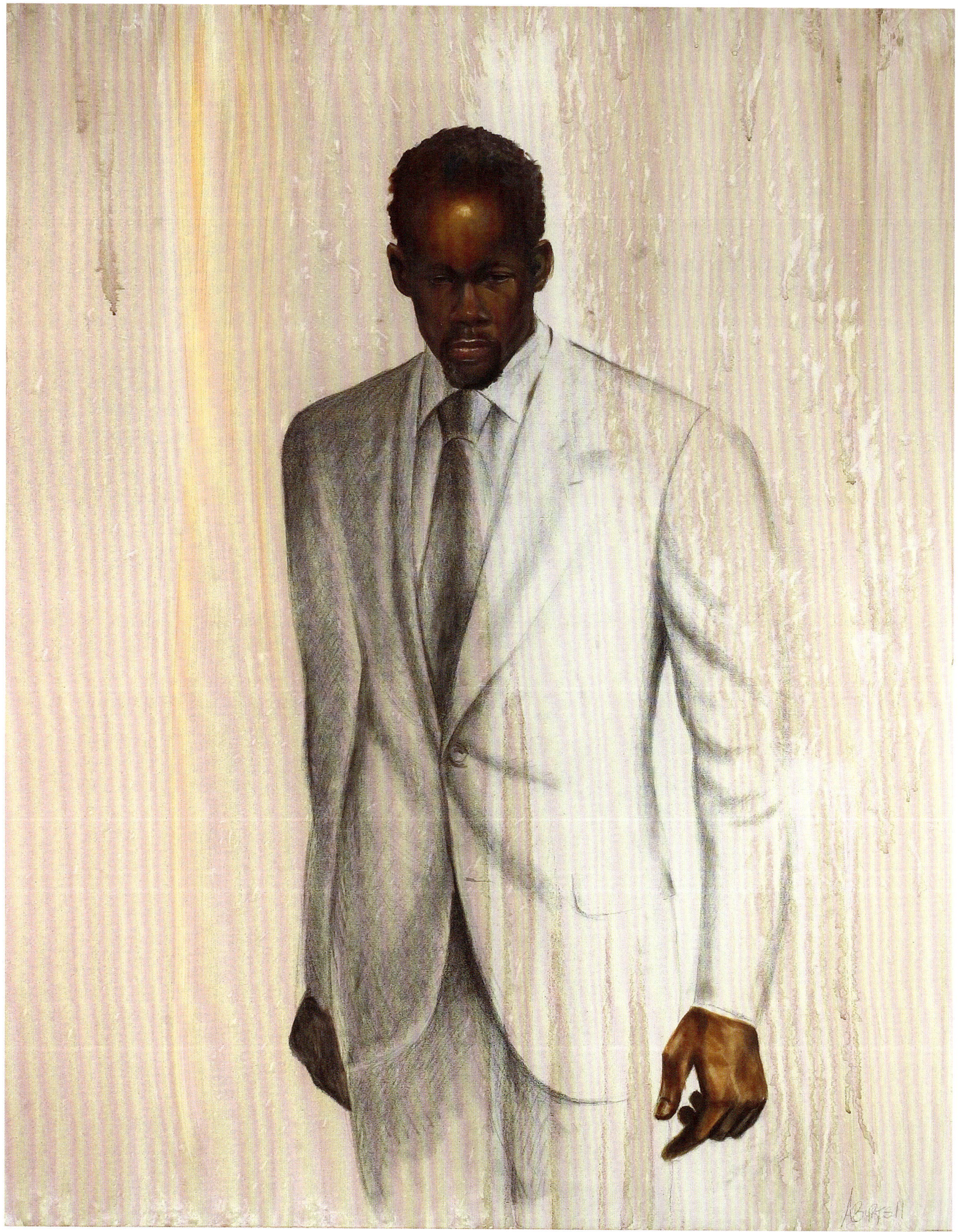

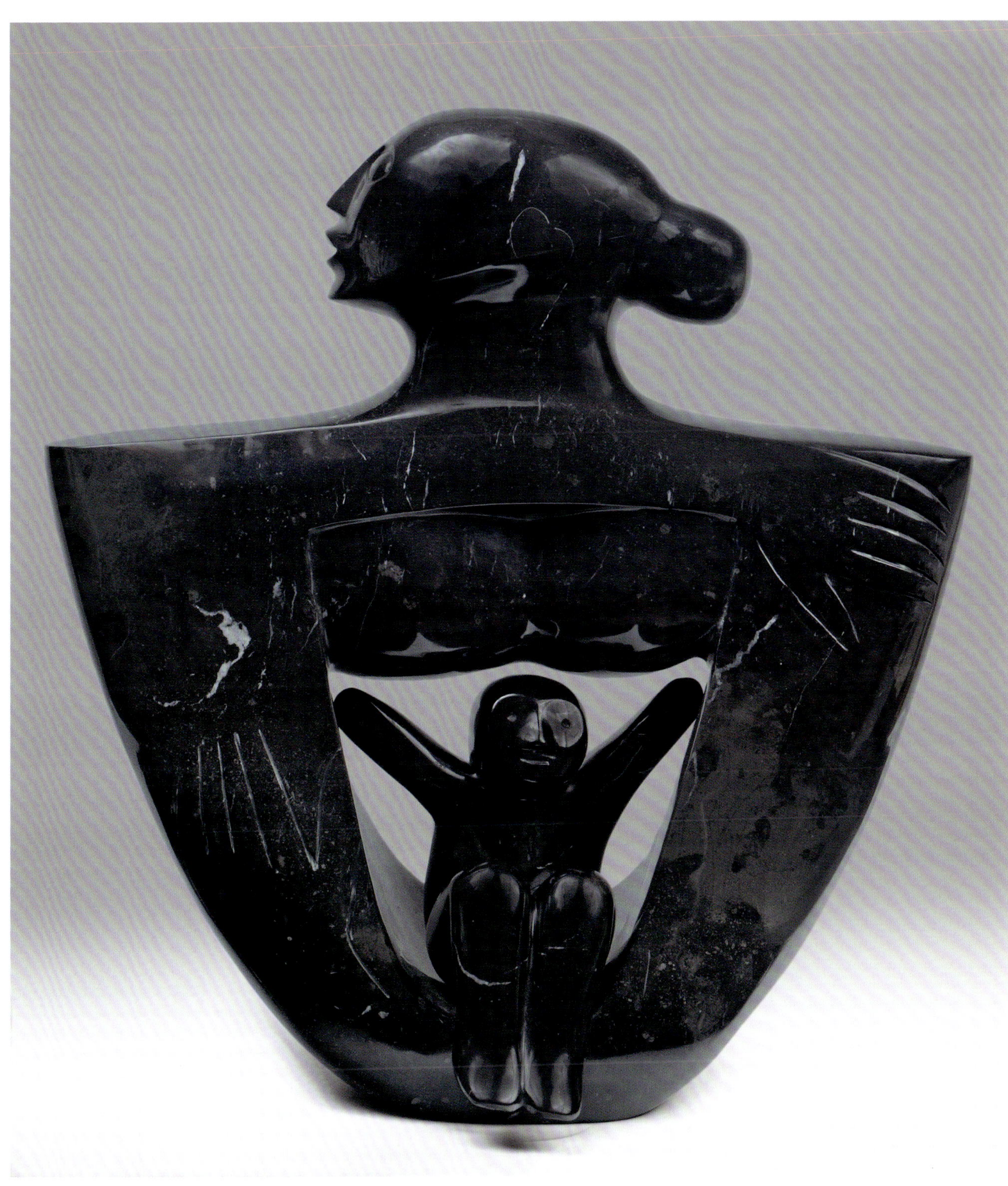

Al Burts
Cinderella Man,
2011, Oil on canvas,
60” × 48” × 2”, Courtesy of the
Eric Key Collection, © Al Burts

Elizabeth Catlett
Maternity, 1980, Marble,
18¾" x 17½" x 8", Courtesy of
the Eric Key Collection, © 2023
Mora-Catlett Family / Licensed
by VAGA at Artists Rights
Society (ARS), NY

untenable restriction for some artists. As more and more Black artists engaged with modernist abstraction in the 1960s and 1970s, the notion that race and figuration should drive their artistry was discredited.[7] In 1969, an all-male panel of Black artists convened at The Metropolitan Museum of Art to discuss the state of the Black artist in America. Hale Woodruff—the elder statesman of the group—talked about the problems that arise with the term "black art." Woodruff spoke specifically about the art of the young Richard Hunt, who was on the panel and is represented in *GATEWAYS* by the 1978 abstract sculpture *Hybrid Figure*. He stated:

> We have a young man here, Richard Hunt, who I think is a great sculptor. The man is an artist. It has nothing to do with race; it is that real spark, unfathomable, and unidentifiable, that is deeply felt. The power of his sculpture is unassailable. Is this Negro art? Is it done by a Negro? It may very well be. Who knows? It's powerful, convincing, compelling art. And this is what I mean. It isn't black, white, green, or blue, but it's great art.[8]

Hunt has consistently revisited the aesthetics of hybridity in his metal sculpture, in which the forms take on different shapes and shifting sensibilities. Hunt's interests begin and end with form and are not fueled by racial considerations.[9] The group hotly debated the value of the formation of Black art as a necessary and cohesive category, versus the freedom to create outside of the confines of racial identification. Abstraction—practiced by artists such as Sam Gilliam, Ed Clark, and Al Loving—is no longer considered a repudiation of the responsibility of a Black artist to tell Black stories or represent some aspect of Black life. While the call for a racially defined definition of Black art remains a constant refrain, African American artists are part of a global community that participates in every form of art-making that exists.

Image-making is essential to reflecting *and* shaping African American life and culture. Many of the works in *GATEWAYS* exhibit the importance of the Black body in a tradition of figurative expression that has been a representational strategy employed by Black artists for more than a century. While the works in the Key Collection vary from figurative to abstract, they come together as a whole to represent the dynamic kaleidoscope of styles, modes, materials, methods, and meanings to be found in the expansive practice of African American artists.

Elizabeth Catlett
Family, 2022, Bronze, 15" × 5½" × 5", Courtesy of the Eric Key Collection, © 2023 Mora-Catlett Family / Licensed by VAGA at Artists Rights Society (ARS), NY

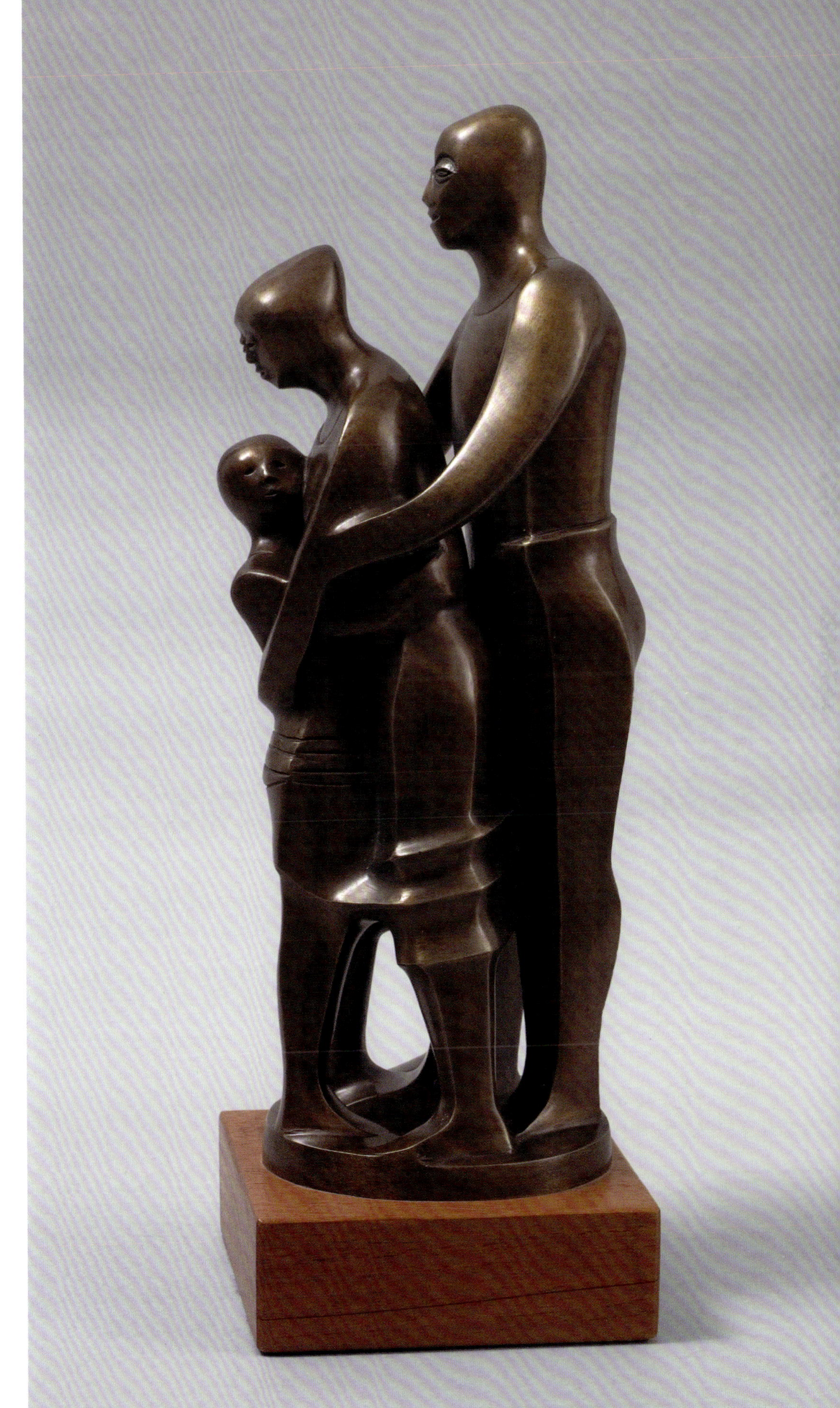

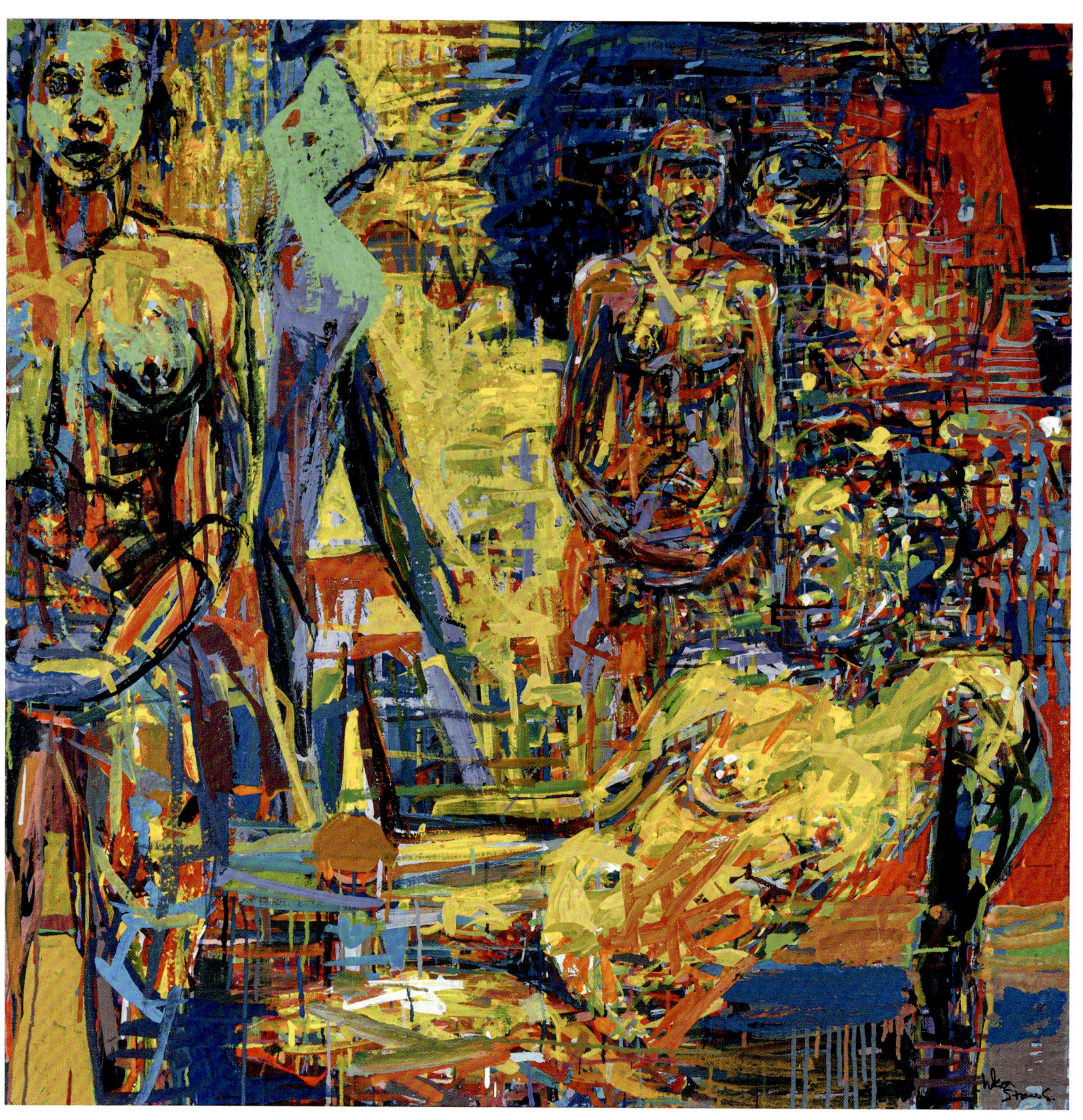

Nelson Stevens
Untitled (nude female),
1980, Oil on canvas,
42" × 42" × 2", Courtesy of
the Eric Key Collection,
© Nelson Stevens

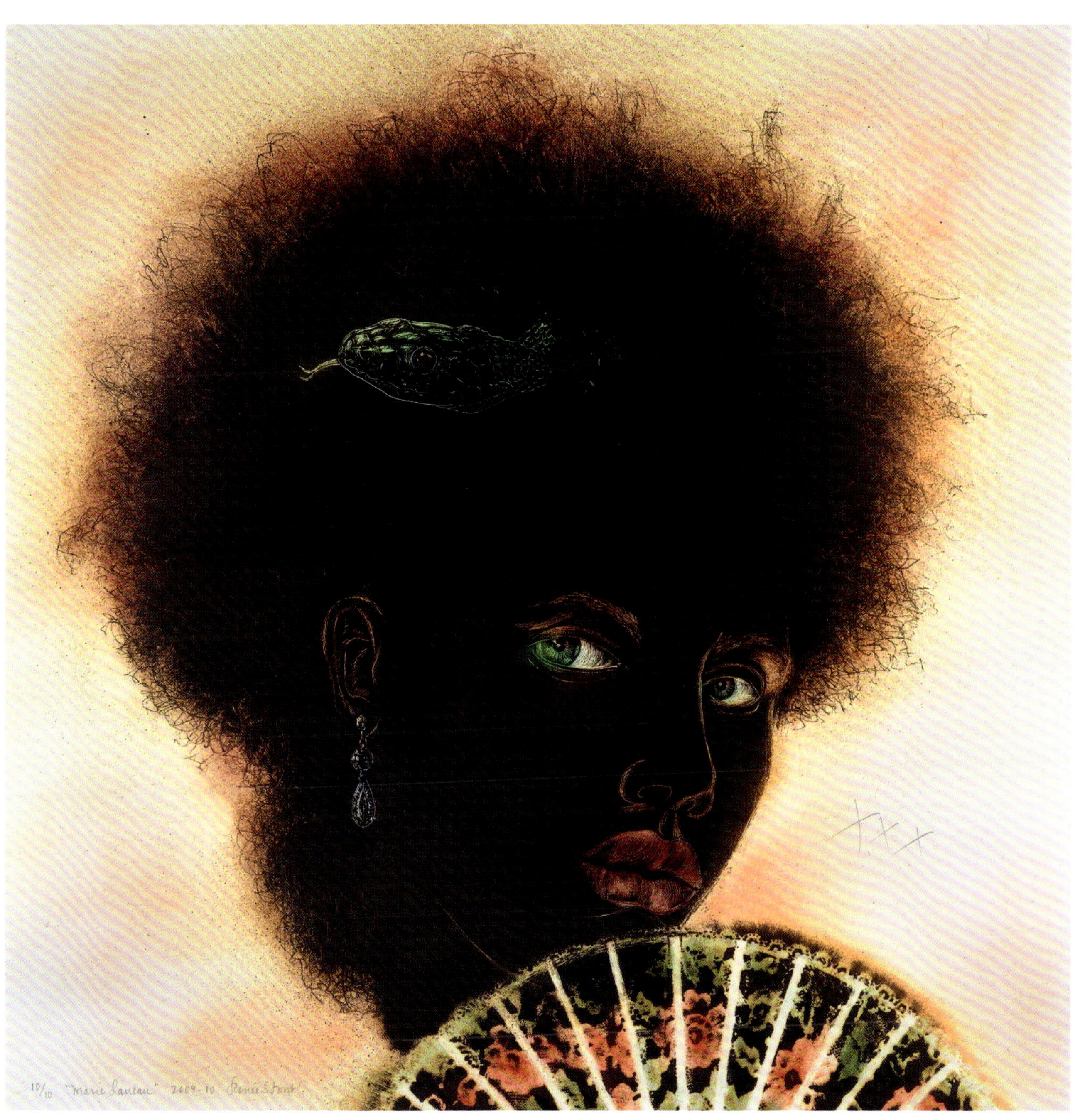

Renée Stout
Marie Laveau, 2009, Color lithograph on paper (10/10), 24" × 24", Courtesy of the Eric Key Collection, © Renée Stout

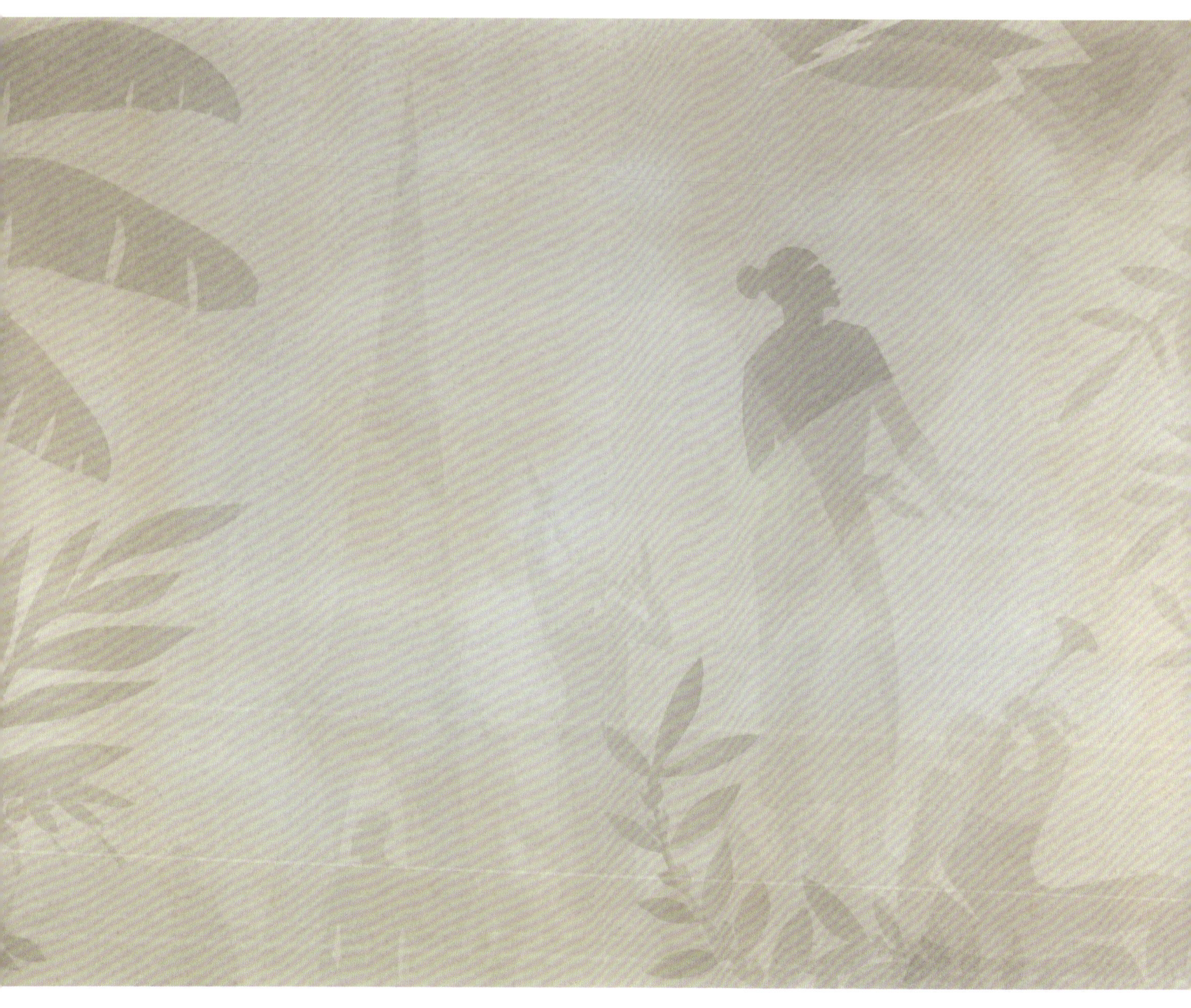

Aaron Douglas
Untitled, 1934, Gouache in grisaille on paper, 17" × 21" × 2", Courtesy of the Eric Key Collection, © 2023 Heirs of Aaron Douglas / Licensed by VAGA at Artists Rights Society (ARS), NY

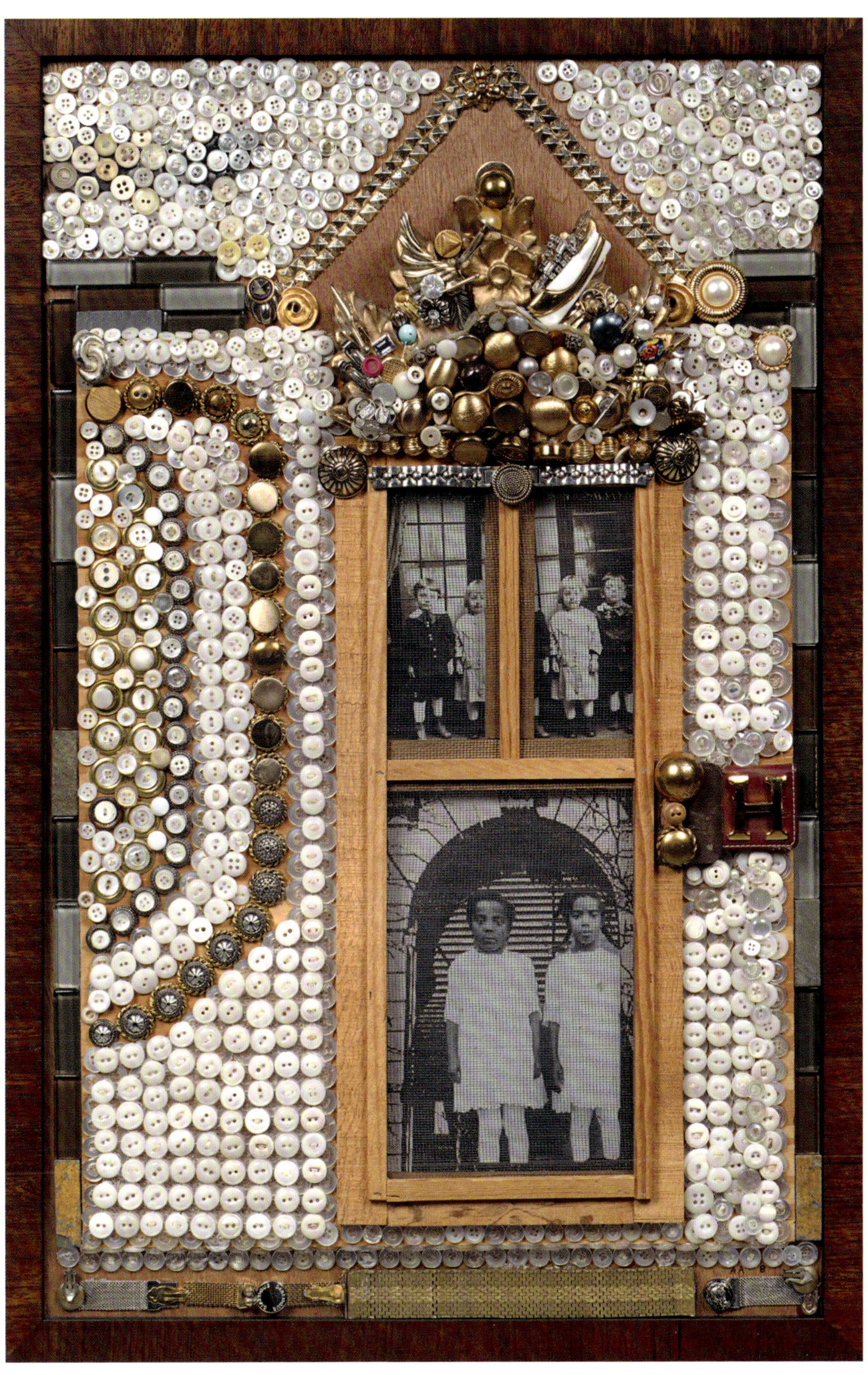

Amalia Amaki
Latch Key, 2018, Mixed media, 30¼" × 20" × 3½", Courtesy of the Eric Key Collection, © Amalia Amaki

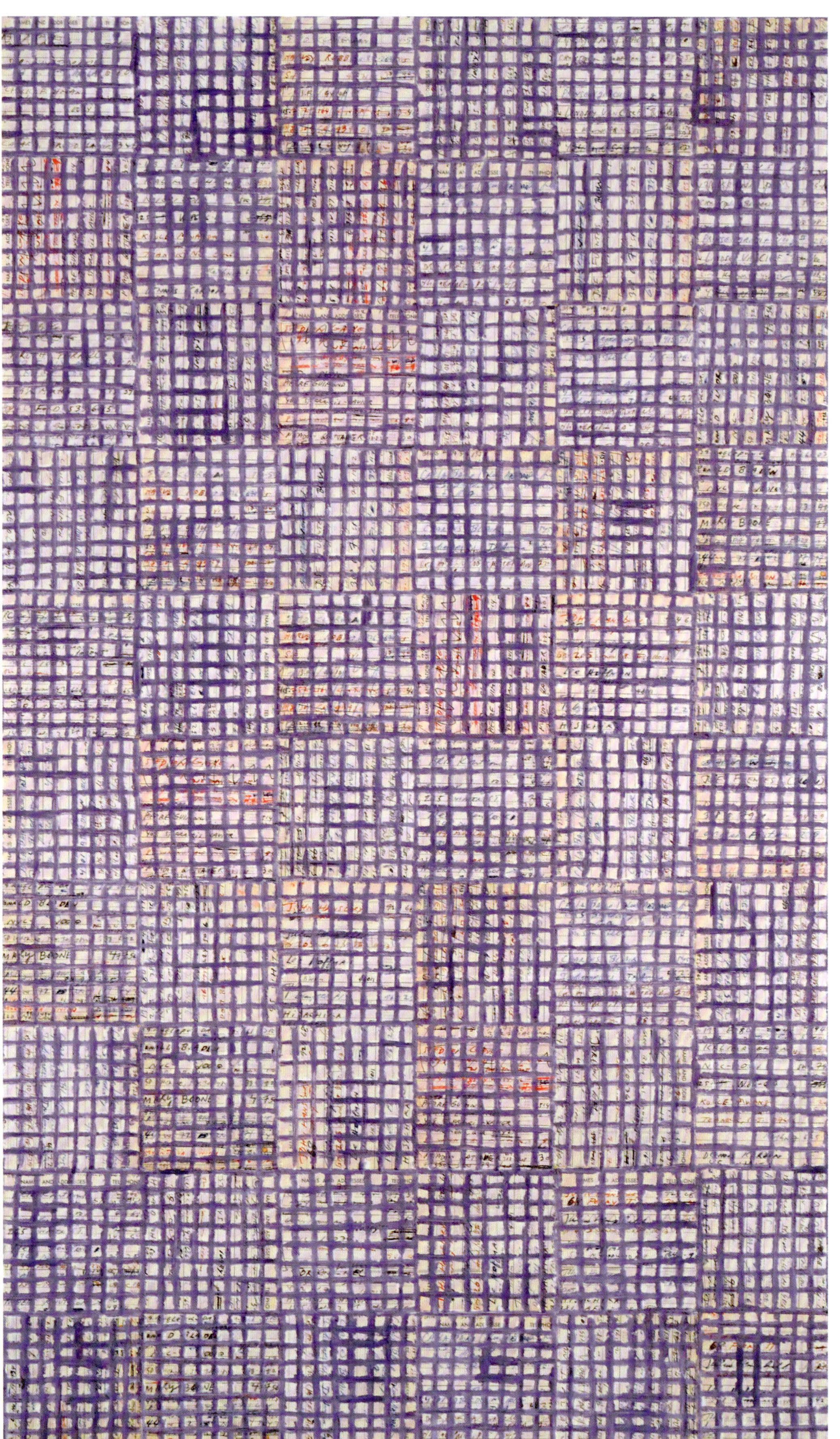

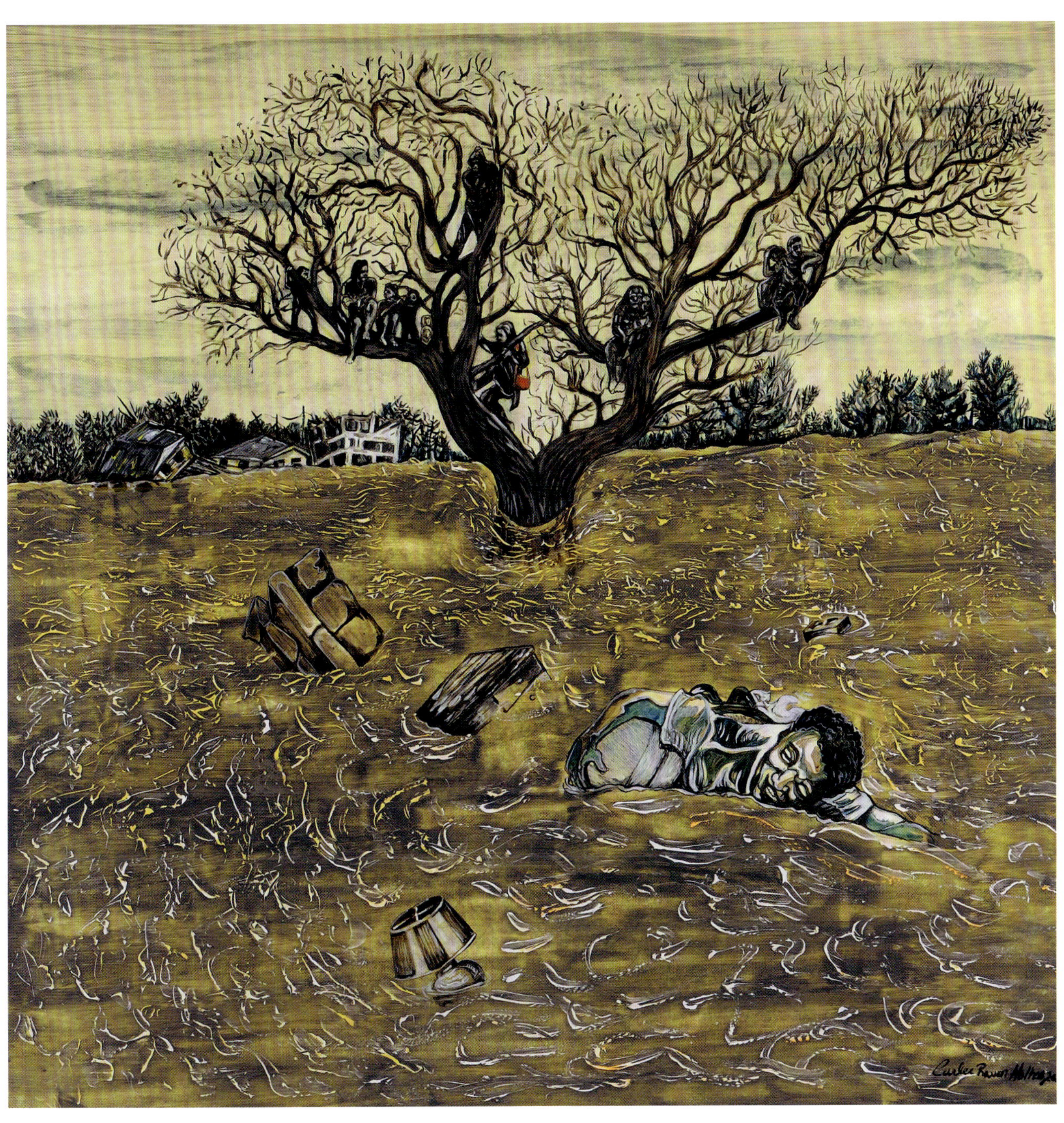

McArthur Binion
DNA Series, 2018,
Mixed media on board,
42" × 25⅞" × 3¼", Courtesy
of the Eric Key Collection,
© McArthur Binion

Curlee Holton
Release, no date, Oil on board,
36" × 36" × 2¼", Courtesy
of the Eric Key Collection,
© Curlee Raven Holton

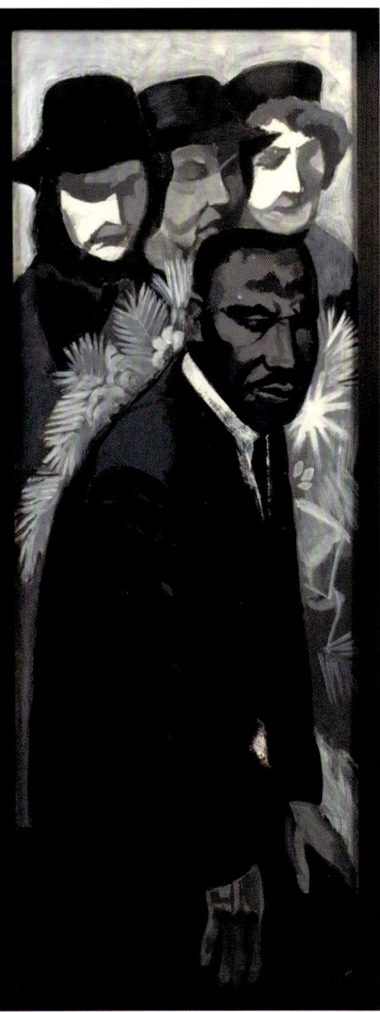
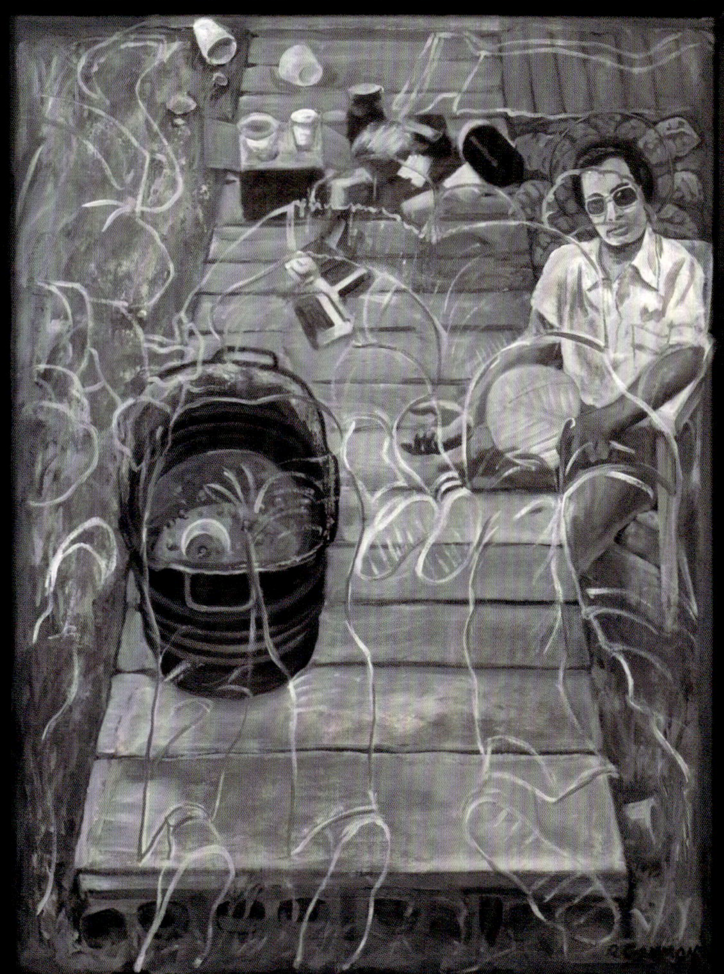
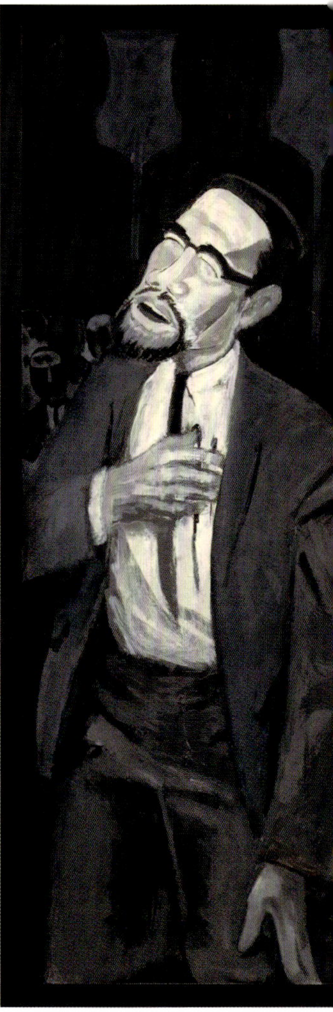

Reginald Gammon
A Triptych for the Black Church (MLK and Mothers), no date, Oil on canvas with gold leaf, 36" × 60" × 2", Courtesy of the Eric Key Collection, © 2023 Estate of Reginald Gammon

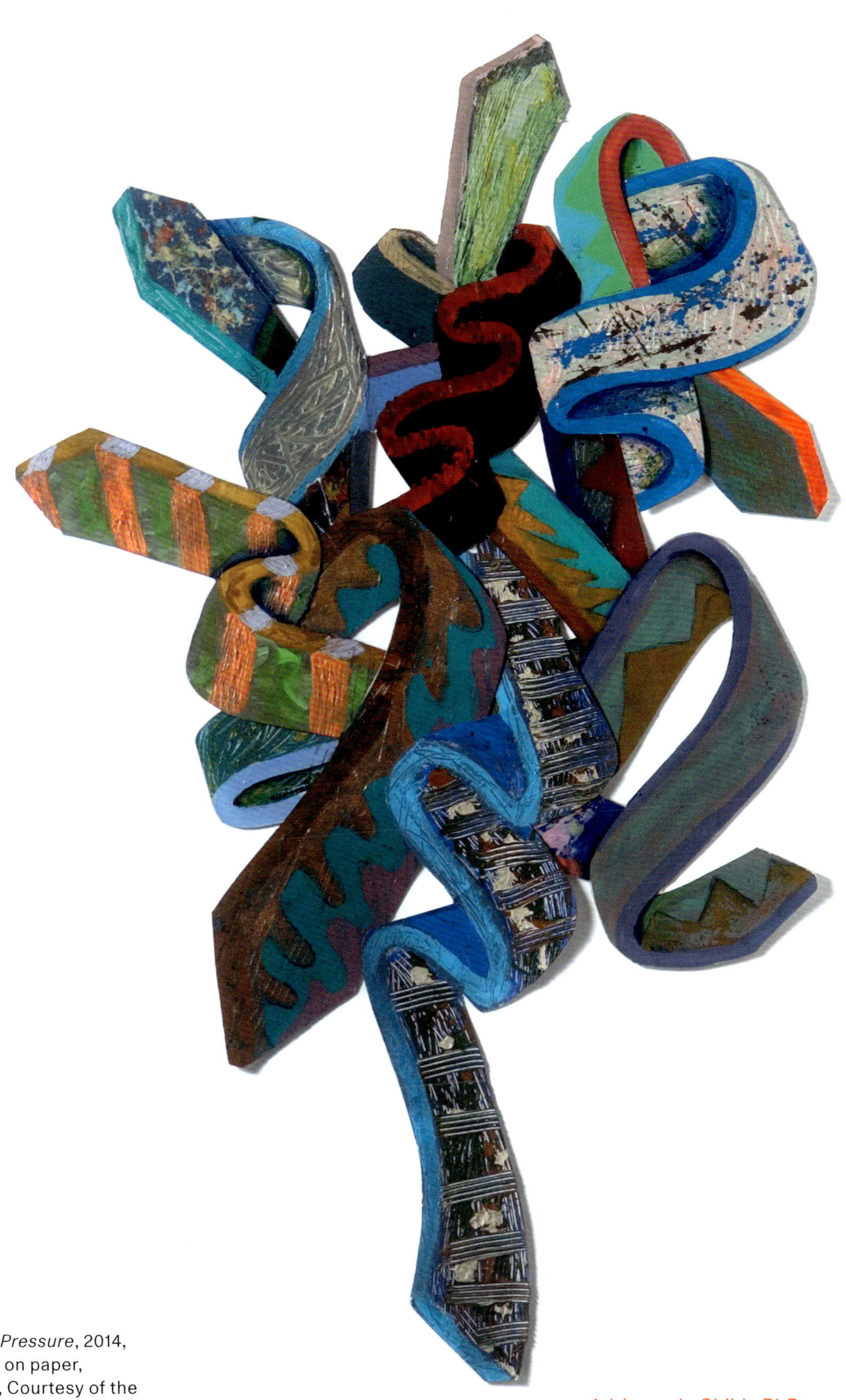

Kevin Cole
Comfort and Pressure, 2014,
Mixed media on paper,
60" × 42" × 2", Courtesy of the
Eric Key Collection, © Kevin Cole

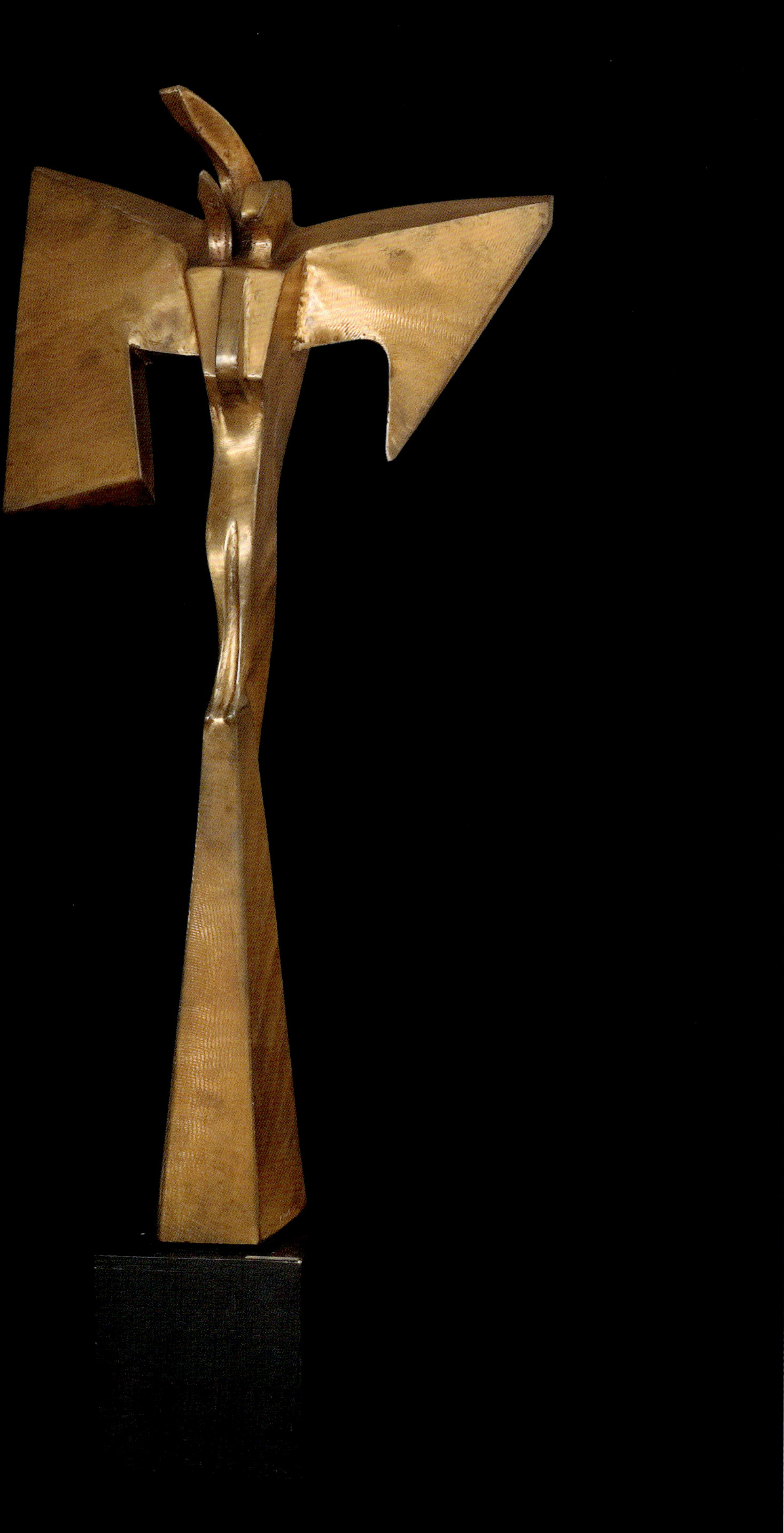

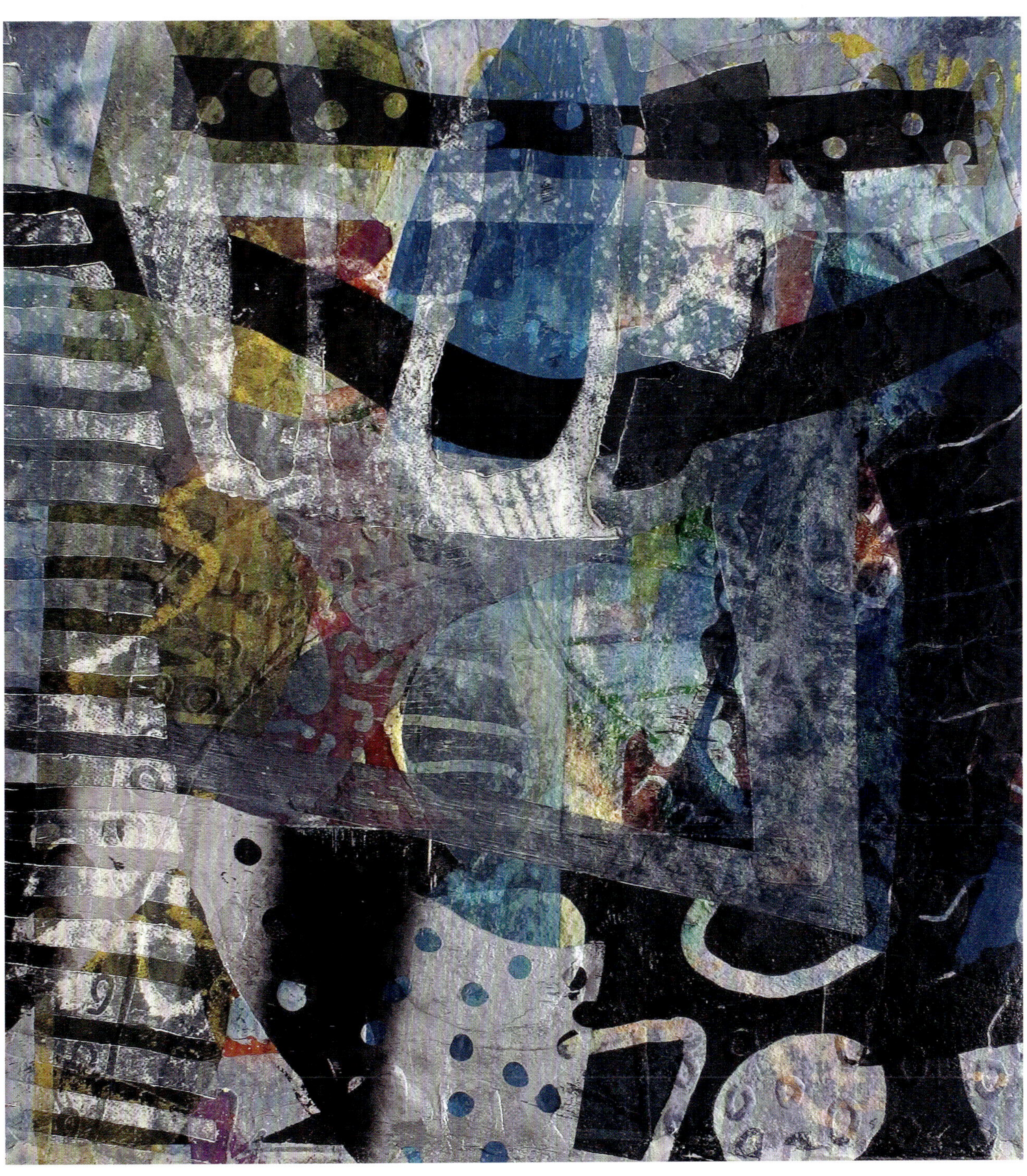

Richard Hunt
Hybrid Figure, 1978,
Welded bronze,
76" × 30" × 12", Courtesy of the Eric Key Collection, © Richard Hunt

Sam Gilliam
Bad River Series, 1988, Mixed media, 50" × 50" × 2", Courtesy of the Eric Key Collection, © 2023 Sam Gilliam / Artists Rights Society (ARS), NY

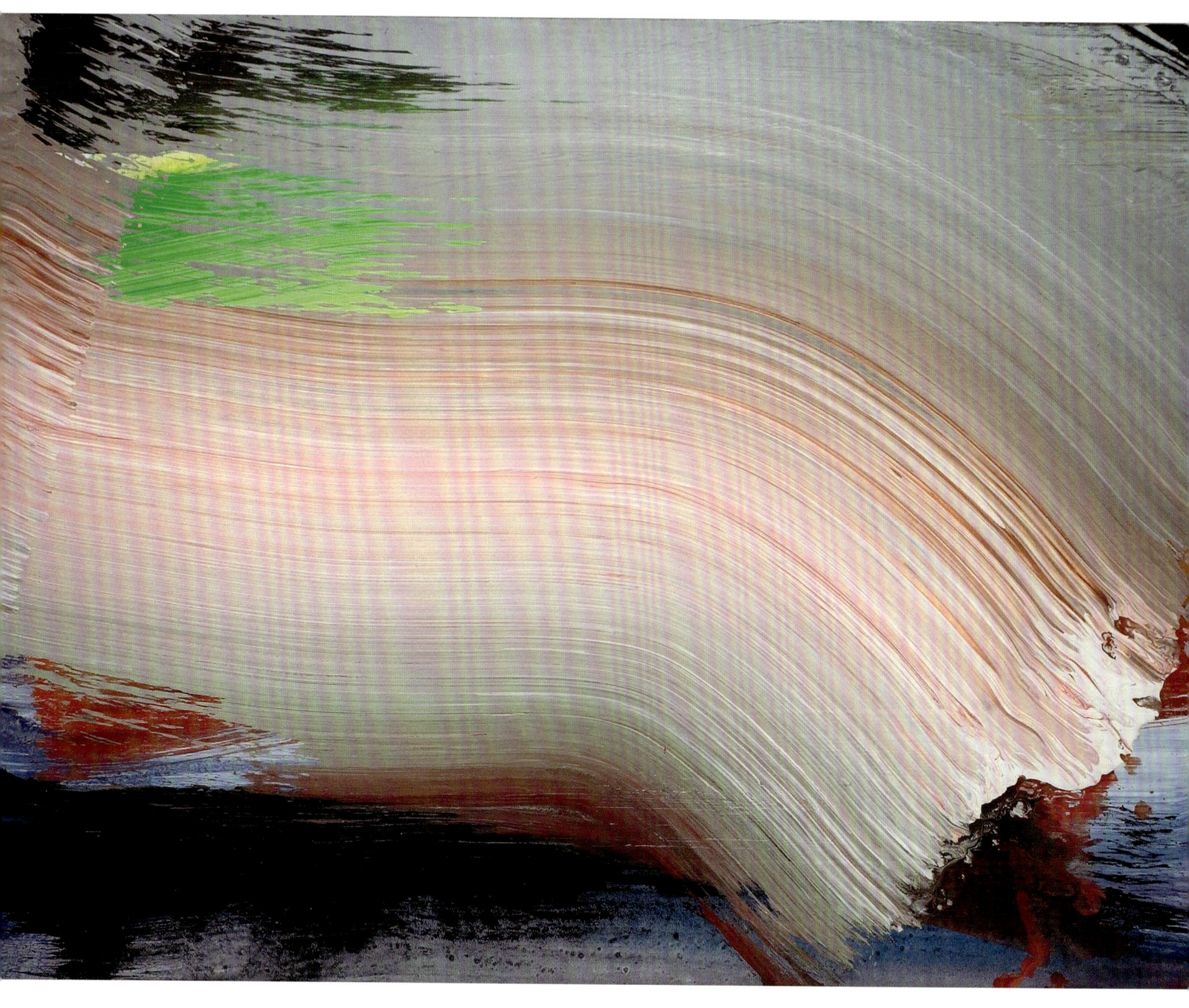

Ed Clark
Untitled (brush painting),
2005, Oil on canvas,
36" × 48" × 2", Courtesy of the
Eric Key Collection, © Ed Clark

Al Loving
Whyte St. #15, 1992,
Mixed media on canvas,
36" × 27" × 2", Courtesy of
the artist and Garth Greenan
Gallery, NY, © Garth Greenan

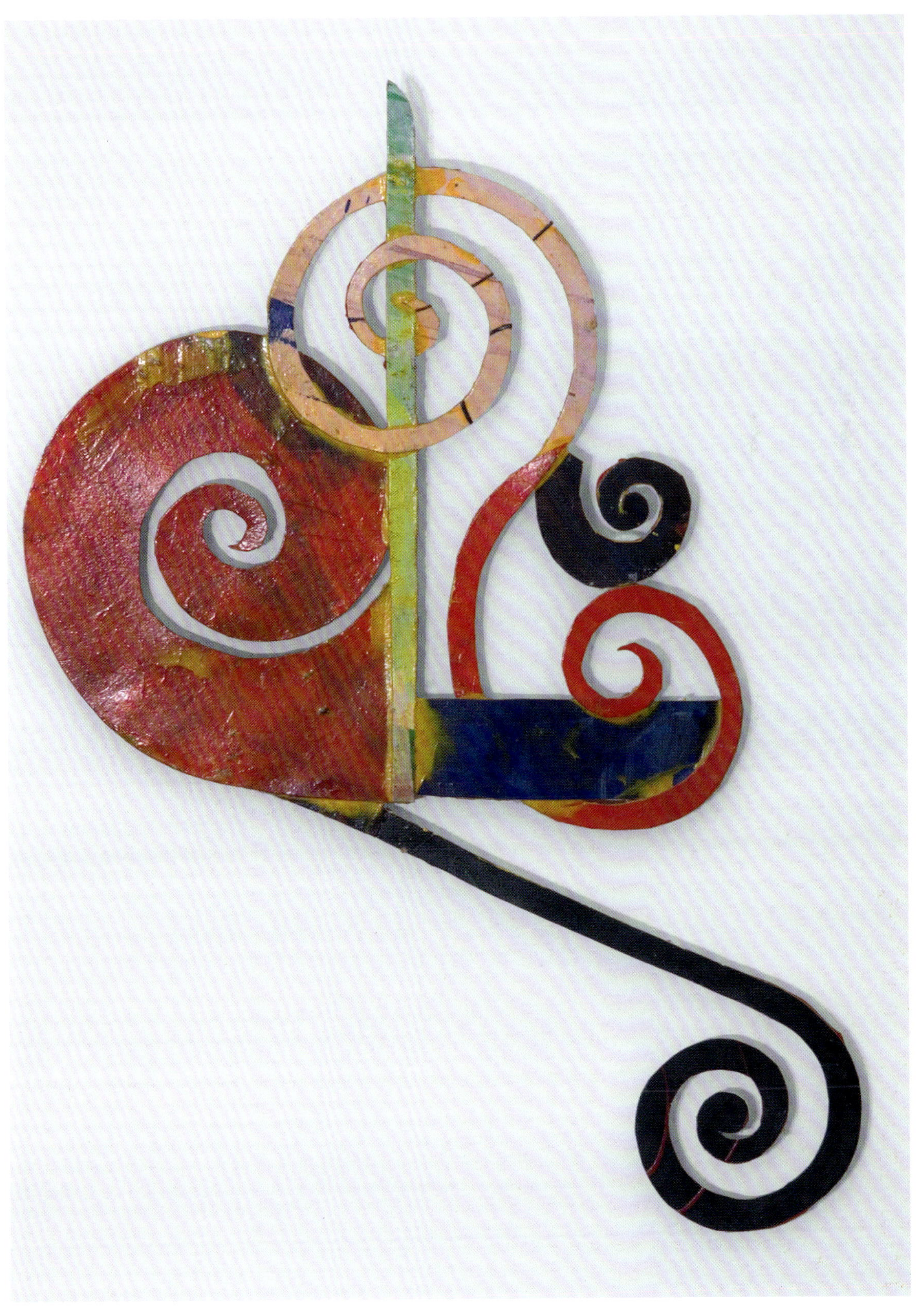

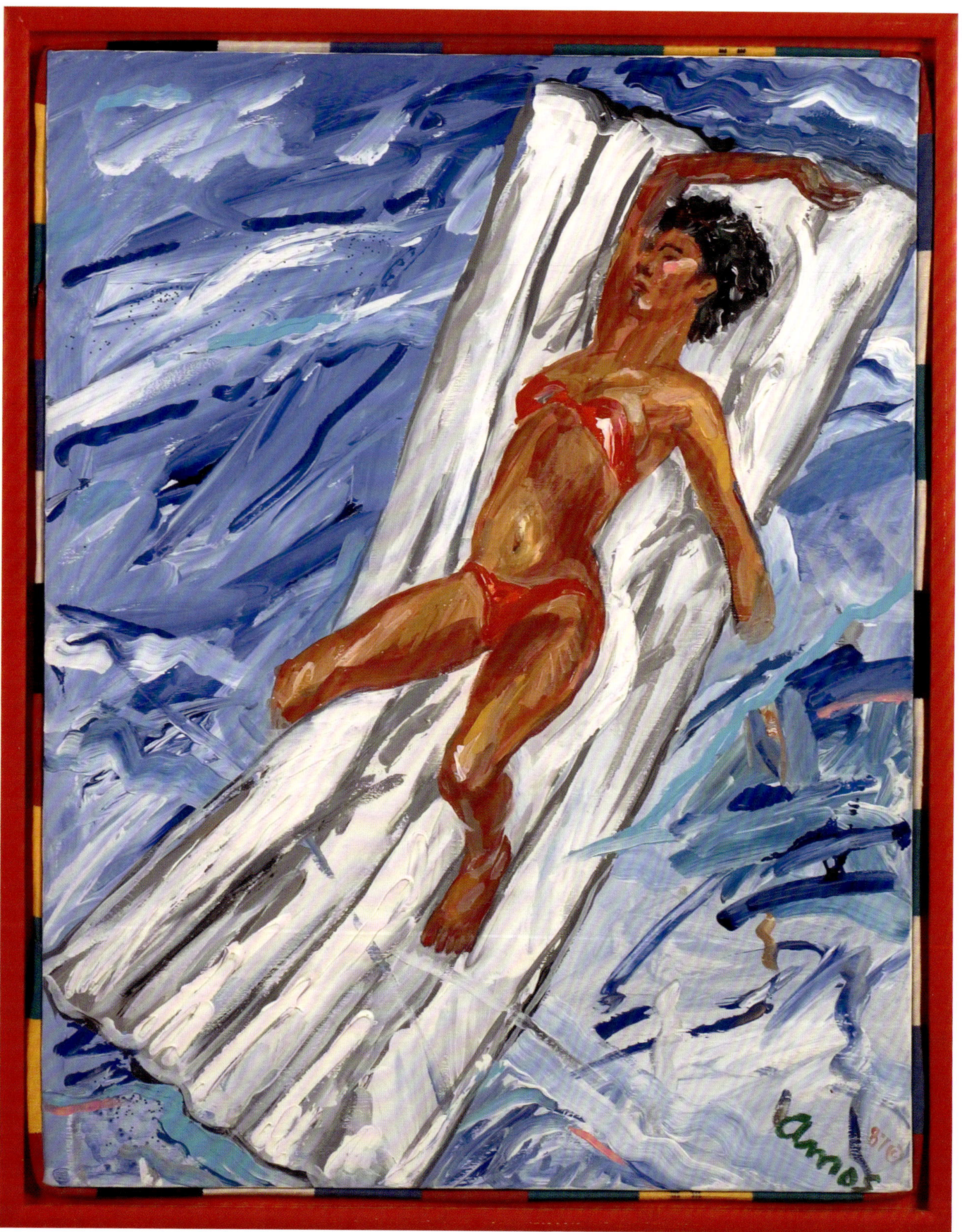

Emma Amos
Sun Babe, 1987, Mixed media on canvas, 30" × 24" × 2", Courtesy of the Eric Key Collection and the Ryan Lee Gallery, NY, © Emma Amos

NOTES

Foreword

1. Freida High Tesfagiorgis, "Afrofemcentrism in the Art of Elizabeth Catlett and Faith Ringgold (a View of Women by Women)," *Sage: A Scholarly Journal on Black Women* 4, no. 1 (1987): 25–32; Lisa Farrington, *Creating Their Own Image: The History of African-American Women Artists* (Oxford: Oxford University Press, 2005); Kellie Jones, "Swimming with E.C.," in *We Wanted a Revolution: Black Radical Women, 1965–85, New Perspectives*, edited by Catherine Morris and Rujeko Hockley (Brooklyn, NY: Brooklyn Museum, 2018).
2. Samella Lewis, interviewed by Karen Anne Mason, UCLA Oral History, 1.2 Tape Number: I Side Two, March 15, 1992, transcript page 32. https://oralhistory.library.ucla.edu/catalog/21198-zz0008zpm5.
3. Christine Y. Kim and Myrtle Elizabeth Andrews, eds., *Black American Portraits: From the Los Angeles County Museum of Art* (Los Angeles, CA: Los Angeles County Museum of Art, 2023); Tricia Hersey, *Rest Is Resistance: A Manifesto*, first ed. (New York: Little, Brown Spark, 2022); Nikki Greene, "Rest: A Pedagogy of Art and Care," Keynote Lecture, Feminist Art History Conference, American University, Washington, DC, September 30, 2023.

Essay 1

1. bell hooks, *Art on My Mind: Visual Politics* (New York: The New Press, 1995).

Essay 2

1. John Stauffer, Zoe Trodd, and Celeste-Marie Bernier, *Picturing Frederick Douglass: An Illustrated Biography of the Nineteenth Century's Most Photographed American* (New York: Liveright Publishing Corporation, 2015), chapter 1, Kindle.
2. See Alain Locke, ed., *The New Negro: An Interpretation* (Mansfield Centre, CT: Martino Publishing, 2015).
3. Barthé's original was sculpted in 1935. In 1986, the Barthé estate issued an edition of 10 bronzes based on the original.
4. James Smalls, "Féral Benga: African Muse of Modernism," *Nka* 41 (November 2017): 45–59.
5. Email communication with the artist, November 14, 2023.
6. Kinitra Brooks, Kameelah L. Martin and LaKisha Simmons, "Conjure Feminism: Toward a Genealogy," *Hypatia* 36, no. 3: 452–461. doi:10.1017/hyp.2021.43. See also Kameelah L. Martin, "Black Feminist Voodoo Aesthetics, Conjure Feminism, and the Arts," in *In the Black Fantastic*, ed. Ekow Eshun (Cambridge, MA: The MIT Press, 2022), 137–144.
7. For more on the issues around abstraction and Black artists in the 1960s and 1970s, see Darby English, *1971: A Year in the Life of Color* (Chicago: The University of Chicago Press, 2016).
8. Hale Woodruff in "The Black Artist in America: A Symposium," *The Metropolitan Museum of Art Bulletin* 27, no. 5 (January 1969): 253.
9. "A Conversation with Richard Hunt and Adrienne L. Childs," in *Richard Hunt* (New York: Gregory R. Miller and Co., 2022), 281–282.

APPENDIX

Additional works from the Key Collection & Exhibition

2

3

1

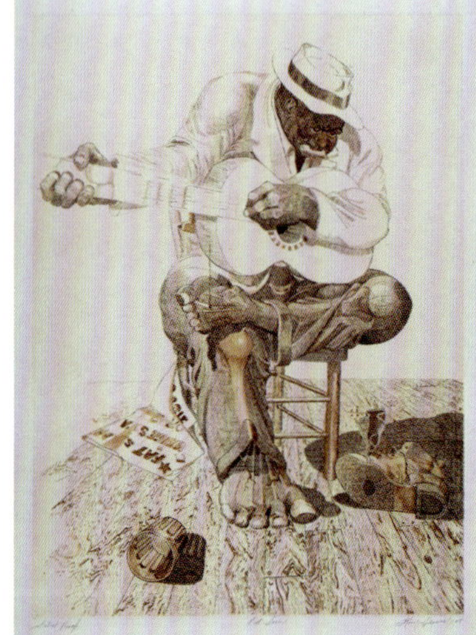

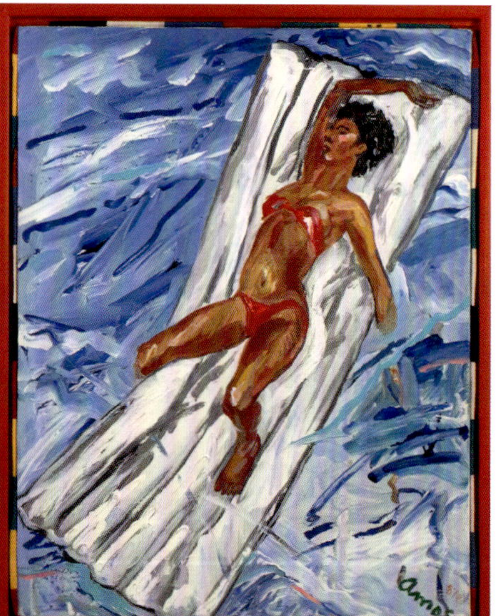

4

5

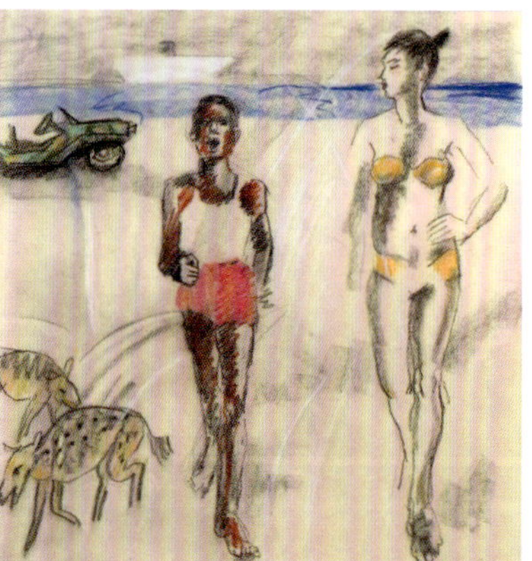

Cat. 1
Ron Adams, *Fat Sam*, 2005, Etching on paper, 30" × 22", Courtesy of the Eric Key Collection, © Ron Adams.

Cat. 2
Ron Adams, *Mr. Blues*, no date, Color etching on paper, 13½" × 13½", Courtesy of the Eric Key Collection, © Ron Adams.

Cat. 3
Amalia Amaki, *Latch Key*, 2018, Mixed media, 30¼" × 20" × 3½", Courtesy of the Eric Key Collection, © Amalia Amaki.

Cat. 4
Emma Amos, *Sun Babe*, 1987, Mixed media on canvas, 30" × 24" × 2", Courtesy of the Ryan Lee Gallery, NY and the Eric Key Collection, © Emma Amos.

Cat. 5
Emma Amos, *The Beach*, 1987, Pastel on paper, 42" × 40" × 2", Courtesy of the Ryan Lee Gallery, NY and the Eric Key Collection, © Emma Amos.

6

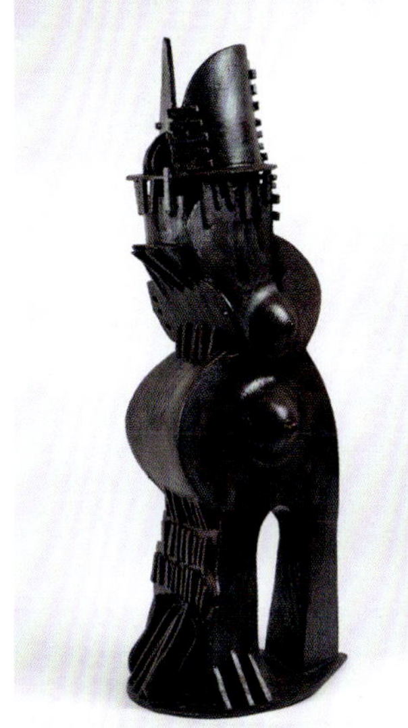

7

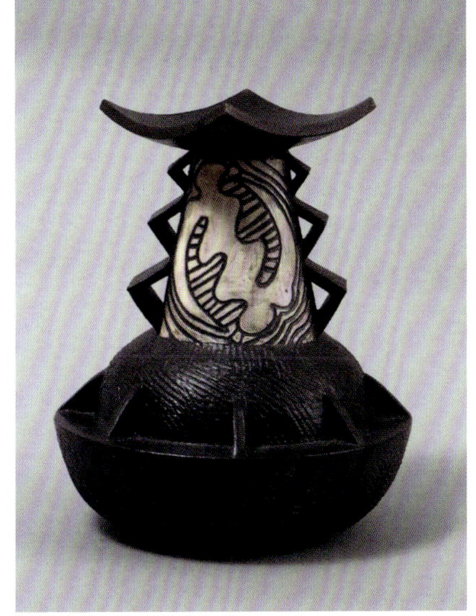

9

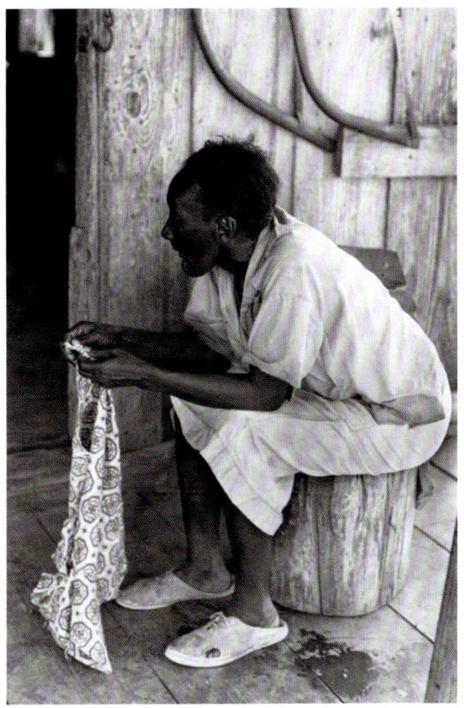

8

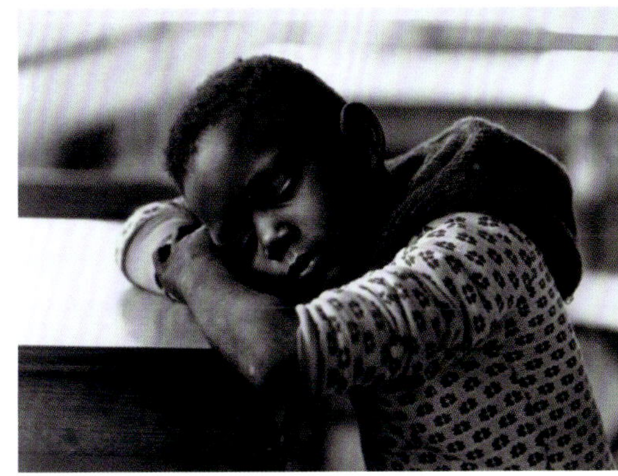

10

Cat. 6
Kwabena Ampofo-Anti, *Bonobodo*, 2002, Ceramic, 34" × 15" × 10", Courtesy of the Eric Key Collection, © Kwabena Ampofo-Anti.

Cat. 7
Kwabena Ampofo-Anti, *Vessel*, 2015, Glazed clay, 8" in diameter, Courtesy of the Eric Key Collection, © Kwabena Ampofo-Anti.

Cat. 8
William Anderson, *Boy Sleeping*, 1968, Photograph, 22" × 21", Courtesy of the Eric Key Collection, © William Anderson.

Cat. 9
William Anderson, *One Minute to Rest*, 1968, Photograph, 22" × 18", Courtesy of the Eric Key Collection, © William Anderson.

Cat. 10
William Anderson, *Untitled (Female wood carving)*, 1970s, Wood, 36" × 25" × 25", Courtesy of the Eric Key Collection, © William Anderson.

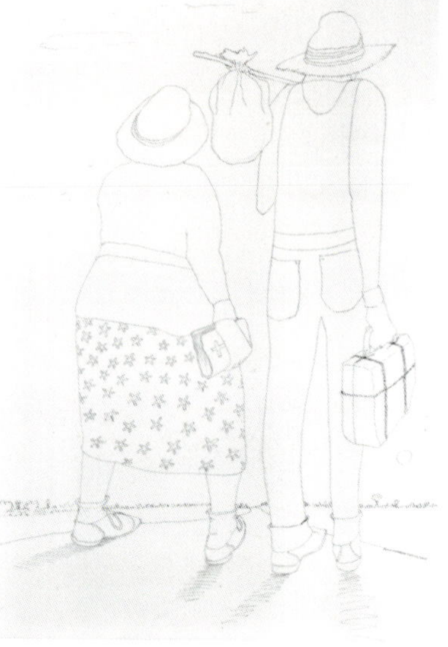

12

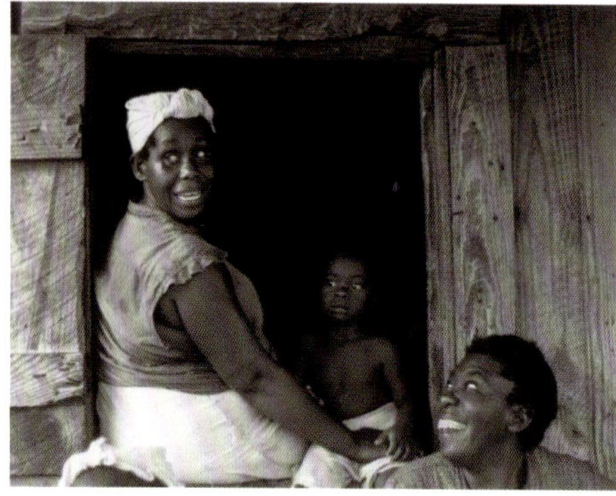

11

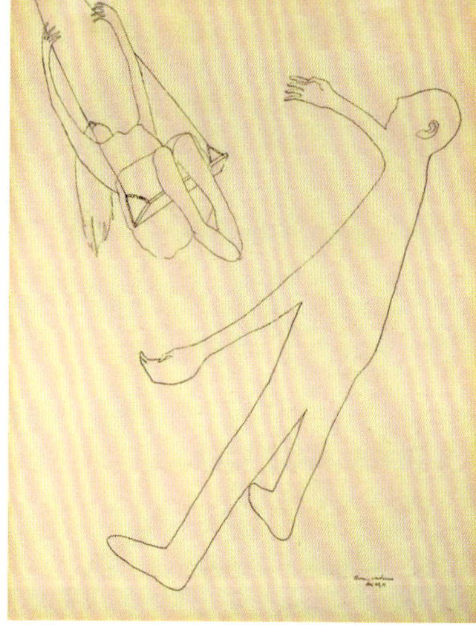

13

14

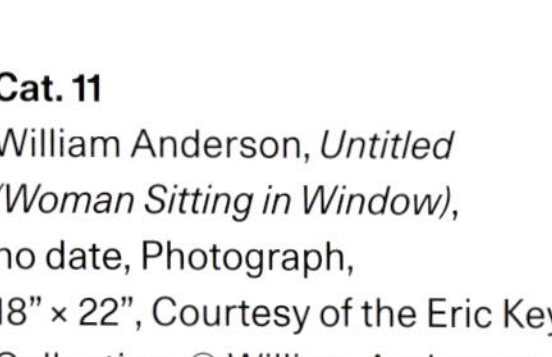

Cat. 11
William Anderson, *Untitled (Woman Sitting in Window)*, no date, Photograph, 18" × 22", Courtesy of the Eric Key Collection, © William Anderson.

Cat. 12
Benny Andrews, *Going North*, 2000, Graphite on paper, 30¼" × 21½", Courtesy of the Eric Key Collection, © 2023 Estate of Benny Andrews / Licensed by VAGA at Artists Rights Society (ARS), NY, Courtesy Michael Rosenfeld Gallery, LLC, New York, NY.

Cat. 13
Benny Andrews, *Untitled*, 1967, Ink on paper, 17" × 14", Courtesy of the Eric Key Collection, © 2023 Estate of Benny Andrews / Licensed by VAGA at Artists Rights Society (ARS), NY, Courtesy Michael Rosenfeld Gallery, LLC,New York, NY.

Cat. 14
Benny Andrews, *Untitled (image seating on rock)*, no date, Etching on paper, 22" × 22", Courtesy of the Eric Key Collection, © 2023 Estate of Benny Andrews / Licensed by VAGA at Artists Rights Society (ARS), NY, Courtesy Michael Rosenfeld Gallery, LLC, New York, NY.

15

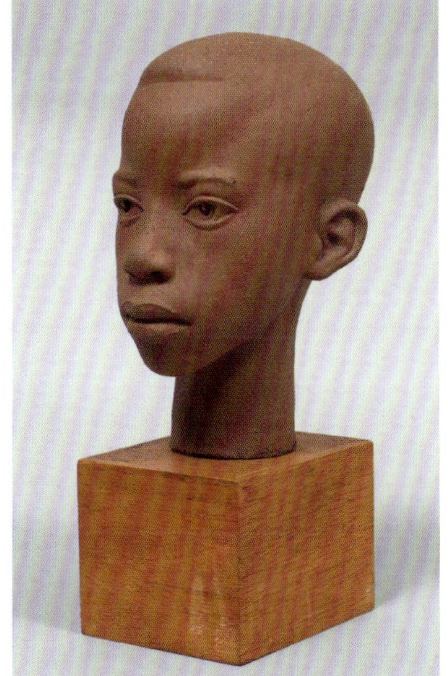

16

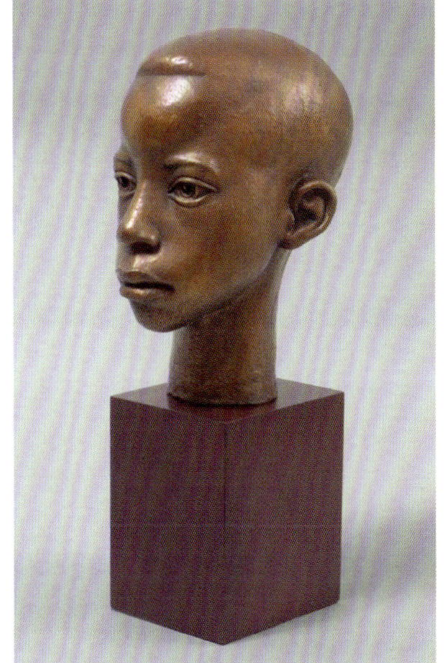

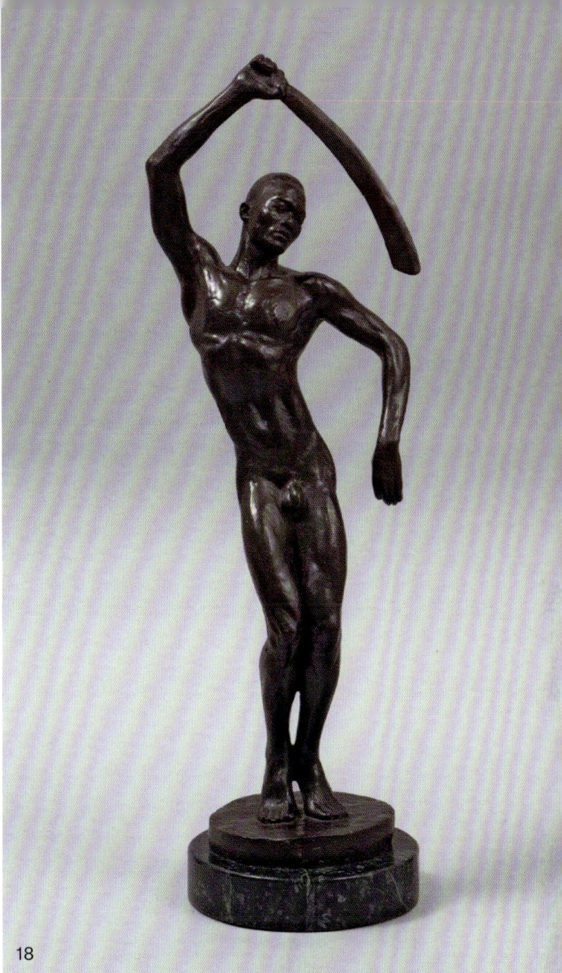

18

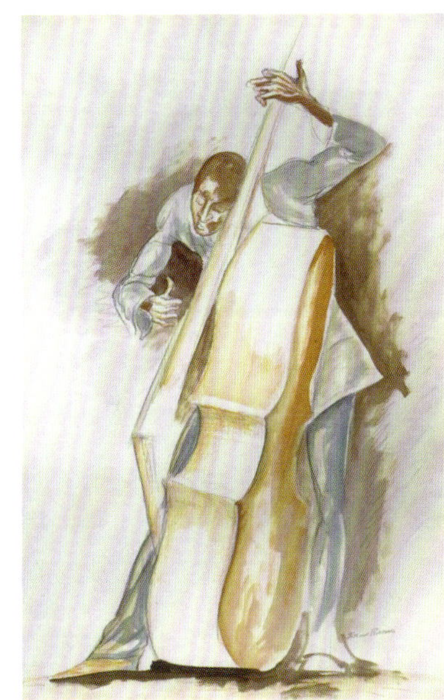

17

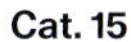

Cat. 15
William E. Artis, *Michael*, 1950, Terra cotta, 9" × 6" × 7", Courtesy of the Eric Key Collection, © William E. Artis.

Cat. 16
William E. Artis, *Michael (bronze Head of a Boy)*, 1950, Bronze, 9" × 6" × 7", Courtesy of the Eric Key Collection, © William E. Artis.

Cat. 17
Ernie Eugene Barnes, *Bass Cello Player*, no date, Watercolor and pencil on paper, 47" × 34" × 2", Courtesy of the Eric Key Collection, © Ernie Eugene Barnes.

Cat. 18
Richmond Barthé, *Feral Benga*, 1986, Bronze, 19" × 4½" × 4½", Courtesy of the Eric Key Collection, © Richmond Barthé.

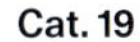

Cat. 19
Richmond Barthé, *Head of a Negro Boy*, no date, Hollow bronze, 6¼" × 4¼" × 4", Courtesy of the Eric Key Collection, © Richmond Barthé.

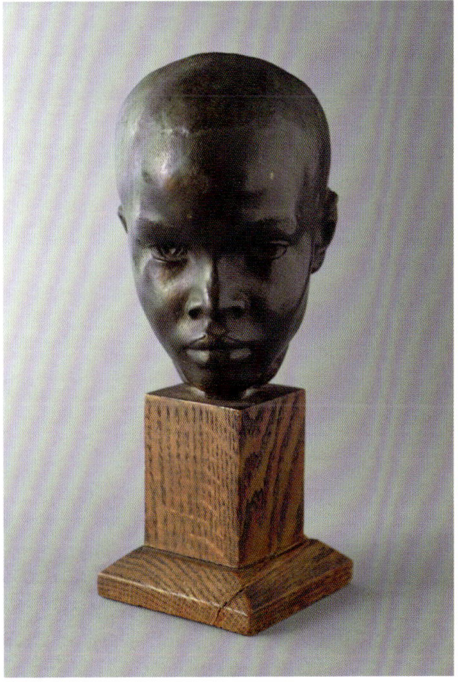

19

21

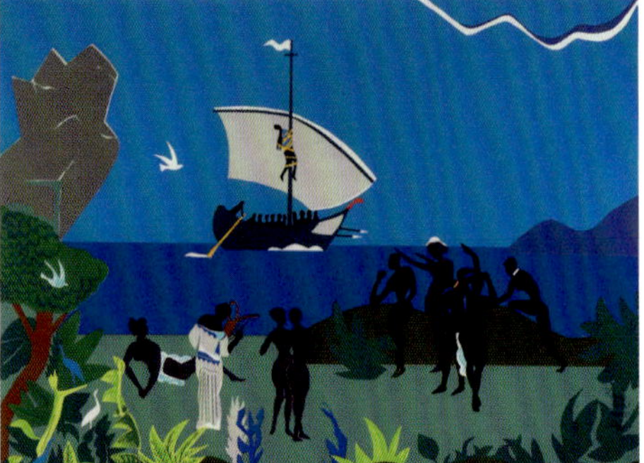

22

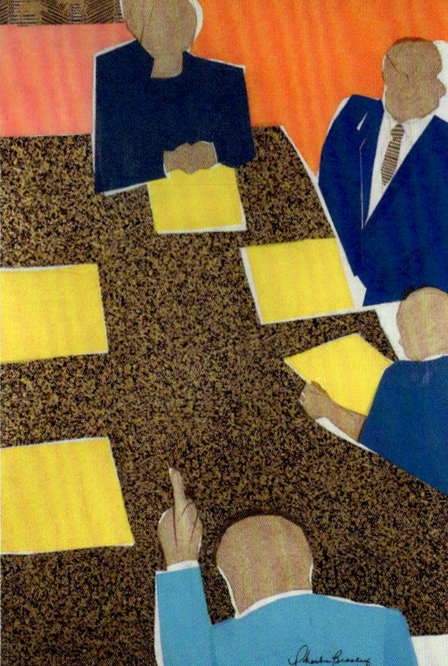

20

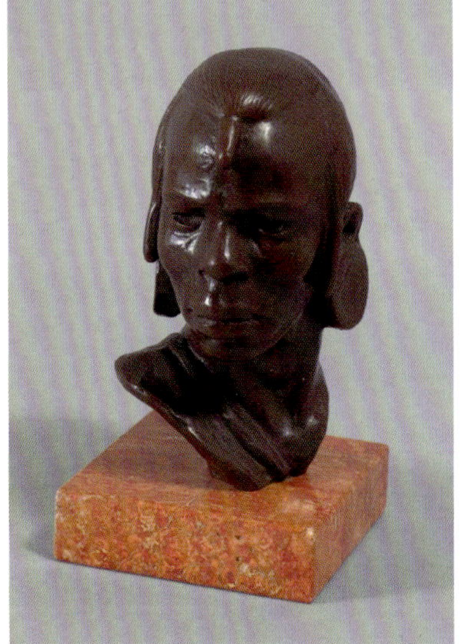

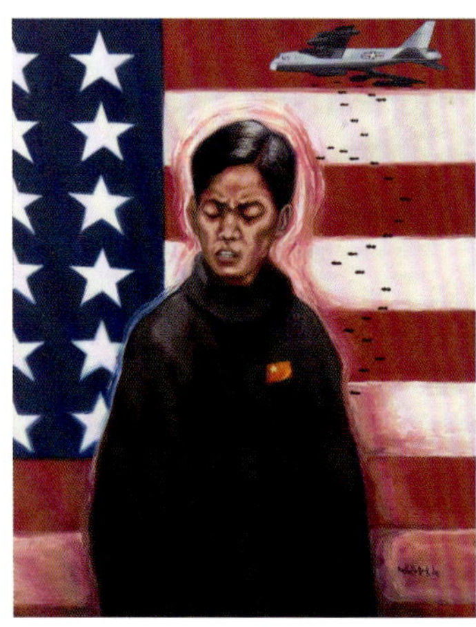

23

24

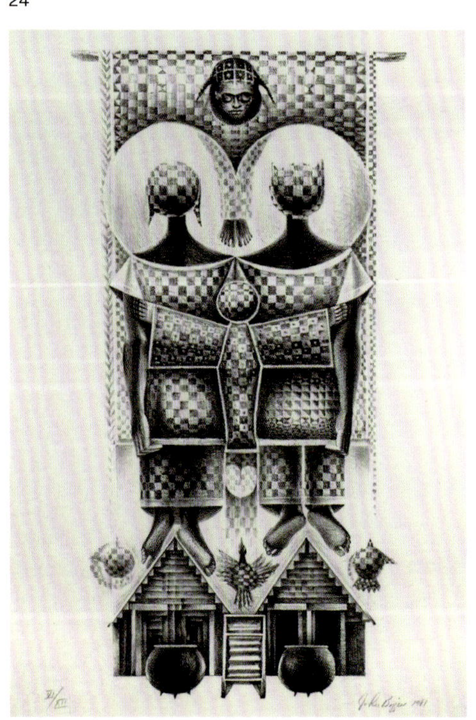

Cat. 20
Richmond Barthé, *Masai Warrior*, 1933, Bronze, 6¼" × 4" × 4½", Courtesy of the Eric Key Collection, © Richmond Barthé.

Cat. 21
Romare Bearden, *Odysseus Series: Odysseus Leaves Nausicaa*, 1979, Color screenprint on wove Lana paper, 26" × 31½", Courtesy of the Eric Key Collection, © 2023 Romare Bearden Foundation / Licensed by VAGA at Artists Rights Society (ARS), NY.

Cat. 22
Phoebe Beasley, *Yellow Legal Pad #3*, 1999, Collage, 36" × 24" × 2", Courtesy of the Eric Key Collection, © Phoebe Beasley.

Cat. 23
Arthello Beck, *Vietnam*, no date, Oil on canvas, 40" × 30", Courtesy of the Eric Key Collection, © Arthello Beck.

Cat. 24
John Biggers, *Quilting Party*, 1981, Lithograph on paper, 35½" × 24", Courtesy of the Eric Key Collection, © 2023 John T. Biggers Estate / Licensed by VAGA at Artists Rights Society (ARS), NY, Estate Represented by Michael Rosenfeld Gallery.

25

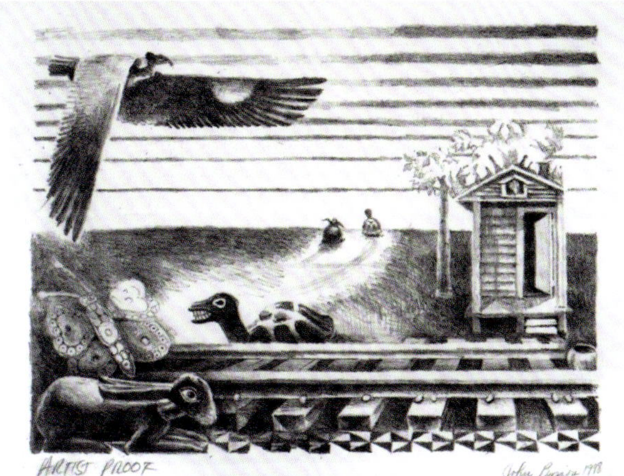

27

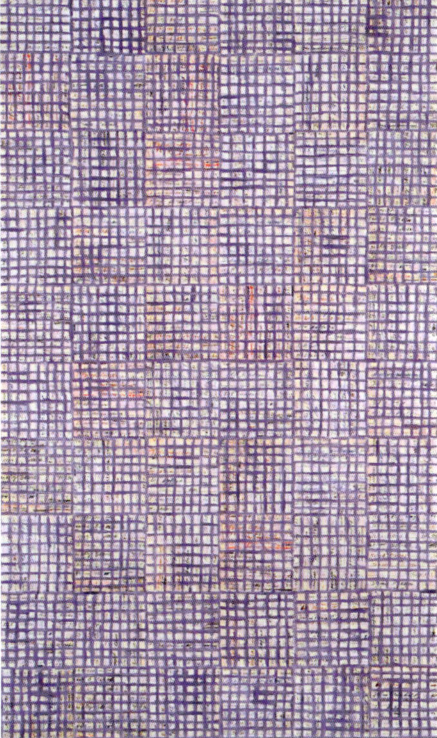

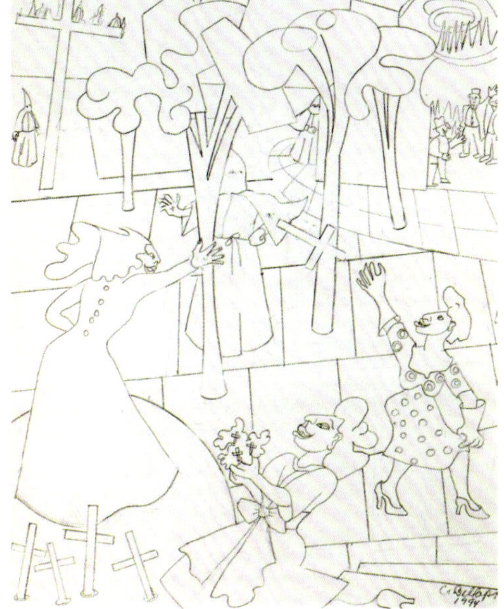

26

28

Cat. 25
John Biggers, *Turtle & Hare*, 1998, Lithograph on paper, 24" × 32", Courtesy of the Eric Key Collection, © 2023 John T. Biggers Estate / Licensed by VAGA at Artists Rights Society (ARS), NY, Estate Represented by Michael Rosenfeld Gallery.

Cat. 26
Camille Billops, *Untitled (The KKK Boutique)*, 1994, Pencil on paper, 19" × 17" × 2", Courtesy of the Eric Key Collection, the estate of the artist, and Ryan Lee Gallery, NY, © Camille Billops.

Cat. 27
McArthur Binion, *DNA Series*, 2018, Mixed media on board, 42" × 25⅞" × 3¼", Courtesy of the Eric Key Collection, © McArthur Binion.

Cat. 28
McArthur Binion, *Driving Through Mississippi in Chicago (Two)*, 2008, Paint stick, Staonal crayon, laser image and sepia ink on masonite, 26" × 24", Courtesy of the Eric Key Collection, © McArthur Binion.

29 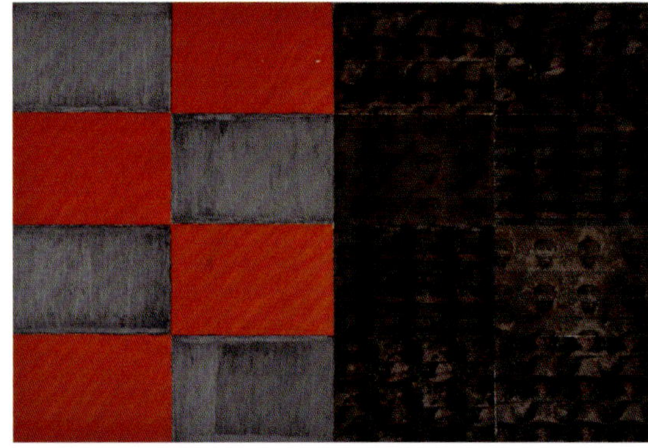

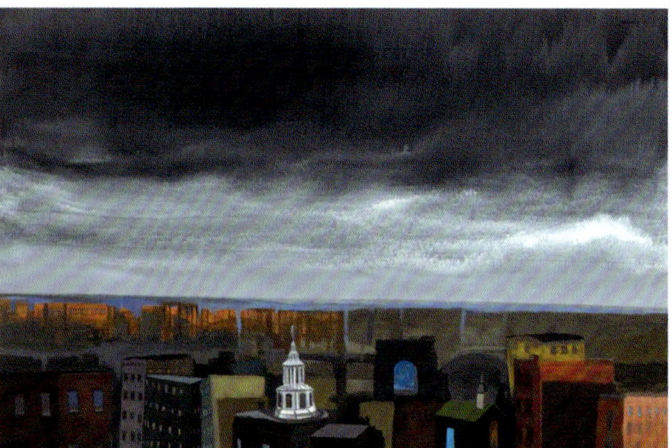 30

31 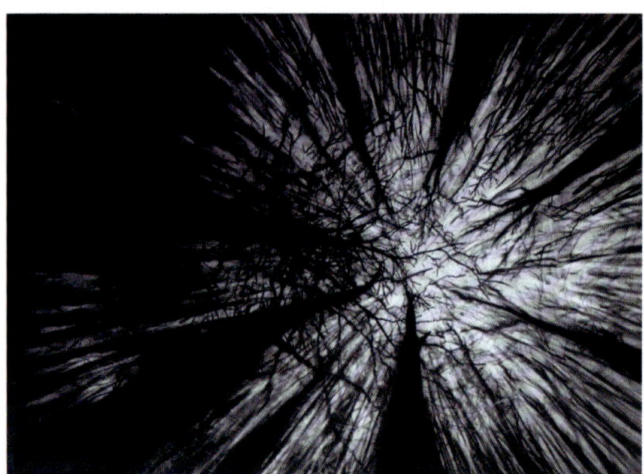

32 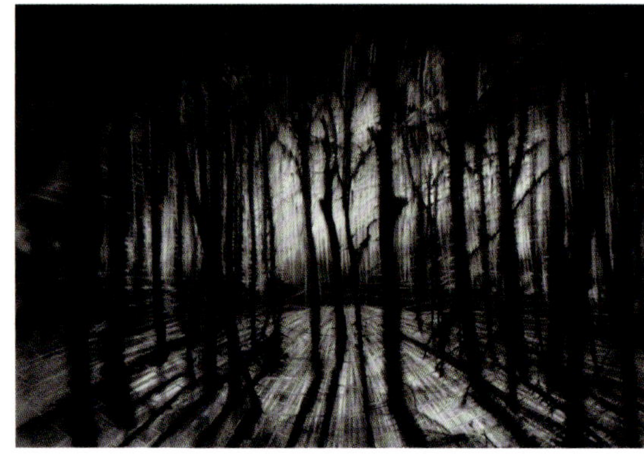

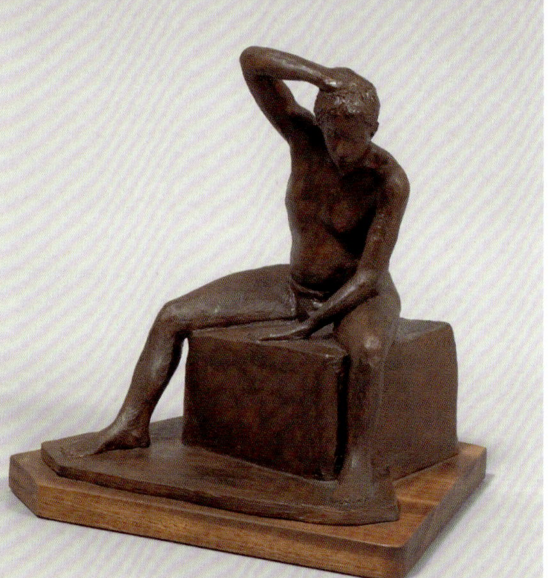 33

Cat. 29
McArthur Binion, *House Work #18*, 2009, Color pencil, ink, laser copy, 27 ¾" × 32", Courtesy of the Eric Key Collection, © McArthur Binion.

Cat. 30
James Brantley, *Balance of Power on the Street Where You Live*, no date, Acrylic on board, 33" × 47" × 2", Courtesy of the Eric Key Collection, © James Brantley.

Cat. 31
Ed Brown, *Light and Shadow*, 2015, Charcoal on paper, 46" × 40" × 2", Courtesy of the Eric Key Collection, © Ed Brown.

Cat. 32
Ed Brown, *Untitled (sun through forest)*, 2010, Charcoal on paper, 39½" × 50", Courtesy of the Eric Key Collection, © Ed Brown.

Cat. 33
Manuelita Brown, *Untitled*, 2012, Bronze, 11" × 10" × 9", Courtesy of the Eric Key Collection, © Manuelita Brown.

34

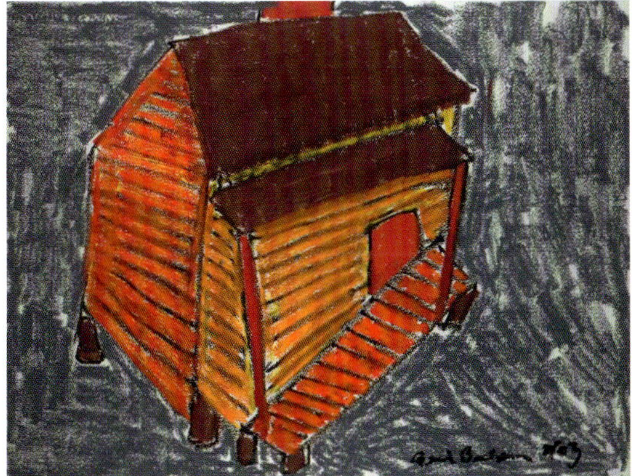

35

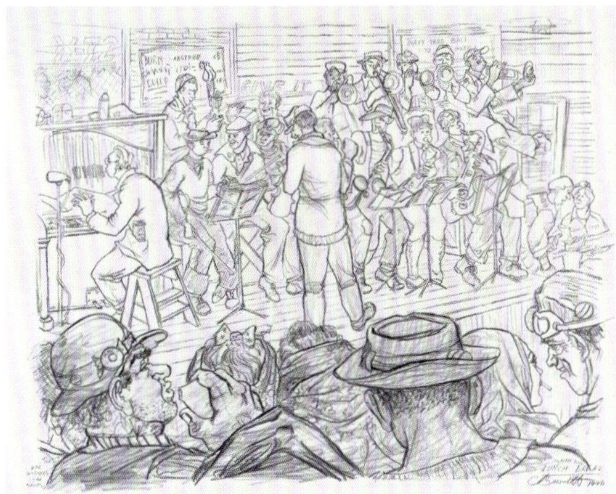

36

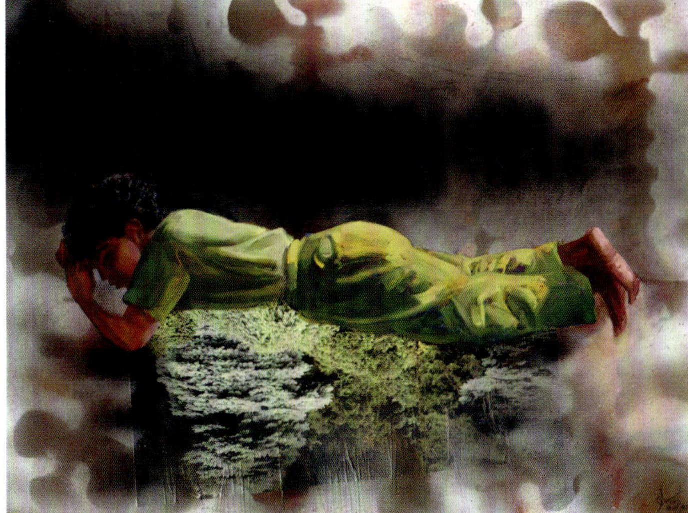

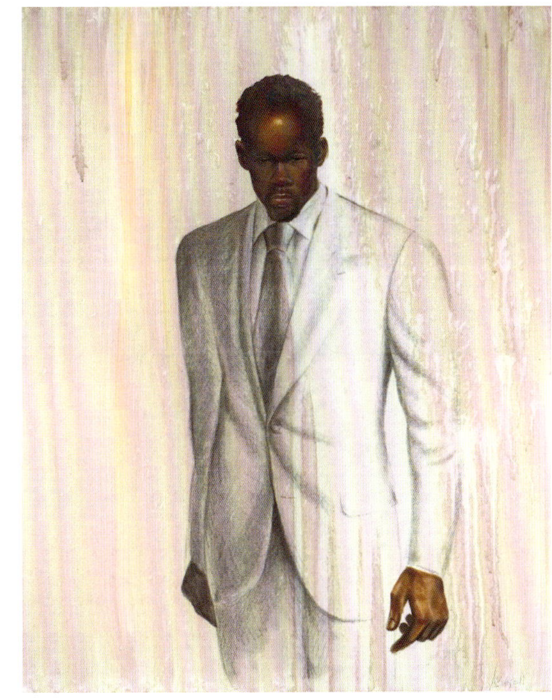

37

Cat. 34
Beverly Buchanan, *Orange Shack*, 2003, Oil pastel on paper, 30½" × 38", Courtesy of the Eric Key Collection, © Beverly Buchanan.

Cat. 35
Calvin Burnett, *Navy Yard Lunch Break, War Worker Series*, 1996, Graphite on paper, 31" × 35", Courtesy of the Eric Key Collection, © 2023 Estate of Calvin Burnett / Licensed by VAGA at Artists Rights Society (ARS), NY.

Cat. 36
Calvin Burnett, *Untitled (boy sleeping)*, 1990, Oil on canvas, 31¼" × 41", Courtesy of the Eric Key Collection, © 2023 Estate of Calvin Burnett / Licensed by VAGA at Artists Rights Society (ARS), NY.

Cat. 37
Al Burts, *Cinderella Man*, 2011, Oil on canvas, 60" × 48" × 2", Courtesy of the Eric Key Collection, © Al Burts.

39

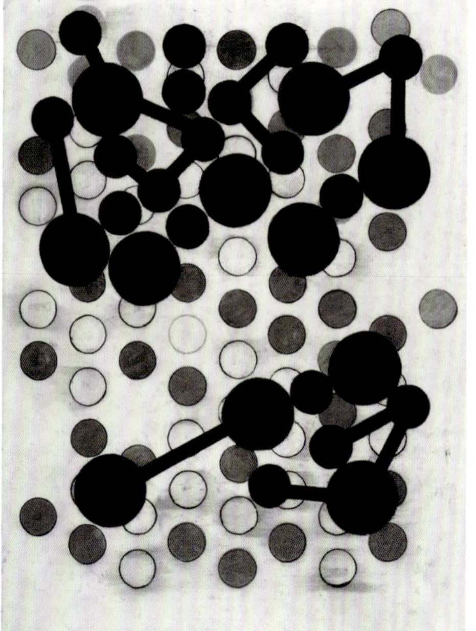

38

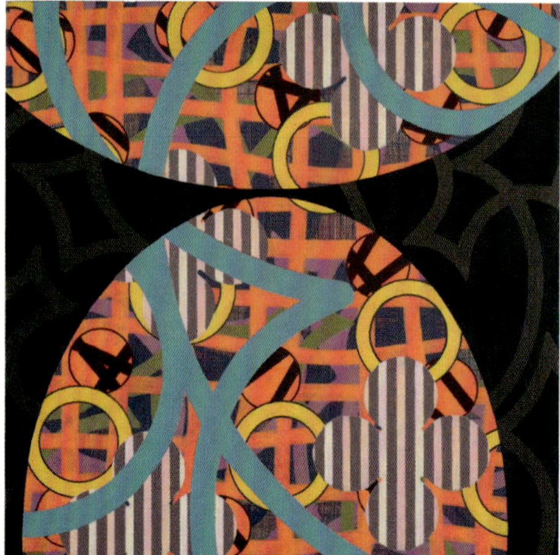

40

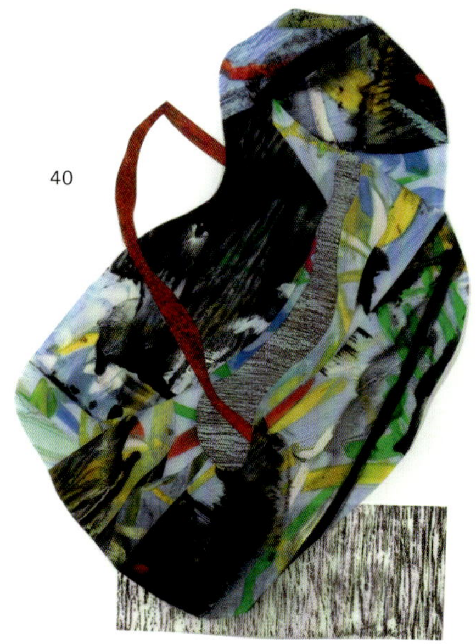

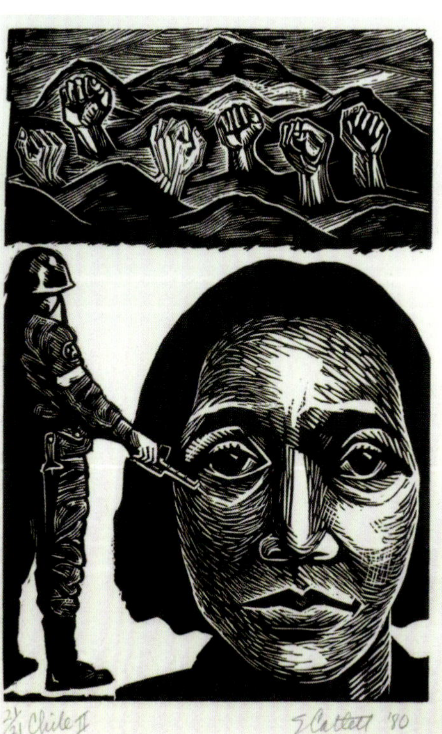

41

Cat. 38
Charles Burwell, *Curved Grid*, 2020, Acrylic on panel, 12" × 12" × 2", Courtesy of the Eric Key Collection, © Charles Burwell.

Cat. 39
Charles Burwell, *Order and Displacement 4-3-2019*, 2020, Acrylic on panel, 18" × 24" × 2", Courtesy of the Eric Key Collection, © Charles Burwell.

Cat. 40
Nanette Carter, *Untitled,* 2007, Paint on Mylar, 14" × 10", Courtesy of the Eric Key Collection, © Nanette Carter.

Cat. 41
Elizabeth Catlett, *Chile II*, 1980, Lithograph, 12" × 8", Courtesy of the Eric Key Collection, © 2023 Mora-Catlett Family / Licensed by VAGA at Artists Rights Society (ARS), NY.

42

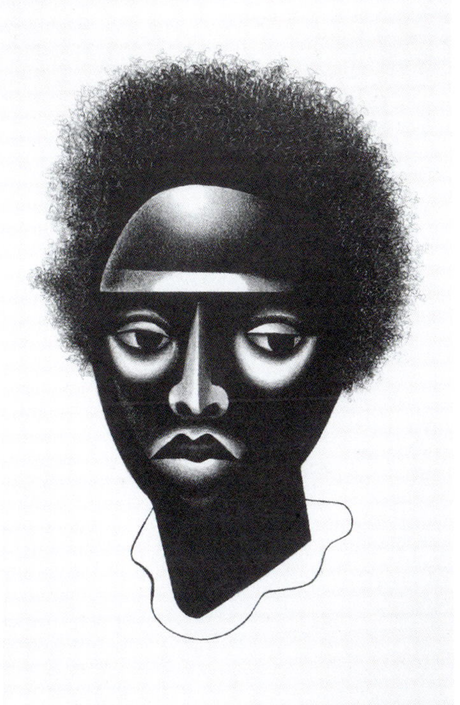

43

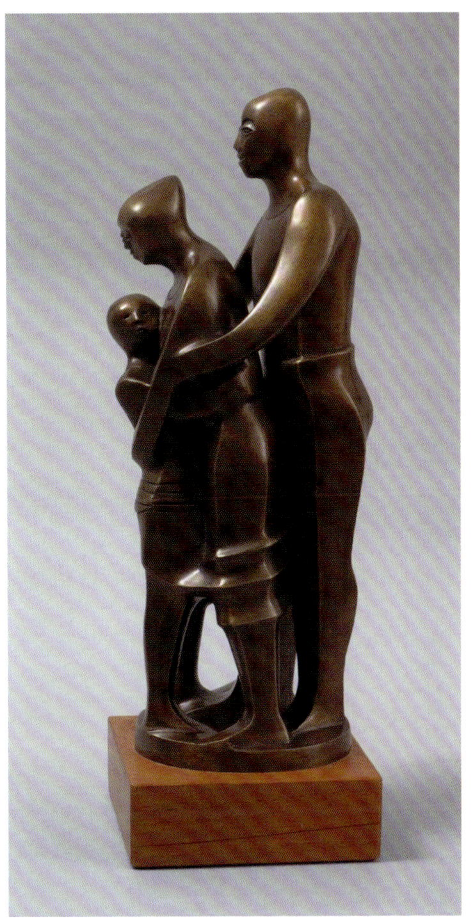

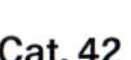

Cat. 42
Elizabeth Catlett, *Clarice (also known as Black Girl)*, 2004, Lithograph on paper, 18" × 12", Courtesy of the Eric Key Collection, © 2023 Mora-Catlett Family / Licensed by VAGA at Artists Rights Society (ARS), NY.

Cat. 43
Elizabeth Catlett, *Family*, 2022, Bronze, 15" × 5½" × 5", Courtesy of the Eric Key Collection, © 2023 Mora-Catlett Family / Licensed by VAGA at Artists Rights Society (ARS), NY.

Cat. 44
Elizabeth Catlett, *Glory*, 1981, Bronze with black patina, 13½" × 8" × 9½", Courtesy of the Eric Key Collection, © 2023 Mora-Catlett Family / Licensed by VAGA at Artists Rights Society (ARS), NY.

Cat. 45
Elizabeth Catlett, *Madonna*, 1982, Lithograph on paper, 42" × 35", Courtesy of the Eric Key Collection, © 2023 Mora-Catlett Family / Licensed by VAGA at Artists Rights Society (ARS), NY.

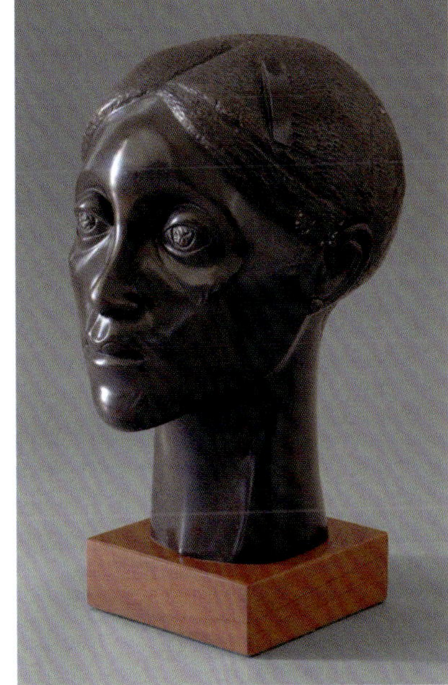

44

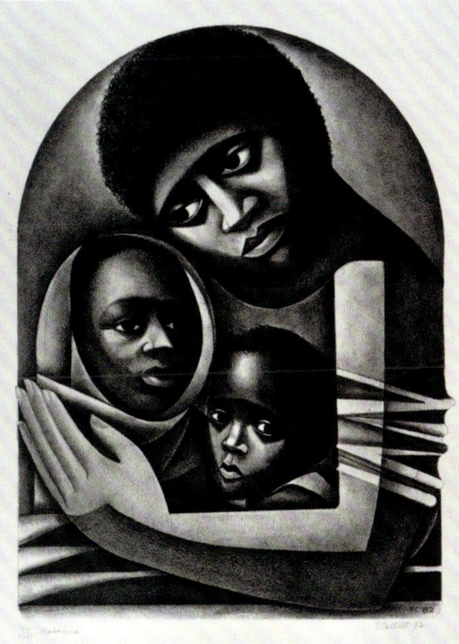

45

46

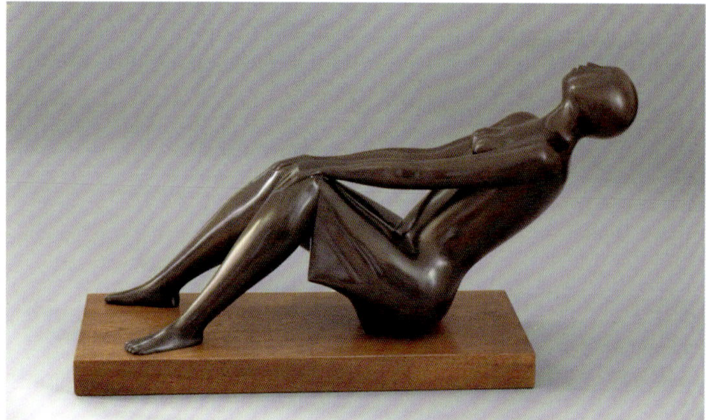

47

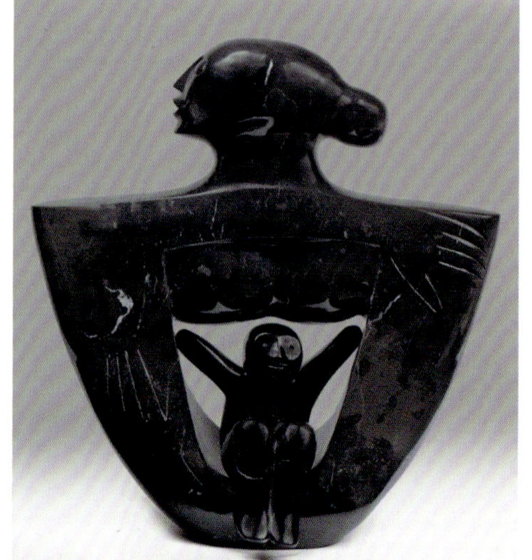

48

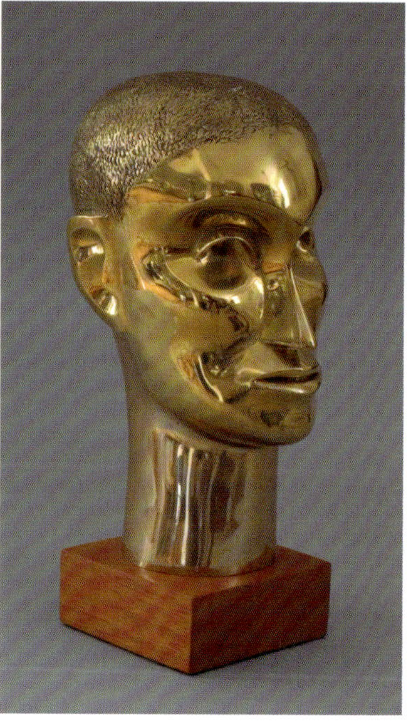

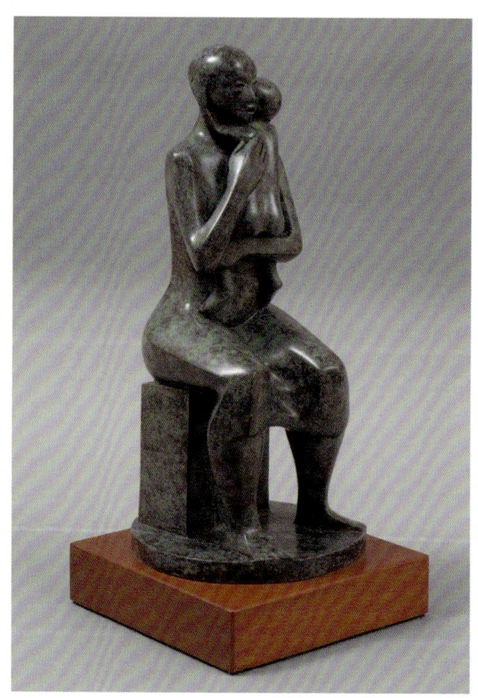

49

Cat. 46
Elizabeth Catlett, *Mahalia*, 2002, Bronze with brown patina, 15" × 11" × 30", Courtesy of the Eric Key Collection, © 2023 Mora-Catlett Family / Licensed by VAGA at Artists Rights Society (ARS), NY.

Cat. 47
Elizabeth Catlett, *Maternity*, 1980, Marble, 18¾" × 17½" × 8", Courtesy of the Eric Key Collection, © 2023 Mora-Catlett Family / Licensed by VAGA at Artists Rights Society (ARS), NY.

Cat. 48
Elizabeth Catlett, *Portrait*, 1973, Polished bronze, 12" × 6¼" × 7¼", Courtesy of the Eric Key Collection, © 2023 Mora-Catlett Family / Licensed by VAGA at Artists Rights Society (ARS), NY.

Cat. 49
Elizabeth Catlett, *Seated Mother and Child*, 1980, Bronze with malaca patina, 16" × 6" × 5½", Courtesy of the Eric Key Collection, © 2023 Mora-Catlett Family / Licensed by VAGA at Artists Rights Society (ARS), NY.

50

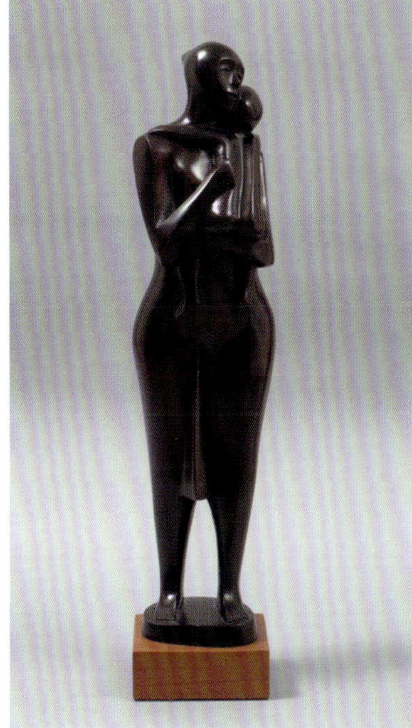

51

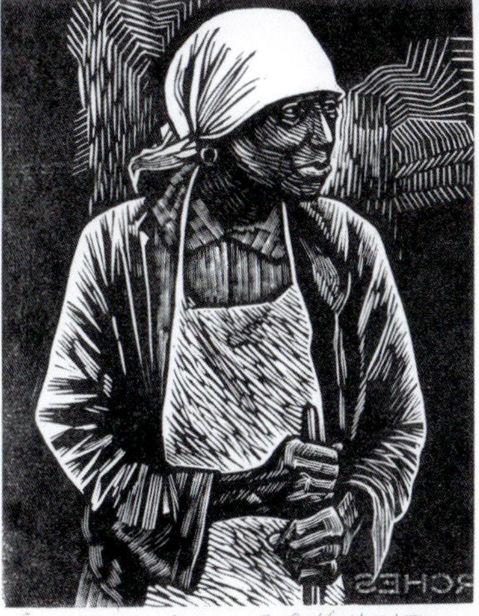

52

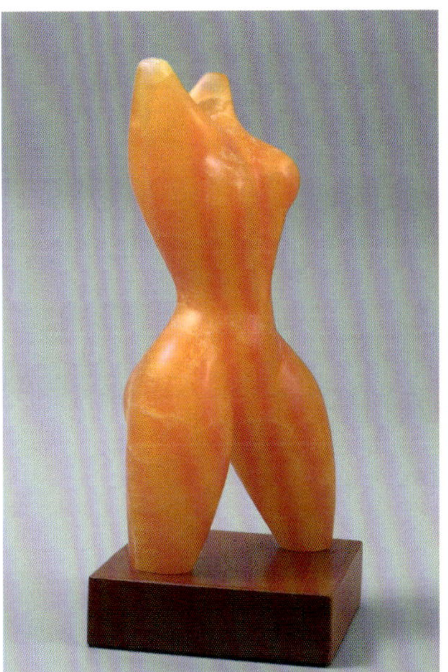

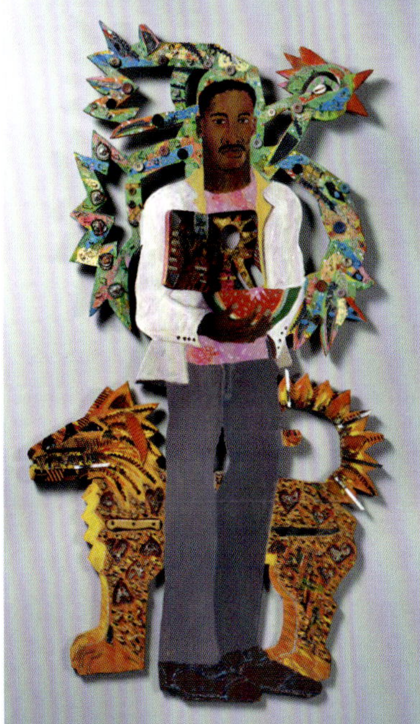

53

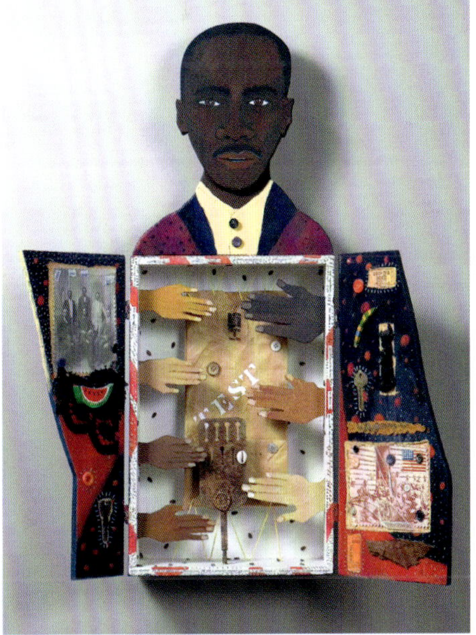

54

Cat. 50
Elizabeth Catlett, *Standing Mother and Child*, 1978, Bronze with black patina, 23" × 6" × 6", Courtesy of the Eric Key Collection, © 2023 Mora-Catlett Family / Licensed by VAGA at Artists Rights Society (ARS), NY.

Cat. 51
Elizabeth Catlett, *Survivor*, 1984, Lithograph on paper, 23" × 19", Courtesy of the Eric Key Collection, © 2023 Mora-Catlett Family / Licensed by VAGA at Artists Rights Society (ARS), NY.

Cat. 52
Elizabeth Catlett, *Torso*, 1970, Orange onyx, 16" × 7¼" × 7¼", Courtesy of the Eric Key Collection, © 2023 Mora-Catlett Family / Licensed by VAGA at Artists Rights Society (ARS), NY.

Cat. 53
Schroeder Cherry, *Bird and Beast*, 1998, Assemblage on wood, 48" × 26" × 1", Courtesy of the Eric Key Collection, © Schroeder Cherry.

Cat. 54
Schroeder Cherry, *Color Test*, 1995, Mixed-media assemblage, 33" × 29" × 5", Courtesy of the Eric Key Collection, © Schroeder Cherry.

57

55

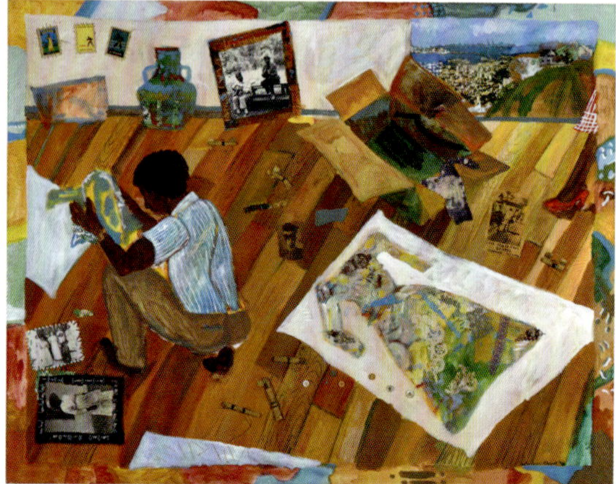

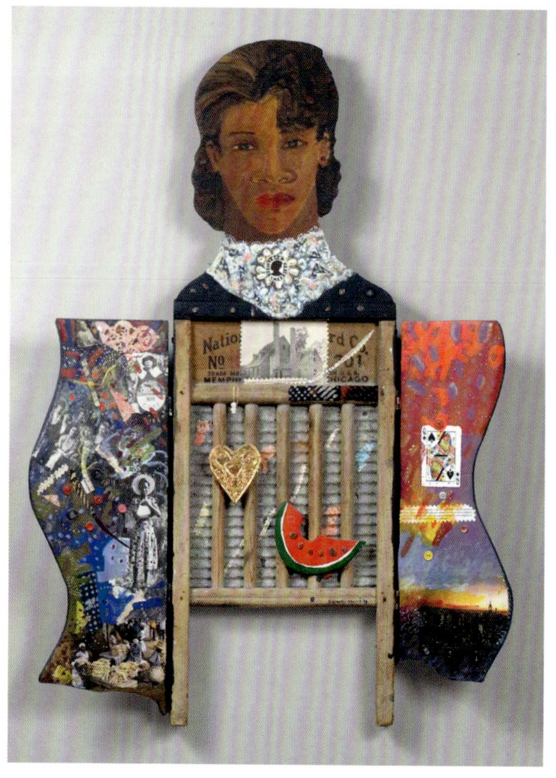

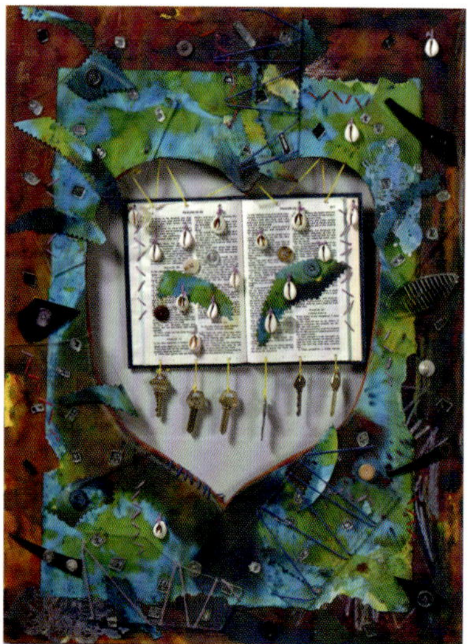

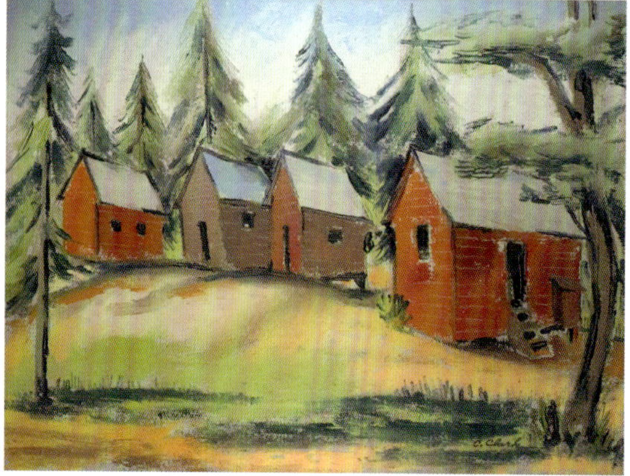

58

56

Cat. 55
Schroeder Cherry, *Hanging the Exhibit*, 2002, Mixed media, 34" × 44", Courtesy of the Eric Key Collection, © Schroeder Cherry.

Cat. 56
Schroeder Cherry, *Psalms*, 2000, Assemblage on wood, 30" × 20¼", Courtesy of the Eric Key Collection, © Schroeder Cherry.

Cat. 57
Schroeder Cherry, *Teacher*, 1991, Assemblage on wood, 39" × 29" × 3", Courtesy of the Eric Key Collection, © Schroeder Cherry.

Cat. 58
Claude Clark, *Cabins at Camp*, 1956, Acrylic on board, 23" × 28", Courtesy of the Eric Key Collection, © Claude Clark.

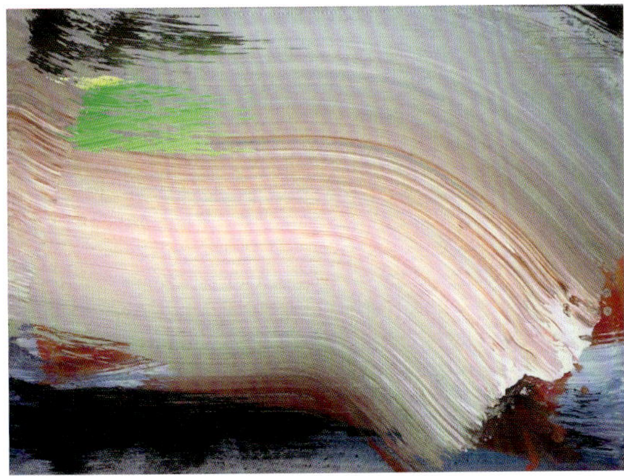

59

60

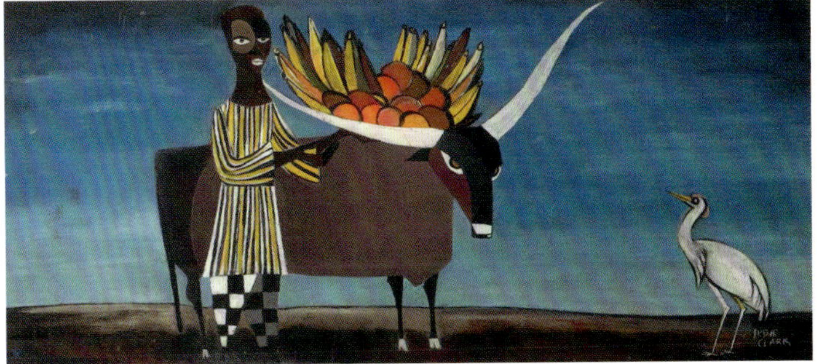

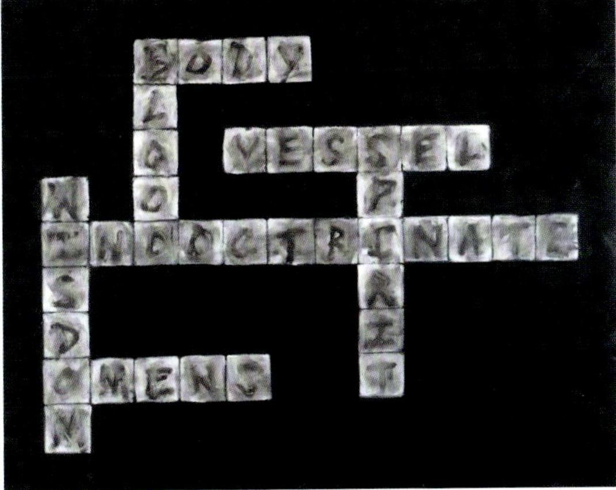

61

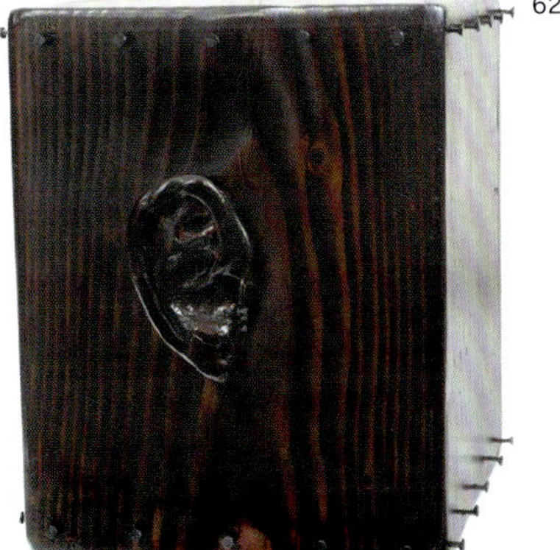

62

63

Cat. 59
Ed Clark, *Untitled (brush painting)*, 2005, Oil on canvas, 36" × 48" × 2", Courtesy of the Eric Key Collection, © Ed Clark.

Cat. 60
Irene Clark, *Man with Bull with Horn*, 1970s, Acrylic on board, 9" × 19½", Courtesy of the Eric Key Collection, © Irene Clark.

Cat. 61
Wesley Clark, *Quiet Moments*, 2023, Acrylic on board, 22" × 28", Courtesy of the Eric Key Collection, © Wesley Clark.

Cat. 62
Wesley Clark, *The Tell-All Earbox: model no.COmmOn3r*, 2019, Wood, stain, metal, tacks, shellac, 8½" × 12½" × 8½", Courtesy of the Eric Key Collection, © Wesley Clark.

Cat. 63
Wesley Clark, *Who are Darker than Blue II*, 2023, Graphite on paper, 22" × 30", Courtesy of the Eric Key Collection, © Wesley Clark.

65

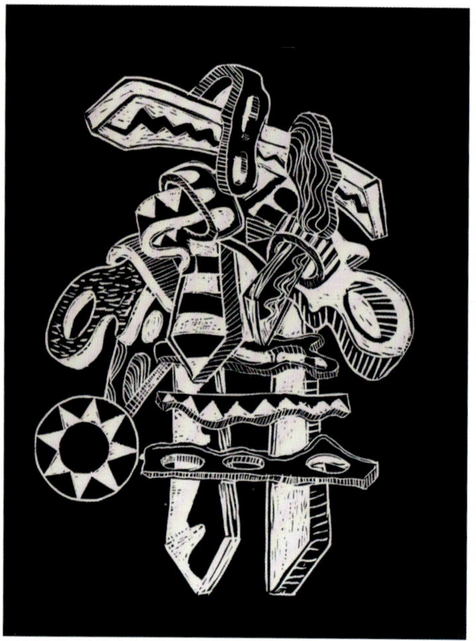

66

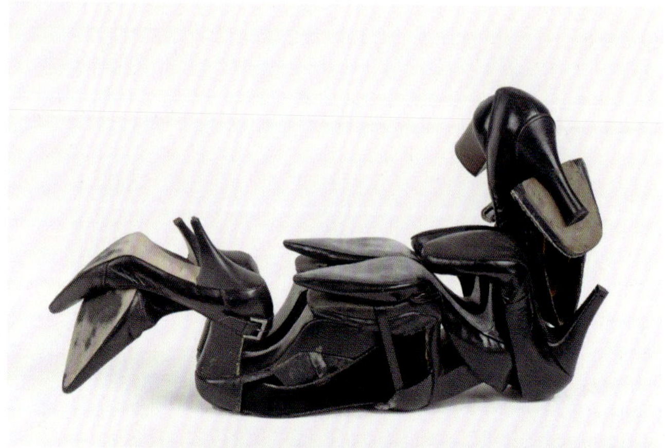

64

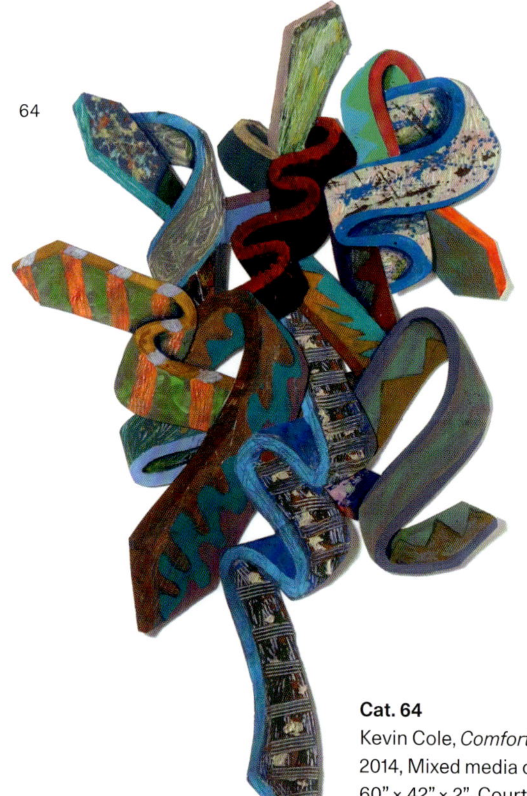

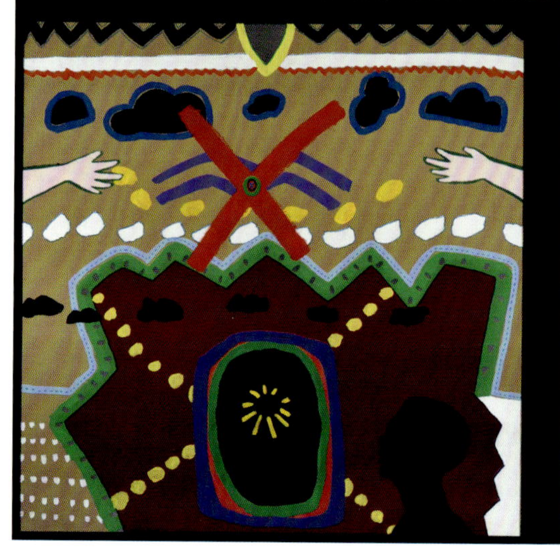

67

Cat. 64
Kevin Cole, *Comfort and Pressure*, 2014, Mixed media on paper, 60" × 42" × 2", Courtesy of the Eric Key Collection, © Kevin Cole.

Cat. 65
Kevin Cole, *Lessons That Lead to Blessing*, 2018, Linocut on paper, 40" × 30" × 2", Courtesy of the Eric Key Collection, © Kevin Cole.

Cat. 66
Willie Cole, *Nicole Miller in Repose*, 2011, Mixed media, 14" × 24" × 8½", Courtesy of the Eric Key Collection, © Willie Cole.

Cat. 67
Floyd Coleman, *Colonial Wars and Things*, 1970–1971, Acrylic on canvas, 61" × 61" × 2", Courtesy of the Eric Key Collection, © Floyd Coleman.

68

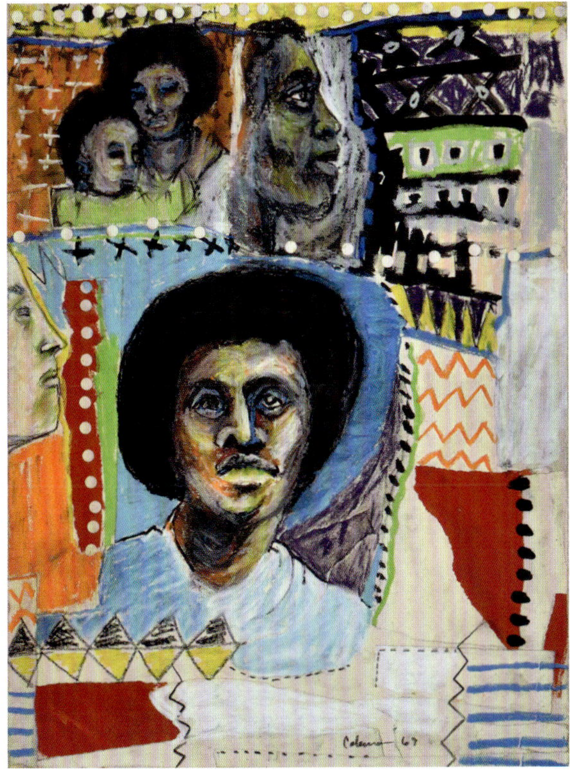

69

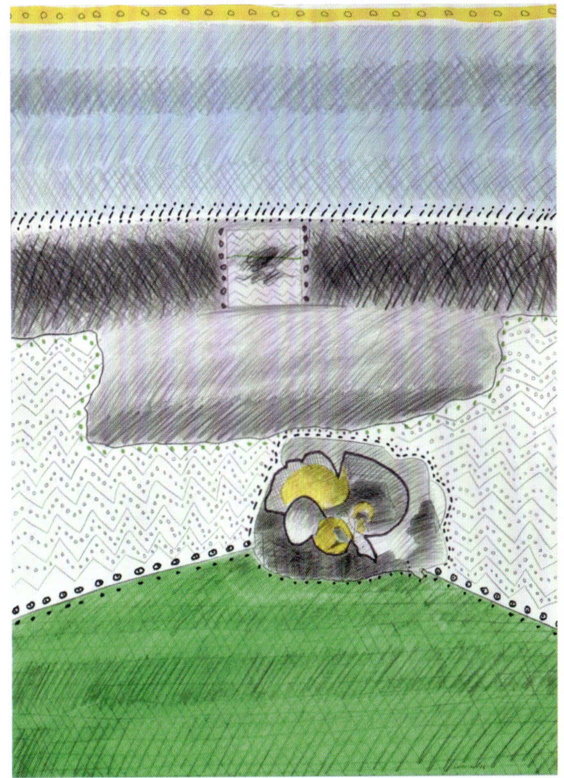

70

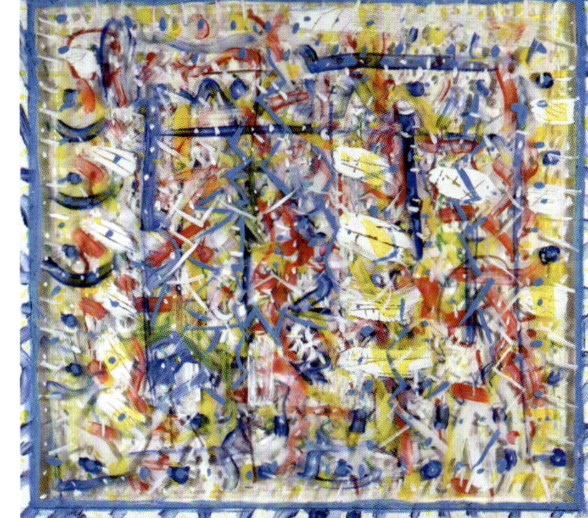

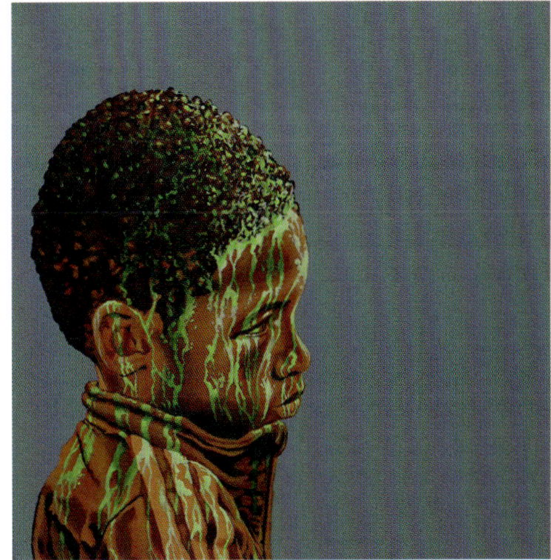

71

Cat. 68
Floyd Coleman, *Family*, 1969, Mixed media on paper, 16" × 11¾", Courtesy of the Eric Key Collection, © Floyd Coleman.

Cat. 69
Floyd Coleman, *Neo-African Series*, 1969, Acrylic on canvas, 39" × 32", Courtesy of the Eric Key Collection, © Floyd Coleman.

Cat. 70
Floyd Coleman, *Went Looking For Africa: Homage to Carrie Mae Weems*, 1993, Acrylic on canvas, 24" × 26¼", Courtesy of the Eric Key Collection, © Floyd Coleman.

Cat. 71
Alfred Conteh, *Snap*, 2019, Acrylic on canvas, 14" × 14" × 3", Courtesy of the Eric Key Collection, Photographed by Alfred Conteh, © Alfred Conteh.

72

73

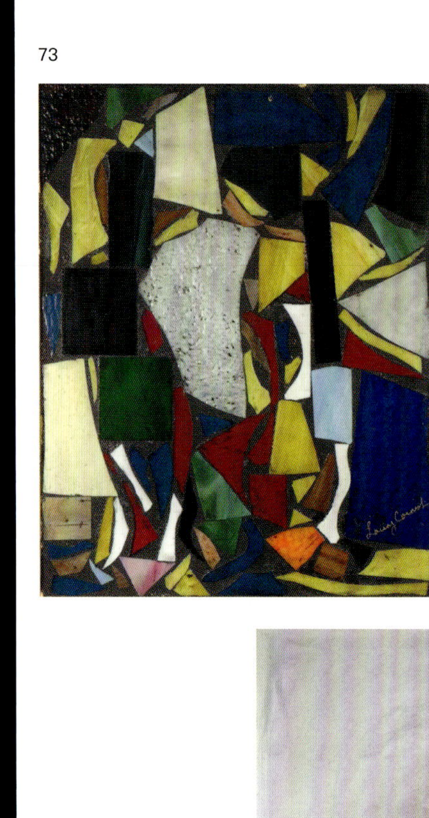

74

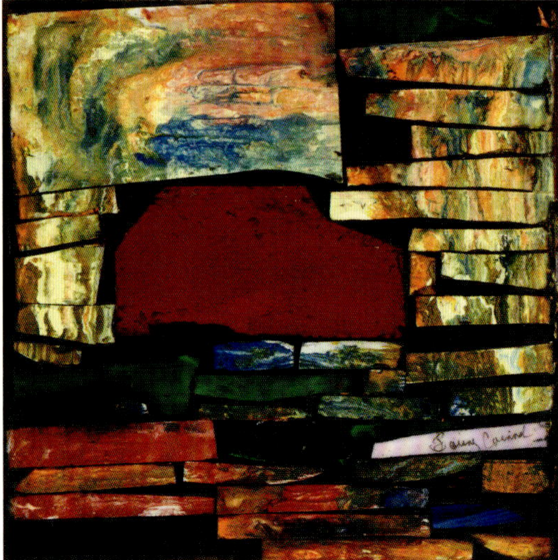

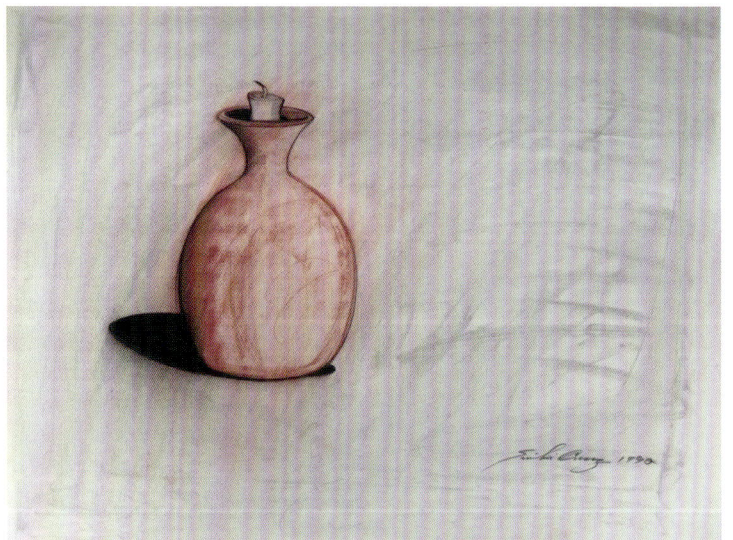

75

Cat. 72
Loring Cornish, *Contemplation*, 2015, Mixed media, 79" × 12" × 1", Courtesy of the Eric Key Collection, © Loring Cornish.

Cat. 73
Loring Cornish, *Untitled*, 2012, Mixed media, 22" × 18½", Courtesy of the Eric Key Collection, © Loring Cornish.

Cat. 74
Loring Cornish, *Untitled (red house)*, 2012, Glass, 17½" × 17½", Courtesy of the Eric Key Collection, © Loring Cornish.

Cat. 75
Emilio Cruz, *Untitled (Vessel with Candle)*, 1992, Charcoal on paper, 28" × 36¼", Courtesy of the Eric Key Collection and the Estate of Emilio Cruz and Corbett vs. Dempsey, Chicago, © Corbett vs. Dempsey.

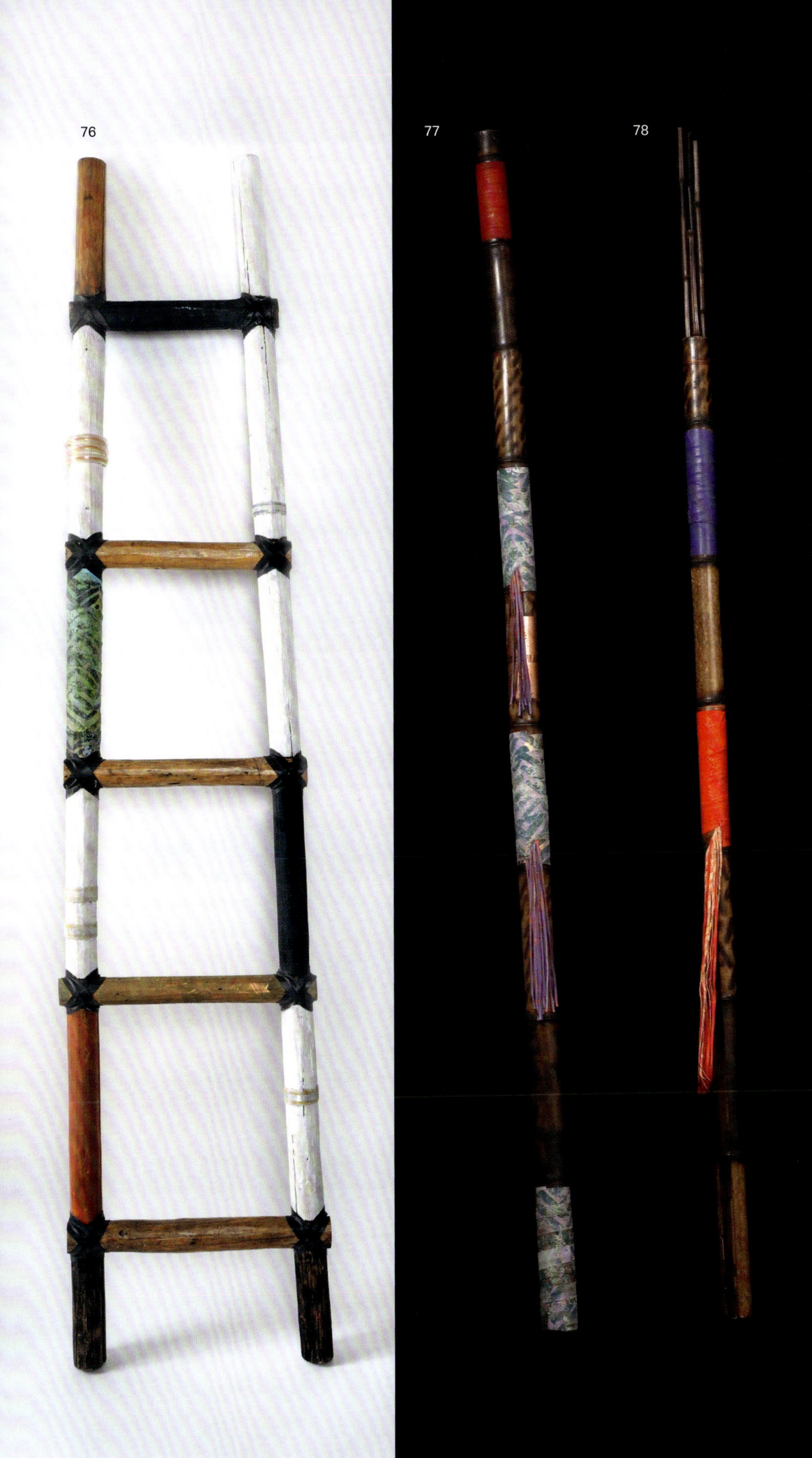

Cat. 76
Alonzo Davis, *Sky Ladder,* no date, Mexican pine with mixed media, 84" × 19" × 3, Courtesy of the Eric Key Collection, © Alonzo Davis.

Cat. 77
Alonzo Davis, *Totem Pole*, 2007, Mixed media on bamboo, 84" × 2½" × 2½", Courtesy of the Eric Key Collection, © Alonzo Davis.

Cat. 78
Alonzo Davis, *Totem Pole (w/small bamboo)*, 2007, Mixed media on bamboo, 88" × 2½" × 2½", Courtesy of the Eric Key Collection, © Alonzo Davis.

79

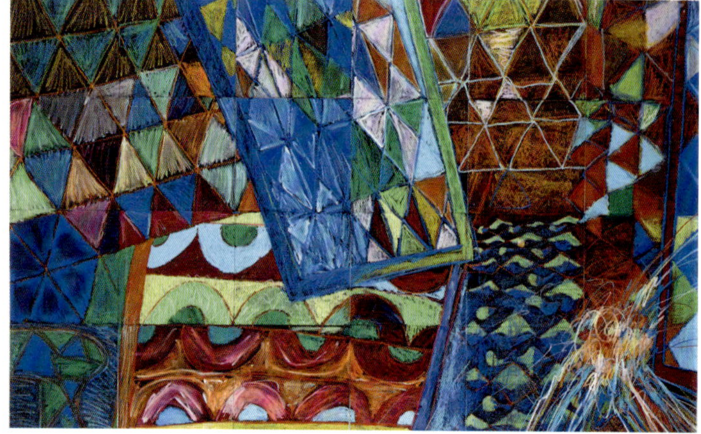

81

80

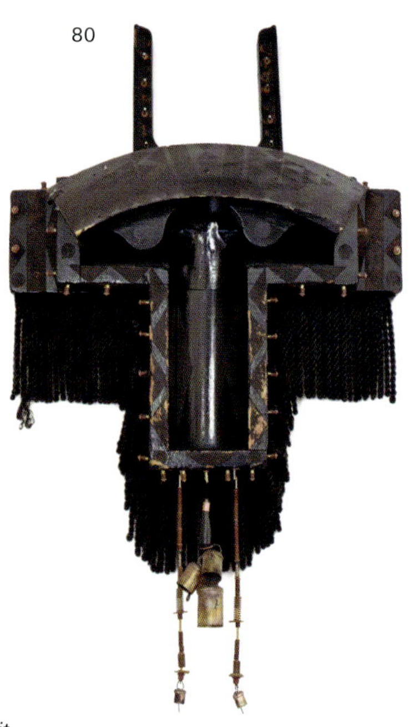

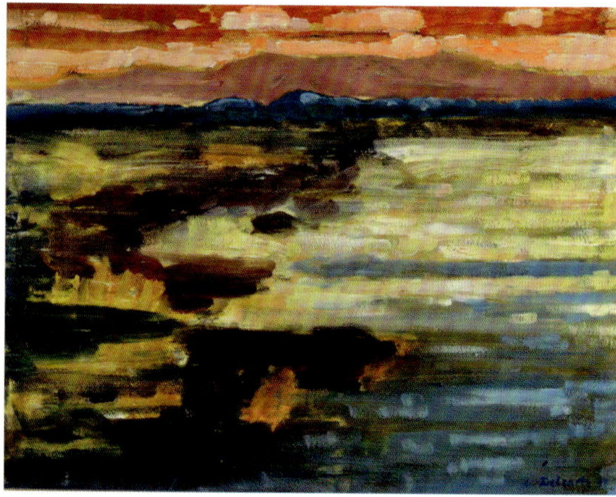

82

Cat. 79
Willis Bing Davis, *Ancestral Spirit Dance*, 2001, Pastel on paper, 43" × 67", Courtesy of the Eric Key Collection, © Willis Bing Davis.

Cat. 80
Willis Bing Davis, *Anti Police Brutality Dance Mask #20*, 2000, Mixed media and found objects, 36" × 21" × 9", Courtesy of the Eric Key Collection, © Willis Bing Davis.

Cat. 81
Louis Delsarte, *Centennial Horizons*, 1991, Oil on canvas, 15¼" × 19 ¼" × 2", Courtesy of the Eric Key Collection, © Louis Delsarte.

Cat. 82
Aaron Douglas, *Untitled*, 1934, Gouache in grisaille on paper, 17" × 21" × 2", Courtesy of the Eric Key Collection, © 2023 Heirs of Aaron Douglas / Licensed by VAGA at Artists Rights Society (ARS), NY.

83

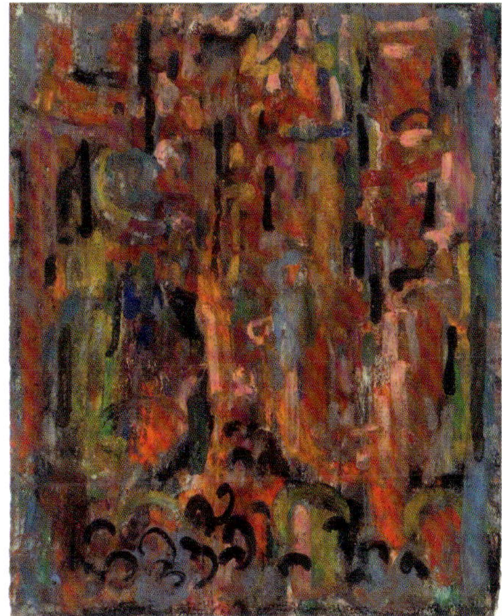

84

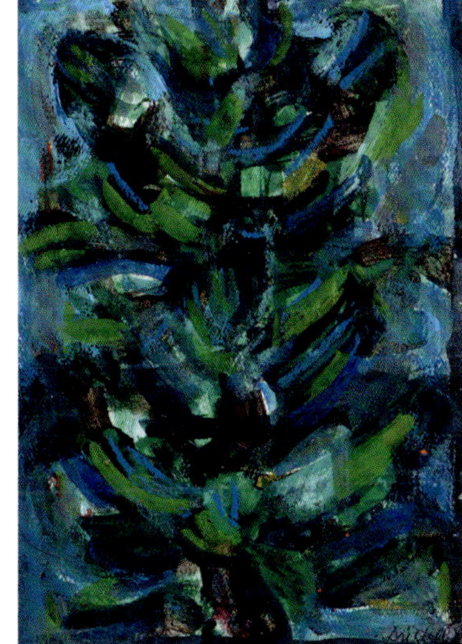

85

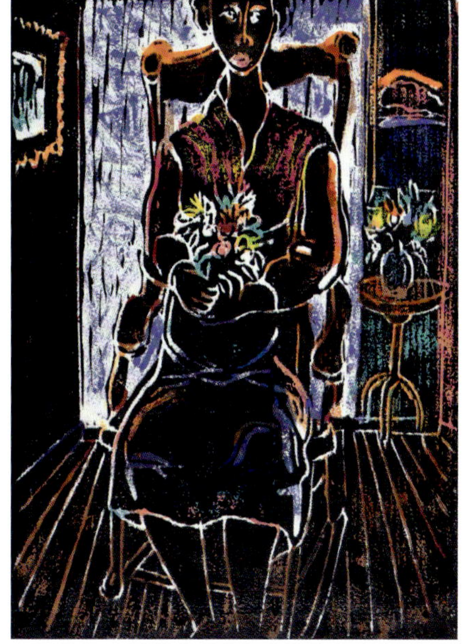

86

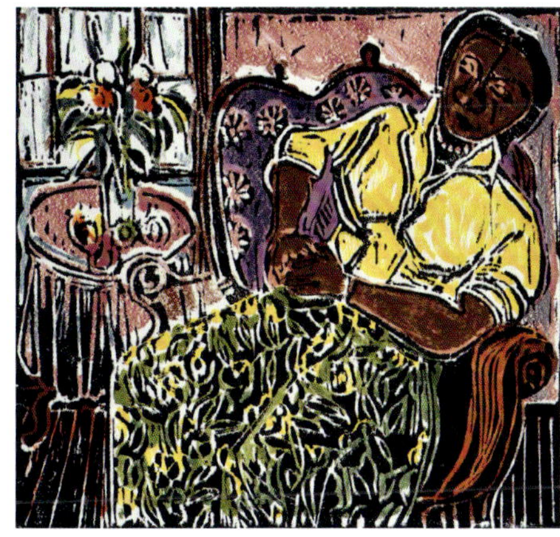

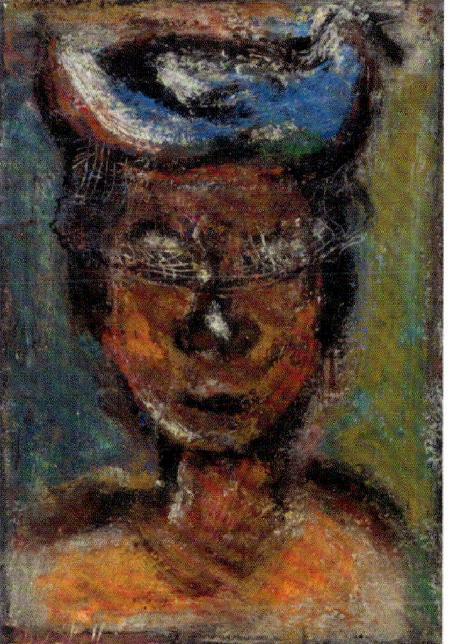

87

Cat. 83
David Driskell, *Landscape*, 1980s, Oil on paper, 14" × 11", Courtesy of the Eric Key Collection, © David Driskell.

Cat. 84
David Driskell, *Pine*, 1971, Acrylic on paper, 20¼" × 16¼" × 2", Courtesy of the Eric Key Collection, © David Driskell.

Cat. 85
David Driskell, *Portfolio "Maine Suite," The Rocker*, 2010–2015, Oil print, 21" × 16½", Courtesy of the Eric Key Collection, © David Driskell.

Cat. 86
David Driskell, *Portfolio "Maine Suite," Woman Resting,* 2010–2015, Oil print, 10½" × 11", Courtesy of the Eric Key Collection, © David Driskell.

Cat. 87
David Driskell, *Untitled (Woman in Hat)*, 1980s, Oil on paper, 19" × 16", Courtesy of the Eric Key Collection, © David Driskell.

89

88

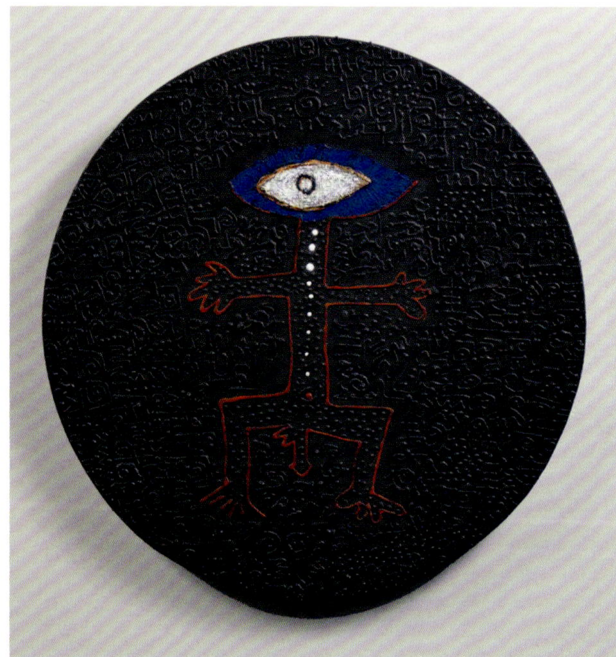

90

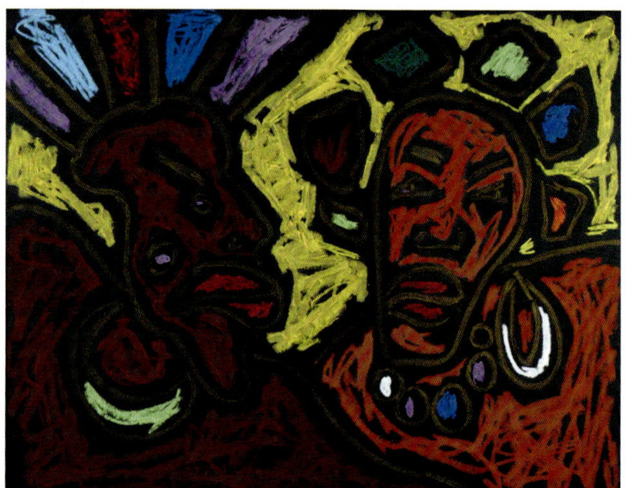

91

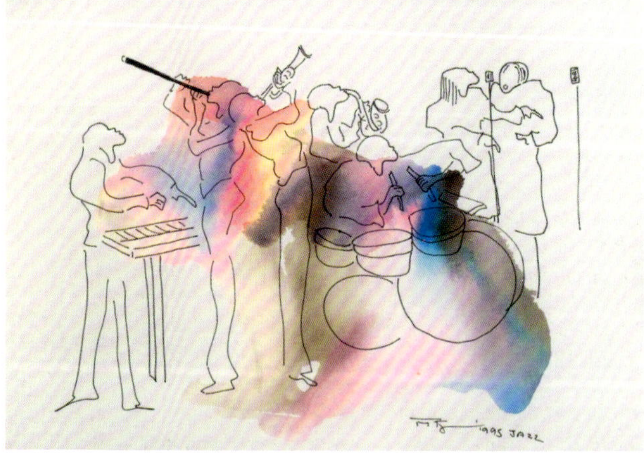

Cat. 88
Victor Ekpuk, *Ojuringba*, 1997, Oil on canvas, 20" in diameter, Courtesy of the Eric Key Collection, © Victor Ekpuk.

Cat. 89
Ted Ellis, *Attitude: Pressure Around Us, Series I*, 1992, Acrylic on board, 28" × 32", Courtesy of the Eric Key Collection, © Ted Ellis.

Cat. 90
Ted Ellis, *Attitude: Pressure Around Us, Series II (frontal view)*, 1992, Acrylic on board, 33" × 38", Courtesy of the Eric Key Collection, © Ted Ellis.

Cat. 91
Frank Frazier, *Jazz*, 1995, Ink and watercolor on paper, 14" × 17", Courtesy of the Eric Key Collection, © Frank Frazier.

92

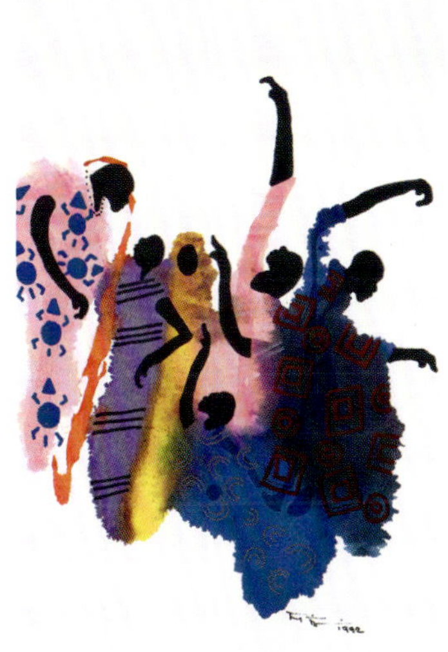

93

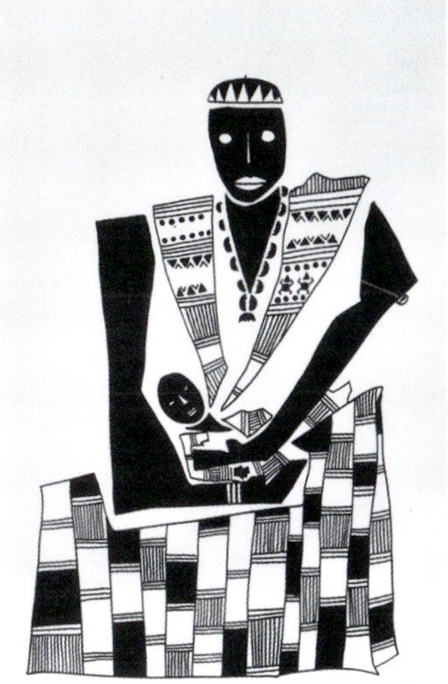

94

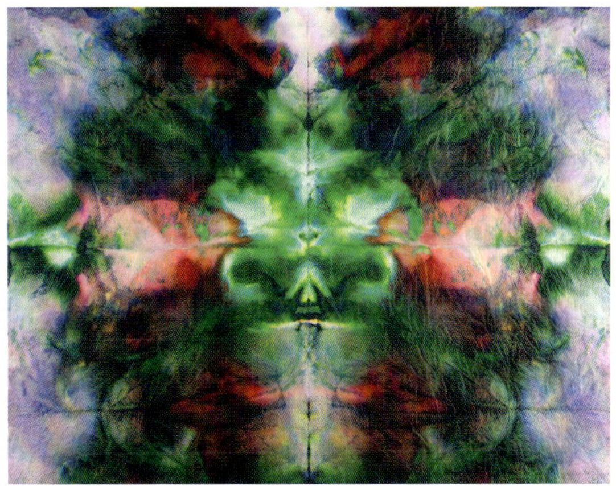

95

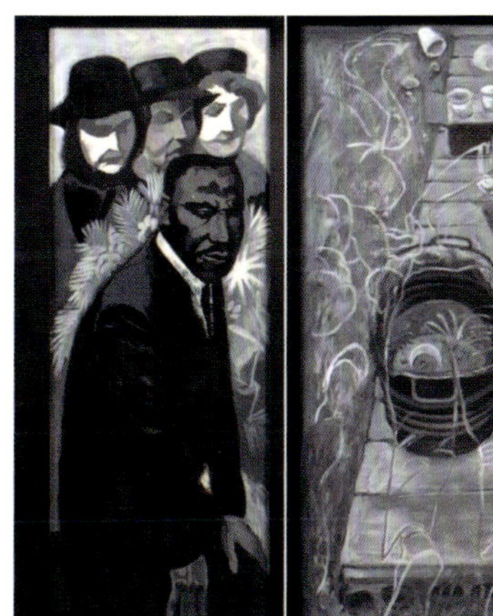

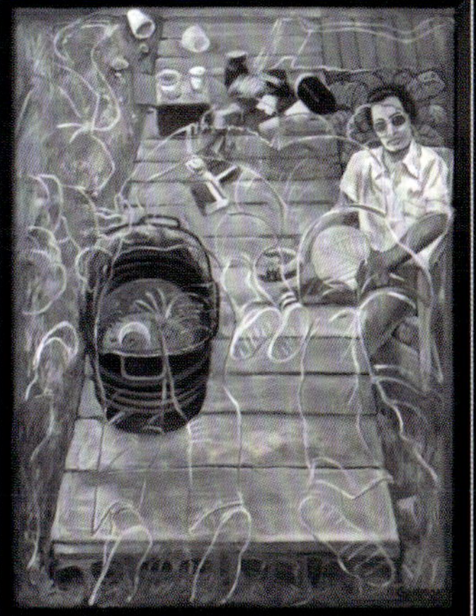

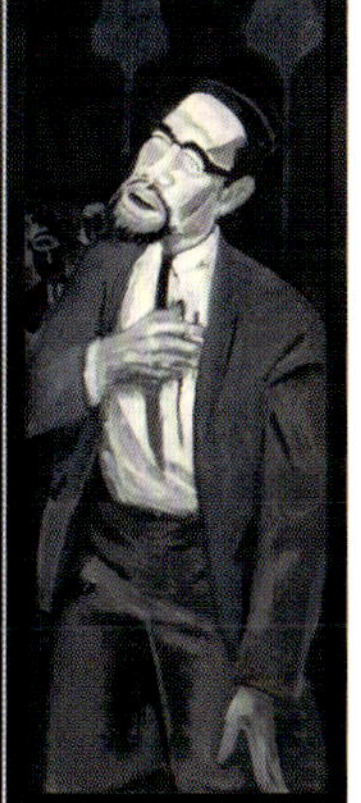

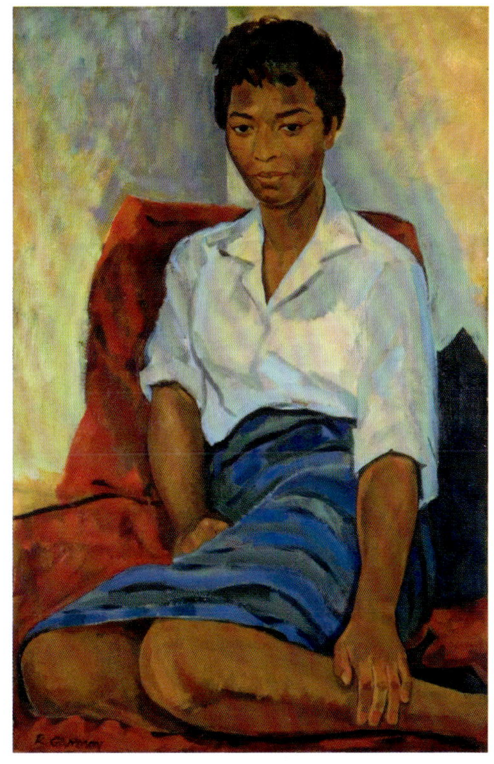

96

Cat. 92
Frank Frazier, *Montsho: Colors/Symbols Series*, 1992, Watercolor on paper, 22½" × 17½" × 1.25", Courtesy of the Eric Key Collection, © Frank Frazier.

Cat. 93
Frank Frazier, *Untitled (father and son)*, 1992, Lithograph on paper, 40" × 30", Courtesy of the Eric Key Collection, © Frank Frazier.

Cat. 94
Maya Freelon, *Balance*, 2017, Watercolor on paper, 37½" × 46" × 2⅓", Courtesy of the Eric Key Collection, © Maya Freelon.

Cat. 95
Reginald Gammon, *A Triptych for the Black Church (MLK and Mothers)*, no date, Oil on canvas with gold leaf, 36" × 60" × 2", Courtesy of the Eric Key Collection, © 2023 Estate of Reginald Gammon.

Cat. 96
Reginald Gammon, *Juanita - A Study*, 1960, Oil on canvas, 36" × 24", Courtesy of the Eric Key Collection, © 2023 Estate of Reginald Gammon.

97

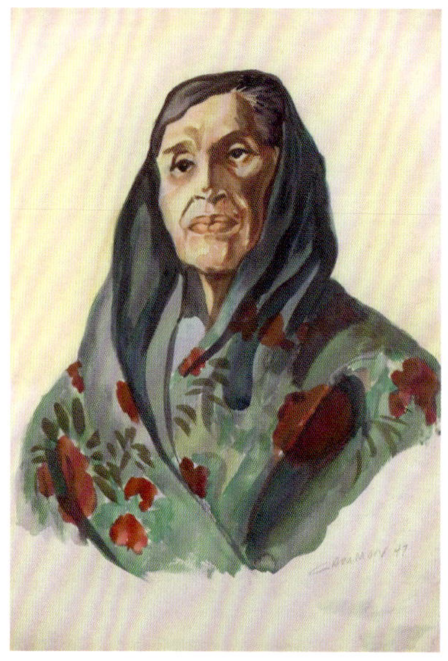

98

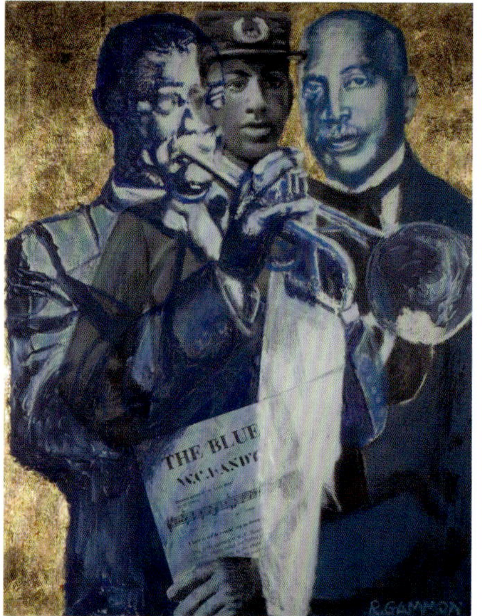

99

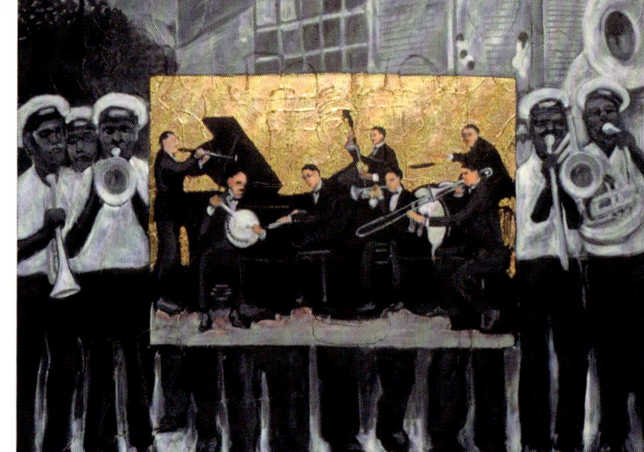

100

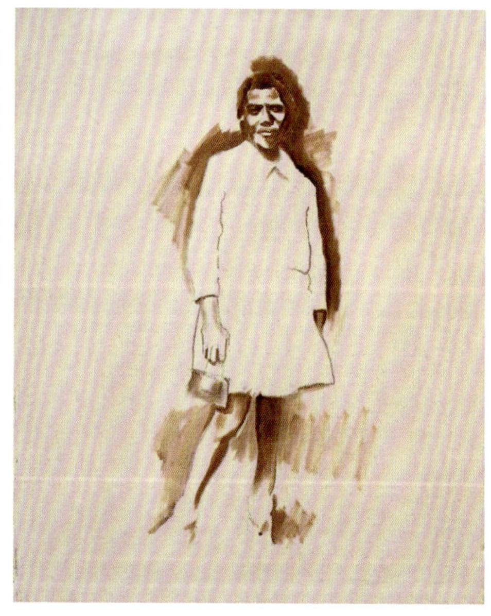

Cat. 97
Reginald Gammon, *Portrait of a Woman*, 1947, Watercolor on paper, 24" × 20", Courtesy of the Eric Key Collection, © 2023 Estate of Reginald Gammon.

Cat. 98
Reginald Gammon, *St. Louis Blues*, no date, Oil on canvas with gold leaf, 28" × 22", Courtesy of the Eric Key Collection, © 2023 Estate of Reginald Gammon.

Cat. 99
Reginald Gammon, *The New Orleans Suite: Storyville Jellyroll Morton and His Red Hot Peppers*, no date, Oil on canvas with gold leaf, 36" × 40", Courtesy of the Eric Key Collection, © 2023 Estate of Reginald Gammon.

Cat. 100
Reginald Gammon, *Young Girl with Purse,* 1975, Oil on canvas, 21½" × 17½", Courtesy of the Eric Key Collection, © 2023 Estate of Reginald Gammon.

101

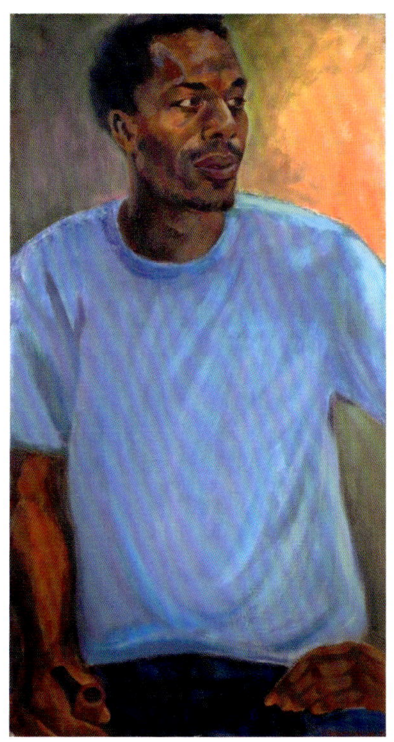

102

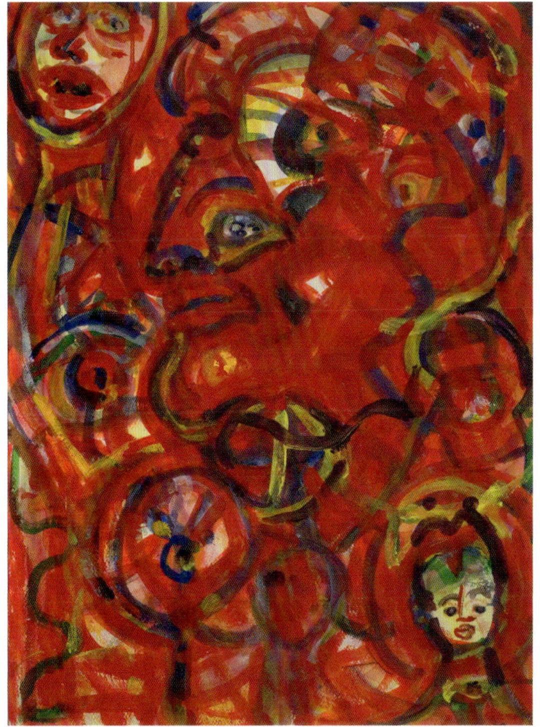

103

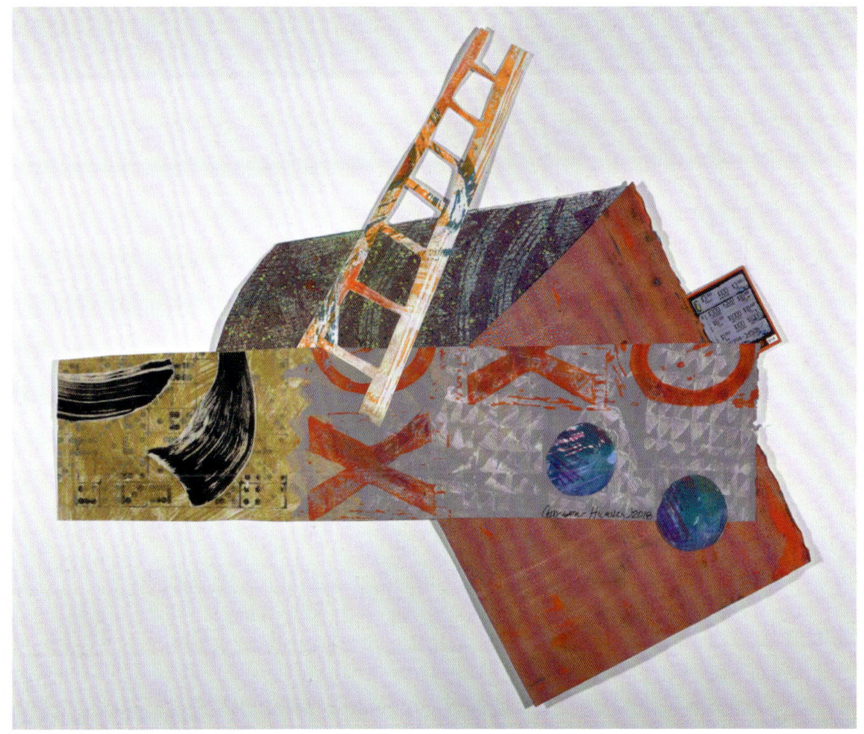

Cat. 101
Reginald Gammon, *Young Man with Pipe*, 1975, Oil on canvas, 32" × 18", Courtesy of the Eric Key Collection, © 2023 Estate of Reginald Gammon.

Cat. 102
Herbert Gentry, *Untitled*, 1980s, Watercolor on paper, 24" × 18", Courtesy of the estate of the artist and the Ryan Lee Gallery, New York © Herbert Gentry.

Cat. 103
Aziza Claudia Gibson-Hunter, *Playing To Win #18 (w/ladder)*, 2018, Mixed media, 20" × 22", Courtesy of the Eric Key Collection, © Aziza Claudia Gibson-Hunter.

105

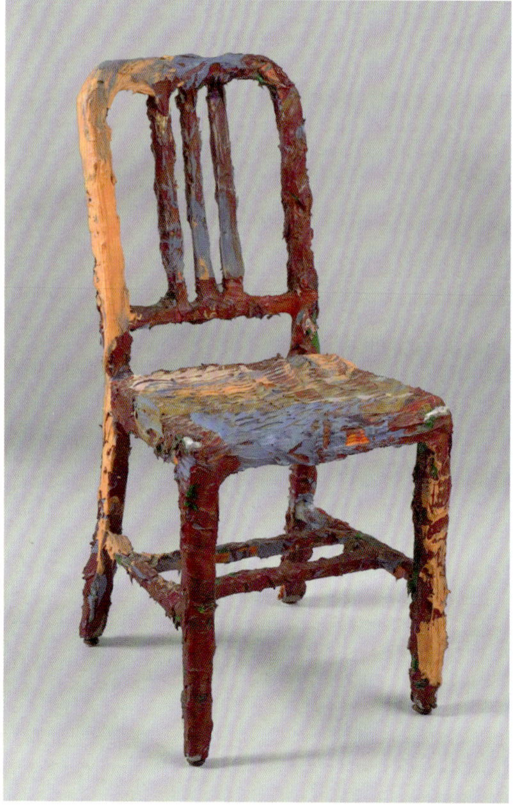

104

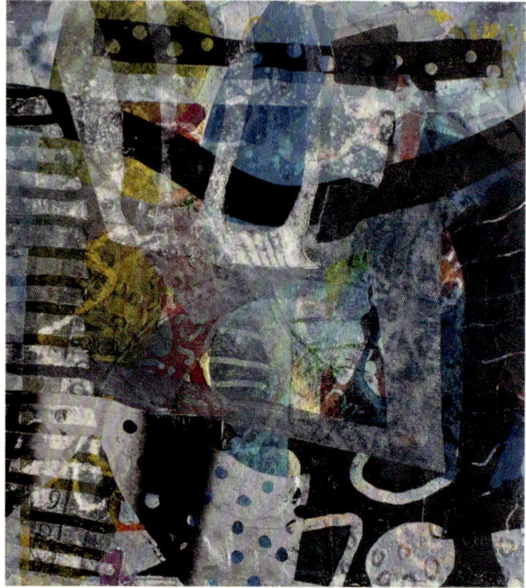

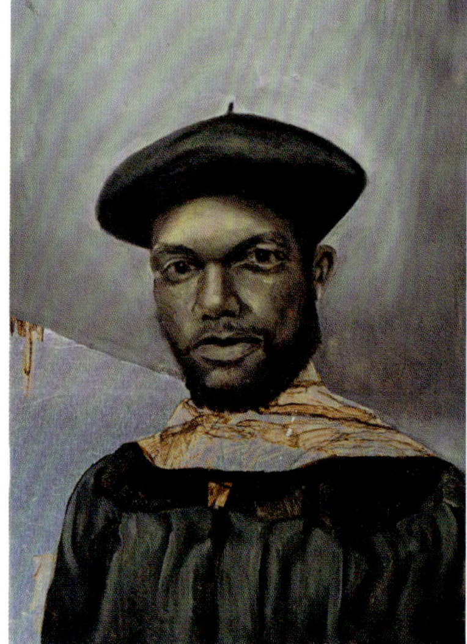

106

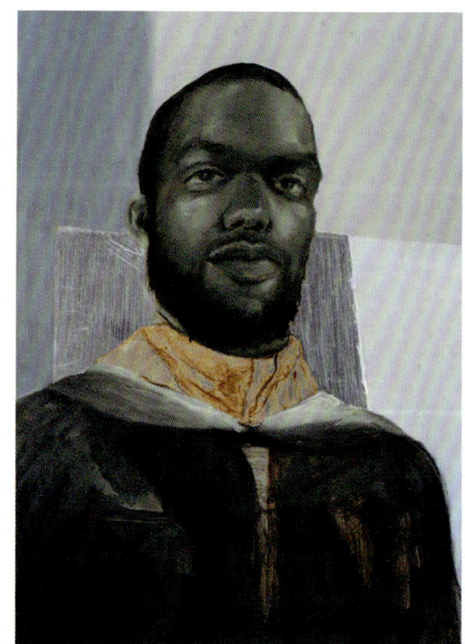

107

Cat. 104
Sam Gilliam, *Bad River Series*, 1988, Mixed media, 50" × 50" × 2", Courtesy of the Eric Key Collection, © 2023 Sam Gilliam / Artists Rights Society (ARS), NY.

Cat. 105
Sam Gilliam, *Untitled (painted chair)*, 1990, Paint on aluminum chair, 35" × 16" × 19", Courtesy of the Eric Key Collection, © 2023 Sam Gilliam / Artists Rights Society (ARS), NY.

Cat. 106
Kyle Hackett, *New Negation 1*, 2018, Oil on aluminum, 7" × 5" × 1", Courtesy of the Eric Key Collection, © Kyle Hackett.

Cat. 107
Kyle Hackett, *New Negation 2*, 2018, Oil on aluminum, 7" × 5" × 1", Courtesy of the Eric Key Collection, © Kyle Hackett.

108

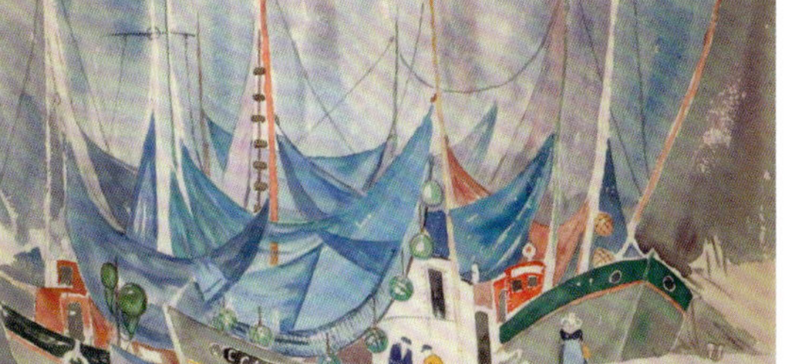

109

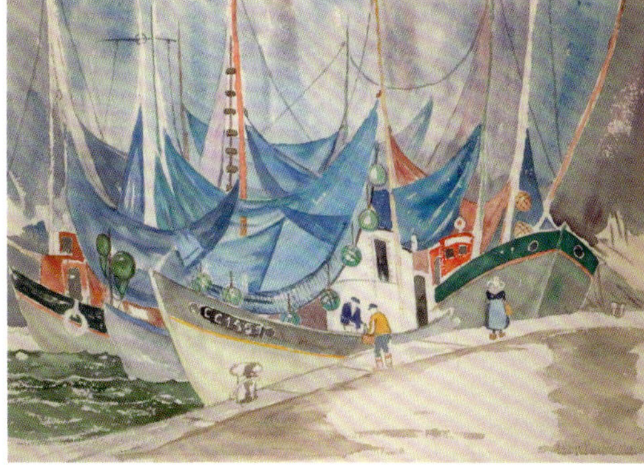

110

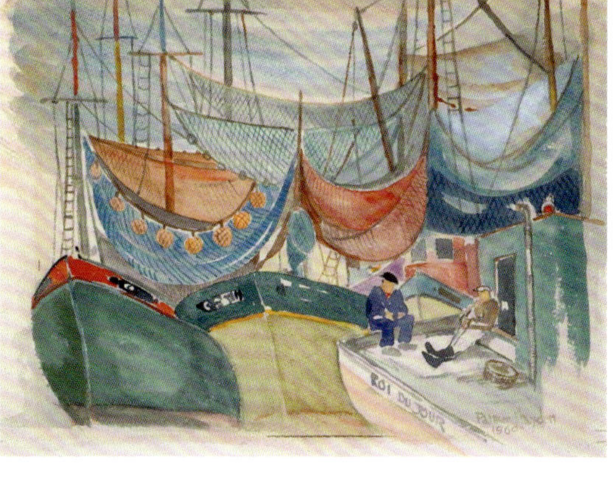

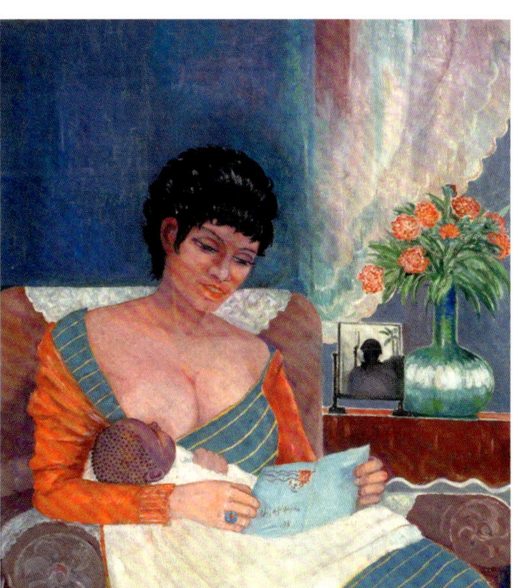

111

Cat. 108
John Wesley Hardwick, *Panoramic Vista*, no date, Oil on board, 12" × 13½" × 2", Courtesy of the Eric Key Collection, © John Wesley Hardwick.

Cat. 109
Palmer Hayden, *Concarneau's New Look*, 1962, Watercolor on paper, 23 ½" × 29 ½", Courtesy Hayden Family Revocable Art Trust and the Eric Key Collection, © Lisa L. Crane, Trustee, Hayden Family Revocable Art Trust.

Cat. 110
Palmer Hayden, *Concarneau's New Look, Le Rio du Jour,* 1960, Watercolor on paper, 17" × 21", Courtesy Hayden Family Revocable Art Trust and the Eric Key Collection, © Lisa L. Crane, Trustee, Hayden Family Revocable Art Trust.

Cat. 111
Palmer Hayden, *G.I. Bride*, 1967, Oil on canvas, 33" × 28" × 2", Courtesy Hayden Family Revocable Art Trust and the Eric Key Collection, © Lisa L. Crane, Trustee, Hayden Family Revocable Art Trust.

112

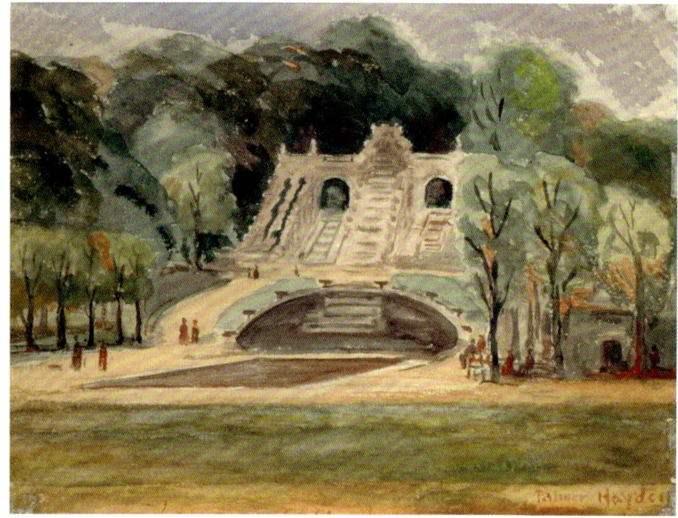

114 

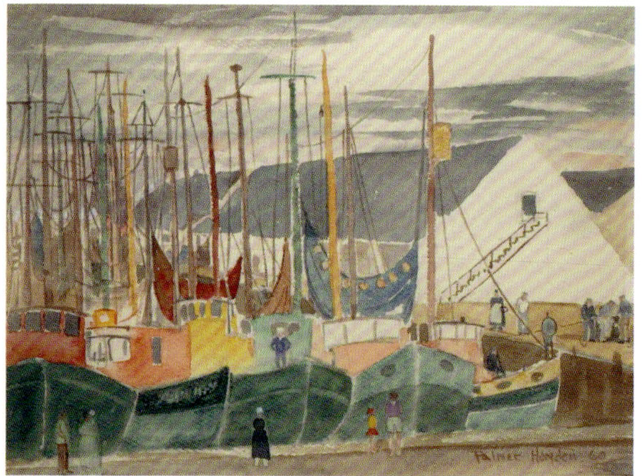

115

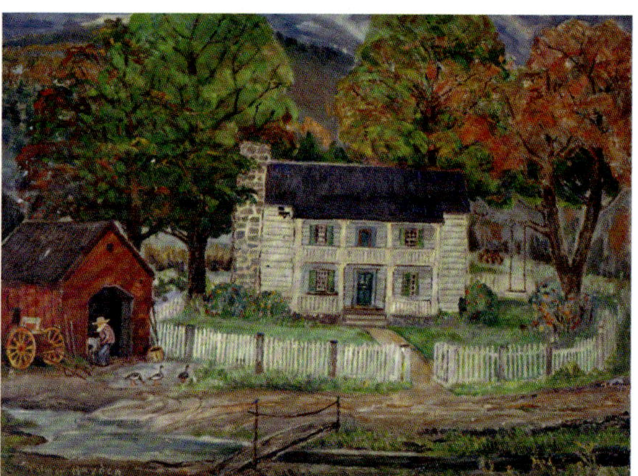

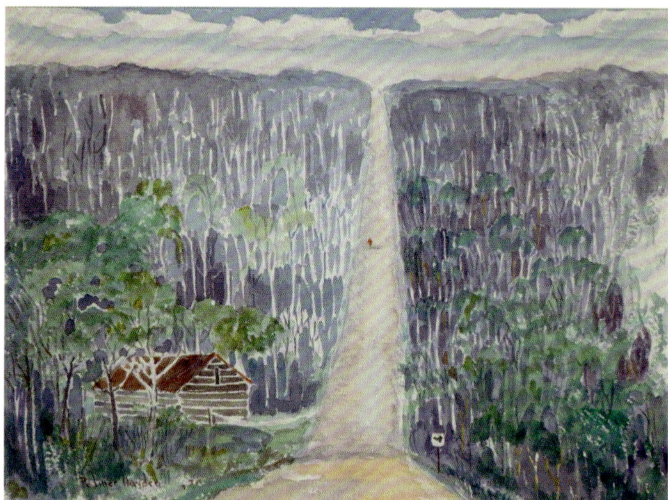

113

Cat. 114
Palmer Hayden, *Untitled (Concarneau)*, 1960, Watercolor on paper, 17" × 21", Courtesy Hayden Family Revocable Art Trust and the Eric Key Collection, © Lisa L. Crane, Trustee, Hayden Family Revocable Art Trust.

Cat. 112
Palmer Hayden, *Old Chateau - St. Cloud*, no date, Watercolor on paper, 15" × 17", Courtesy Hayden Family Revocable Art Trust and the Eric Key Collection, © Lisa L. Crane, Trustee, Hayden Family Revocable Art Trust.

Cat. 113
Palmer Hayden, *Road in New Brunswick*, no date, Watercolor on paper, 18" × 21½", Courtesy Hayden Family Revocable Art Trust and the Eric Key Collection, © Lisa L. Crane, Trustee, Hayden Family Revocable Art Trust.

Cat. 115
Palmer Hayden, *White House at Great Bend*, 1940s, Oil on canvas, 22" × 30", Courtesy Hayden Family Revocable Art Trust and the Eric Key Collection, © Lisa L. Crane, Trustee, Hayden Family Revocable Art Trust.

116

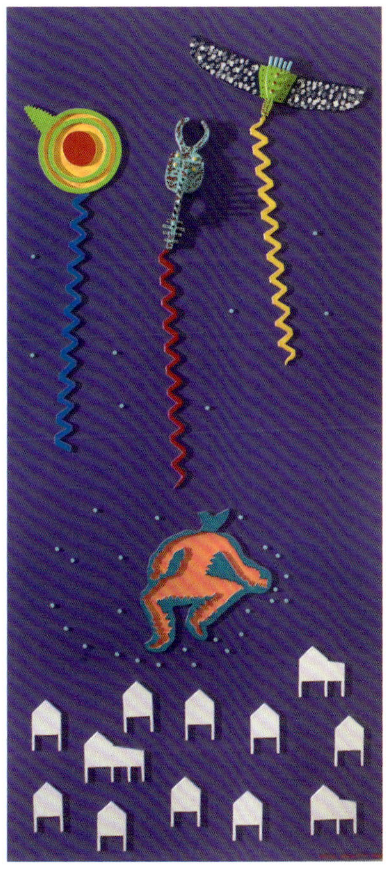

117

118

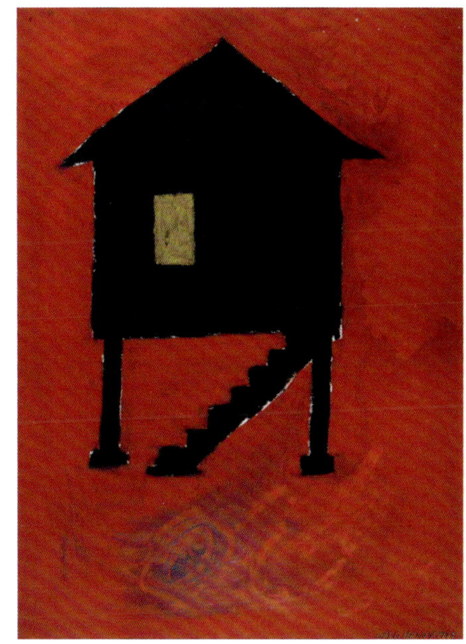

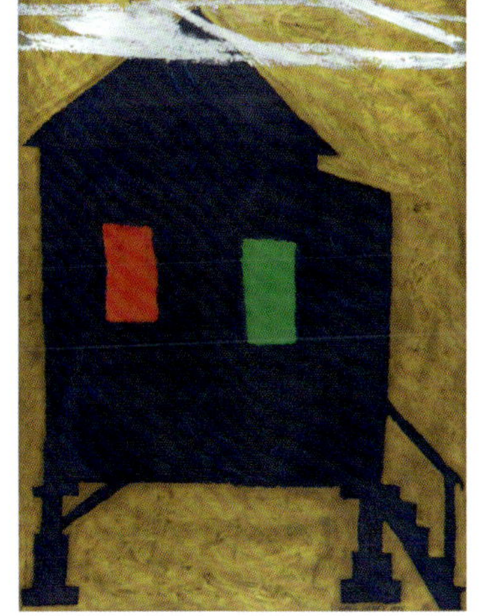

119

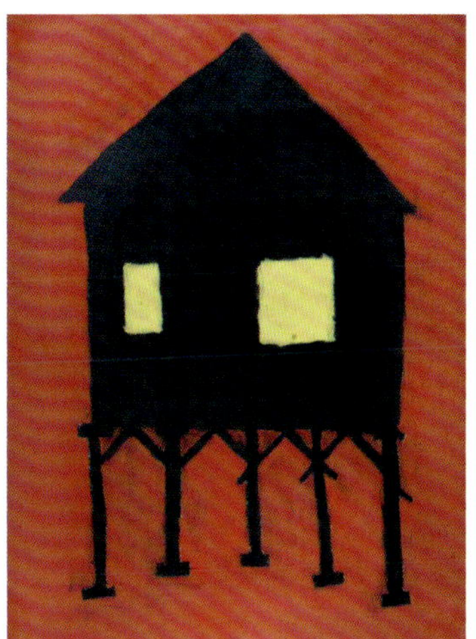

120

Cat. 116
Gregory A. Henry, *Kite in the Sky*, 1995, Painted wood, 72" × 32" × 1", Courtesy of the Eric Key Collection, © Gregory A. Henry.

Cat. 117
Gregory A. Henry, *Sunning*, 1999, Woodcut on paper (edition A/P), 45½" × 33½", Courtesy of the Eric Key Collection, © Gregory A. Henry.

Cat. 118
Gregory A. Henry, *Untitled (house with gold window)*, 1998, Acrylic on paper, 37¼" × 29¼", Courtesy of the Eric Key Collection, © Gregory A. Henry.

Cat. 119
Gregory A. Henry, *Untitled (house with red and green windows)*, 1998, Acrylic on paper, 39½" × 31½", Courtesy of the Eric Key Collection, © Gregory A. Henry.

Cat. 120
Gregory A. Henry, *Untitled (House with Yellow Windows)*, 1998, Acrylic on paper, 39½" × 31½", Courtesy of the Eric Key Collection, © Gregory A. Henry.

122

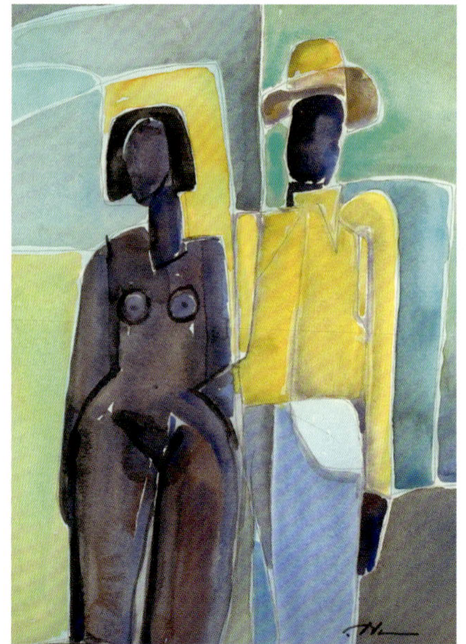

121

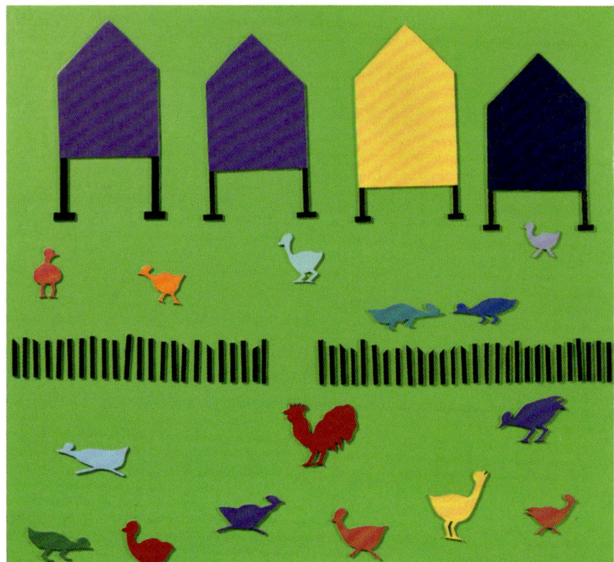

123

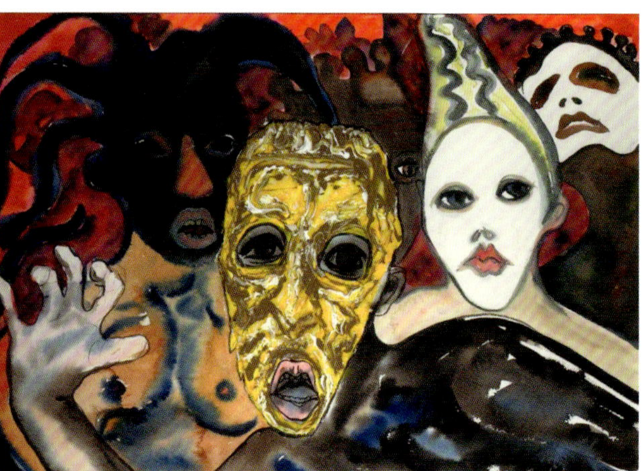

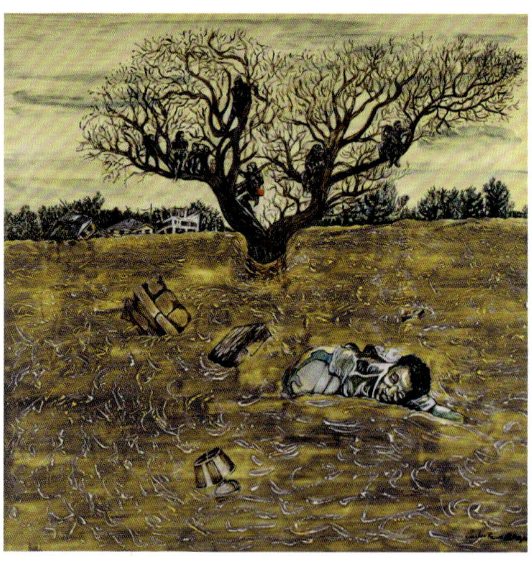

124

Cat. 121
Gregory A. Henry, *Waiting for the Afternoon*, 1995, Wood, paint, 37" × 41" × 2", Courtesy of the Eric Key Collection, © Gregory A. Henry.

Cat. 122
Joseph Holston, *Couple*, 2008, Watercolor on paper, 29" × 24", Courtesy of the Eric Key Collection, © Joseph Holston.

Cat. 123
Curlee Holton, *Farewell to the Flesh*, 1997, Watercolor and oil on paper, 22" × 26", Courtesy of the Eric Key Collection, © Curlee Raven Holton.

Cat. 124
Curlee Holton, *Release*, no date, Acrylic on board, 36" × 36" × 2¼", Courtesy of the Eric Key Collection, © Curlee Raven Holton.

125

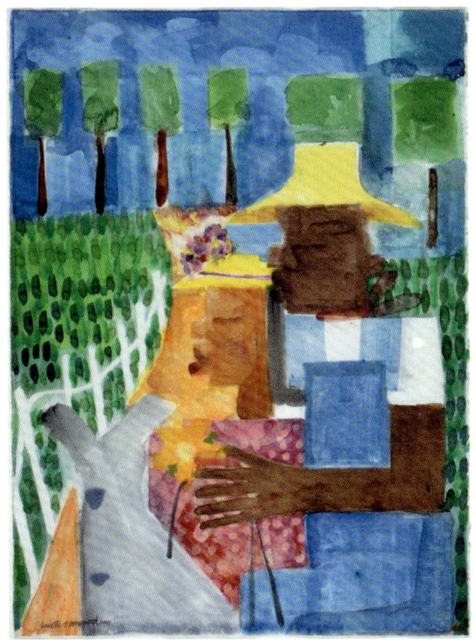

127

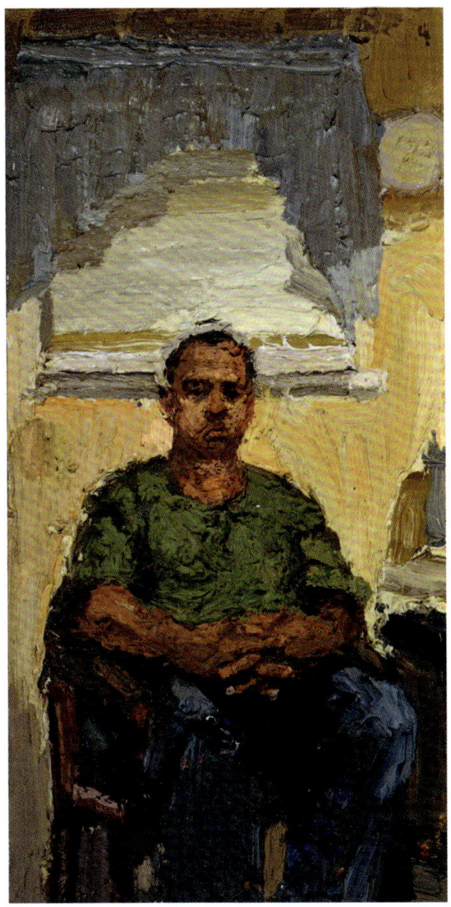

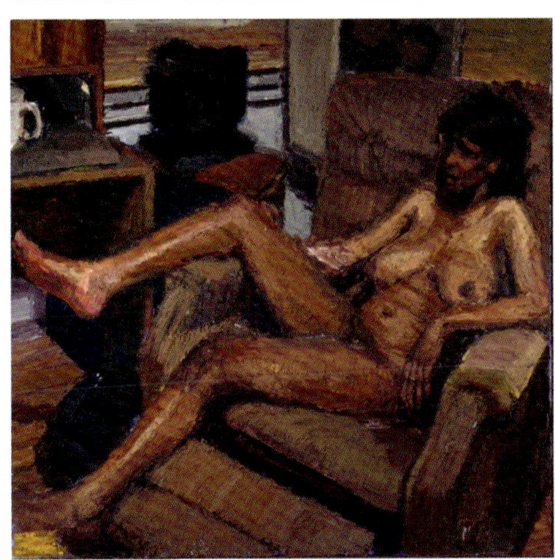

126

128

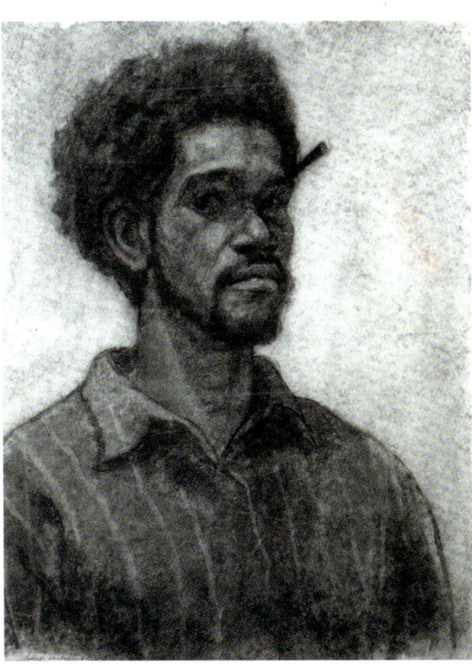

Cat. 125
Varnette Honeywood, *Elope*, 1999, Watercolor on paper, 37½" × 33" × 2", Courtesy of the Eric Key Collection, © Varnette Honeywood.

Cat. 126
Sedrick Huckaby, *Reclining Nude in Chair*, 1990s, Oil on canvas, 29" × 29", Courtesy of the Eric Key Collection, © Sedrick Huckaby.

Cat. 127
Sedrick Huckaby, *Seated Man*, 1999, Oil on canvas, 12" × 6", Courtesy of the Eric Key Collection, © Sedrick Huckaby.

Cat. 128
Sedrick Huckaby, *Self Portrait*, 2001, Charcoal on paper, 30½" × 24¾" × 2", Courtesy of the Eric Key Collection, © Sedrick Huckaby.

129

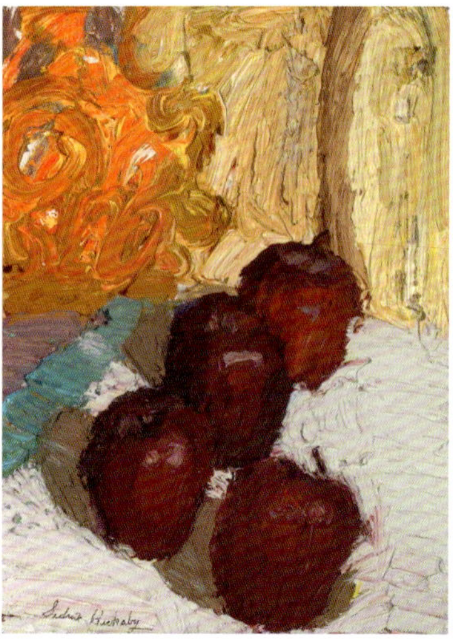

130

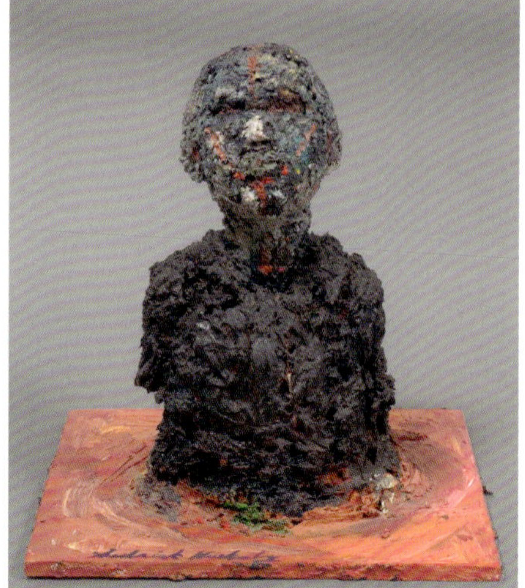

131

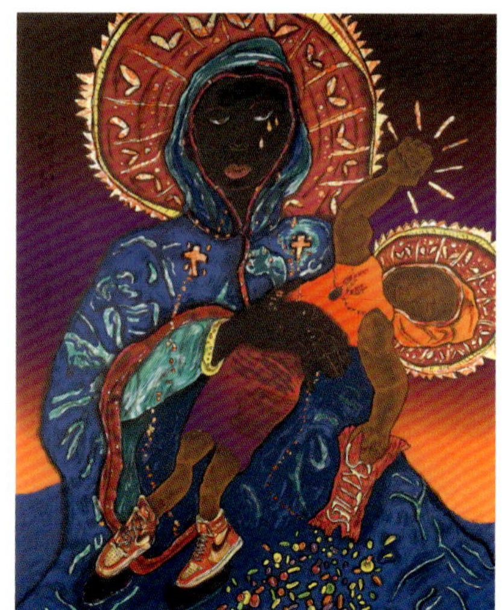

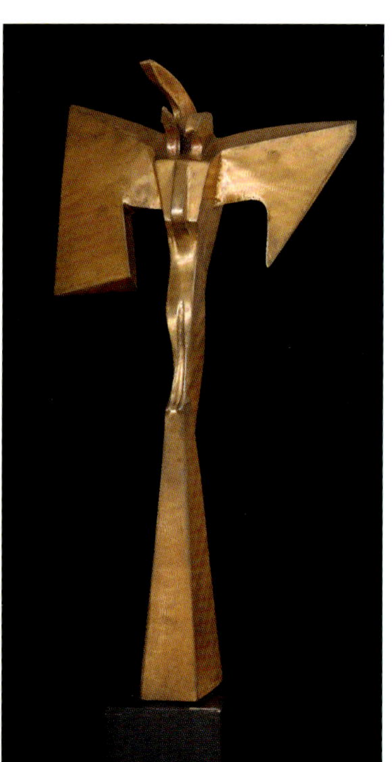

132

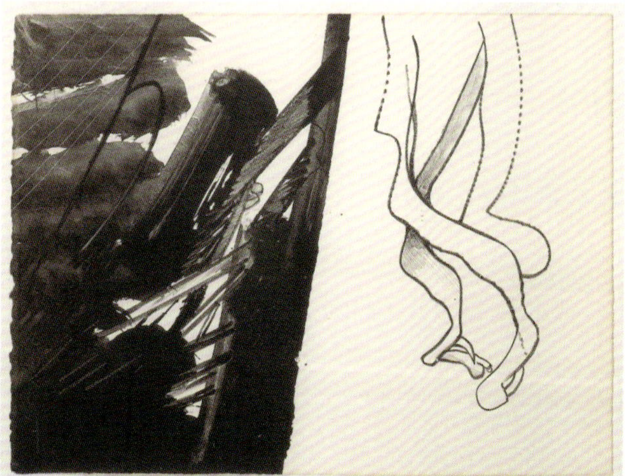

133

Cat. 129
Sedrick Huckaby, *Still Life*, 1997, Oil pastel on paper, 30" × 24", Courtesy of the Eric Key Collection, © Sedrick Huckaby.

Cat. 130
Sedrick Huckaby, *Untitled (Head of Man)*, no date, Newspaper and wood pulp over wire armature, board, 15" × 14" × 14", Courtesy of the Eric Key Collection, © Sedrick Huckaby.

Cat. 131
Margo Humphrey, *The Black Madonna (26/30)*, 2013, Color lithograph with gold leaf on paper, 27" × 22", Courtesy of the Eric Key Collection, © Margo Humphrey.

Cat. 132
Richard Hunt, *Hybrid Figure*, 1978, Welded bronze, 76" × 30" × 12", Courtesy of the Eric Key Collection, © Richard Hunt.

Cat. 133
Richard Hunt, *Untitled*, 1972, Lithograph on paper, 13" × 9", Courtesy of the Eric Key Collection, © Richard Hunt.

134

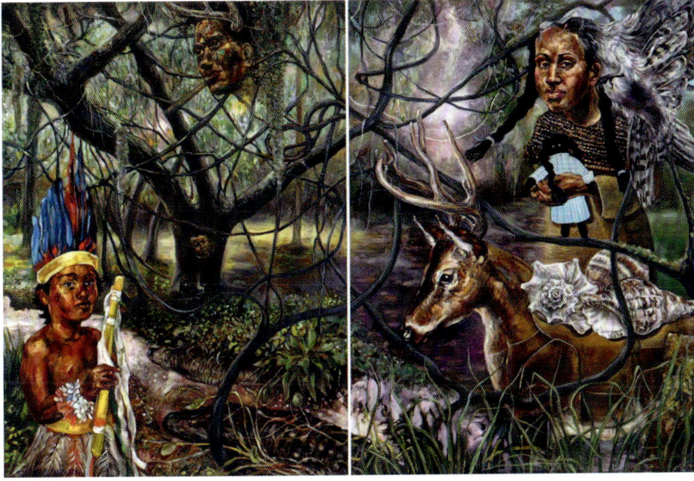

135

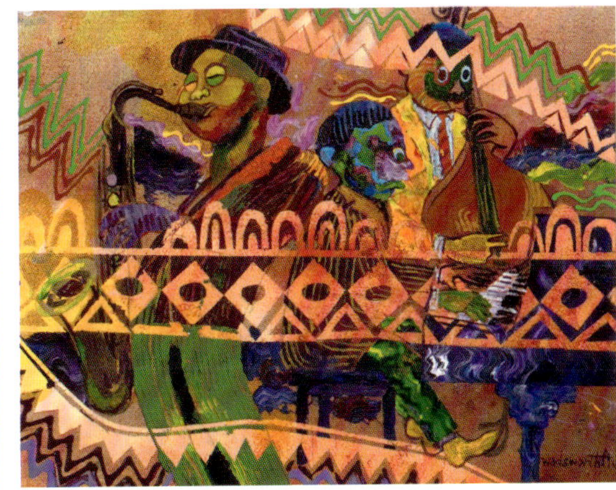

136

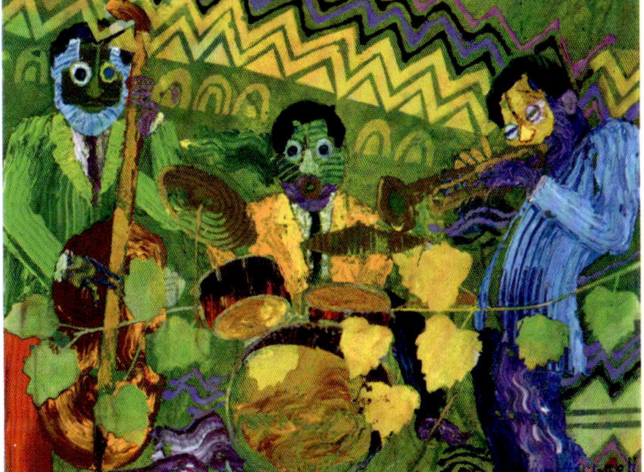

137

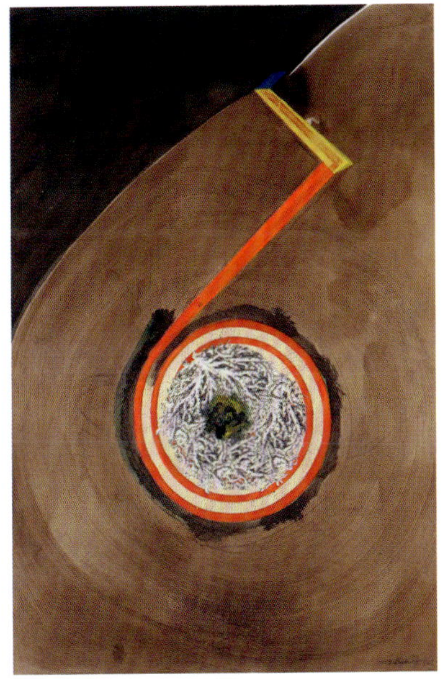

138

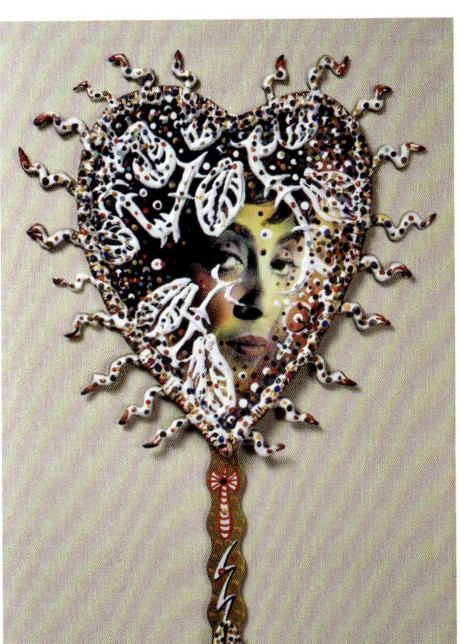

Cat. 134
Stefanie Jackson, *ZAPALA, Estuary of Regret*, 2017, Oil on canvas, 48" × 72" × 2", Courtesy of the Eric Key Collection, © Stefanie Jackson.

Cat. 135
Wadsworth Jarrell, *James Carter Trio*, 1999, Acrylic on board, 18" × 20", Courtesy of the Eric Key Collection, © Wadsworth Jarrell.

Cat. 136
Wadsworth Jarrell, *Miles Davis Group*, 2006, Acrylic on board, 15½" × 18½", Courtesy of the Eric Key Collection, © Wadsworth Jarrell.

Cat. 137
Martha Jackson Jarvis, *Ideograph #3*, 2018, Mixed media, 65½" × 45½" × 2", Courtesy of the Eric Key Collection, © Martha Jackson Jarvis.

Cat. 138
Ben Jones, *Untitled (Fan)*, 2001, Mixed media, 22¼" × 15¼" × 3", Courtesy of the Eric Key Collection, © Ben Jones.

139

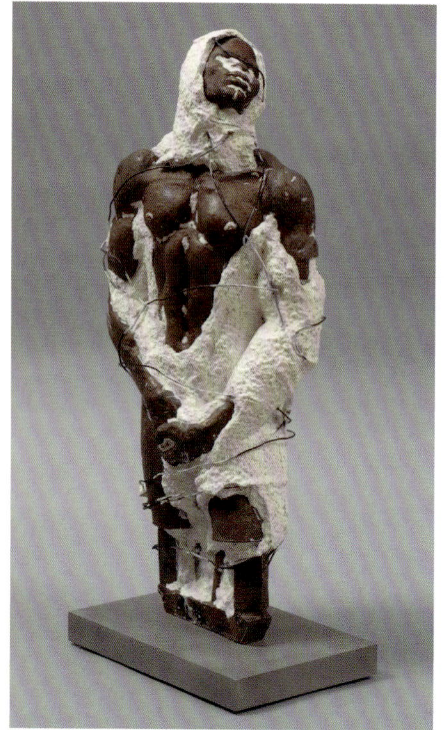

140

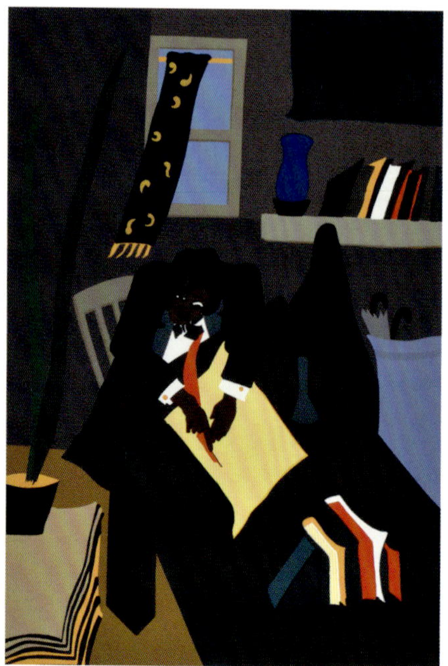

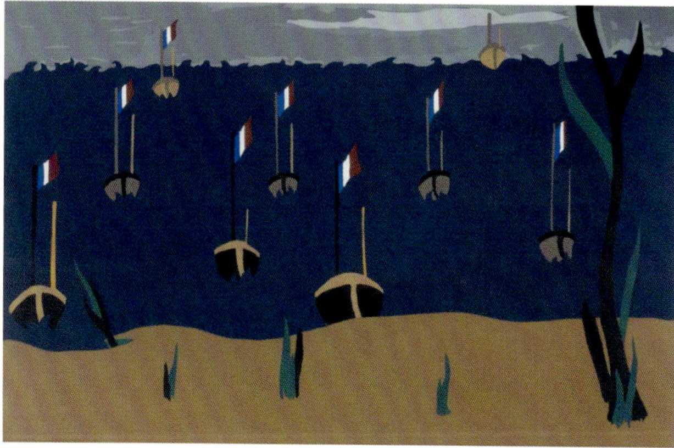

141

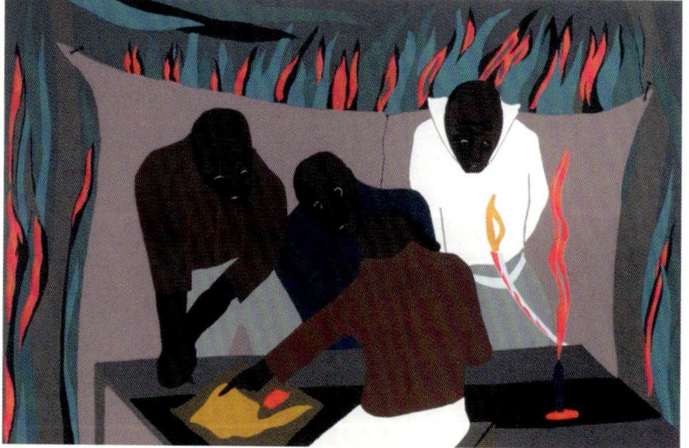

142

Cat. 139
Artis Lane, *Emerging into Spirit*, 1993, Bronze, wire, resin, 21" × 9¼" × 6¼", Courtesy of the Eric Key Collection, © Artis Lane.

Cat. 140
Jacob Lawrence, *Douglass*, 1999, Silkscreen on paper, 32" × 22", Courtesy of the Eric Key Collection, © 2023 The Jacob and Gwendolyn Knight Lawrence Foundation, Seattle / Artists Rights Society (ARS), NY.

Cat. 141
Jacob Lawrence, *Flotilla*, 1996, Silkscreen on paper (92/120), 18" × 28" × 2", Courtesy of the Eric Key Collection, © 2023 The Jacob and Gwendolyn Knight Lawrence Foundation, Seattle / Artists Rights Society (ARS), NY.

Cat. 142
Jacob Lawrence, *Strategy*, 1999, Silkscreen on paper (12/120), 18" × 28" × 2", Courtesy of the Eric Key Collection, © 2023 The Jacob and Gwendolyn Knight Lawrence Foundation, Seattle / Artists Rights Society (ARS), NY.

143

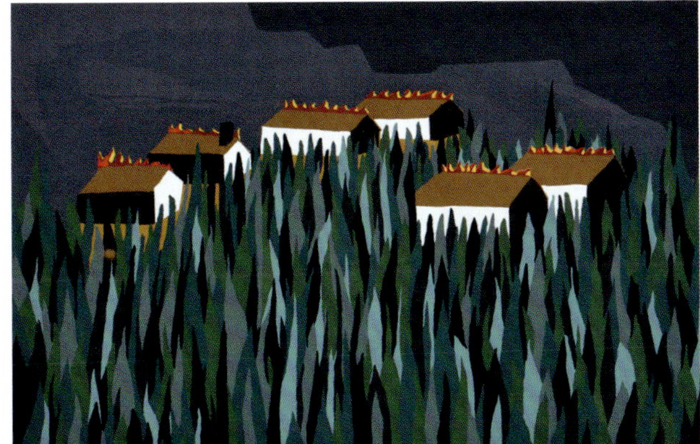

144

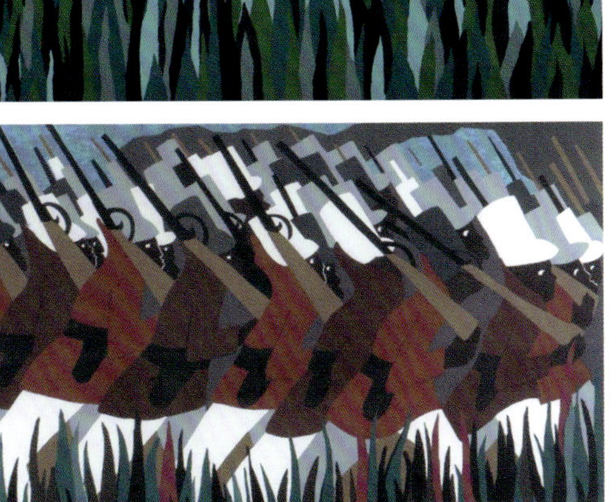

145

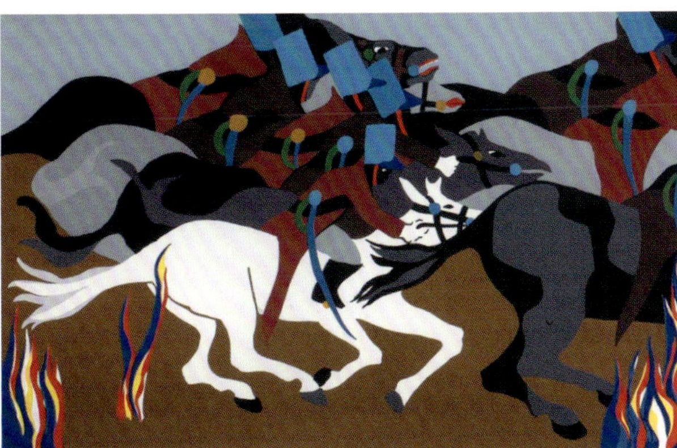

146

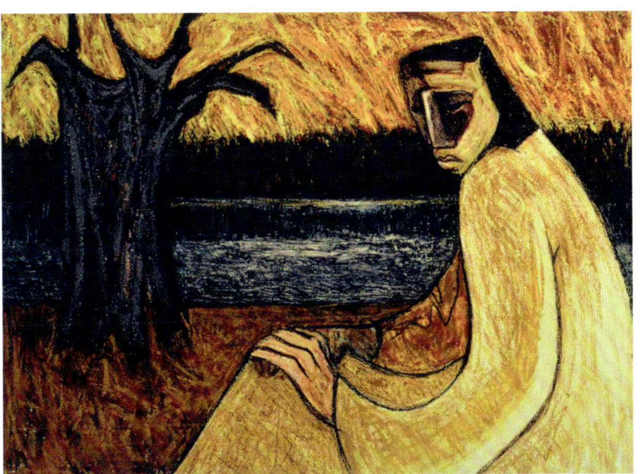

147

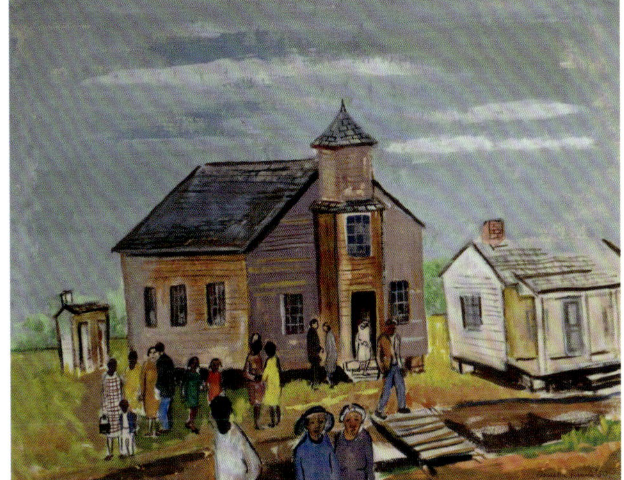

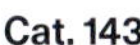

Cat. 143
Jacob Lawrence, *The Burning*, 1999, Silkscreen on paper, 35½" × 45", Courtesy of the Eric Key Collection, © 2023 The Jacob and Gwendolyn Knight Lawrence Foundation, Seattle / Artists Rights Society (ARS), NY.

Cat. 144
Jacob Lawrence, *The March*, 1995, Silkscreen on paper (99/120), 18" × 28" × 2", Courtesy of the Eric Key Collection, © 2023 The Jacob and Gwendolyn Knight Lawrence Foundation, Seattle / Artists Rights Society (ARS), NY.

Cat. 145
Jacob Lawrence, *Toussaint at Ennery*, 1989, Silkscreen on paper, 18" × 29" × 2", Courtesy of the Eric Key Collection, © 2023 The Jacob and Gwendolyn Knight Lawrence Foundation, Seattle / Artists Rights Society (ARS), NY.

Cat. 146
Samella Lewis, *Bayou Woman*, 1999, Oil stick on paper, 24" × 30", Courtesy of the Eric Key Collection, © 2023 Samella Lewis / Licensed by VAGA at Artists Rights Society (ARS), NY.

Cat. 147
Samella Lewis, *Church Gathering*, 1972, Watercolor on paper, 20¼" × 23", Courtesy of the Eric Key Collection, © 2023 Samella Lewis / Licensed by VAGA at Artists Rights Society (ARS), NY.

148
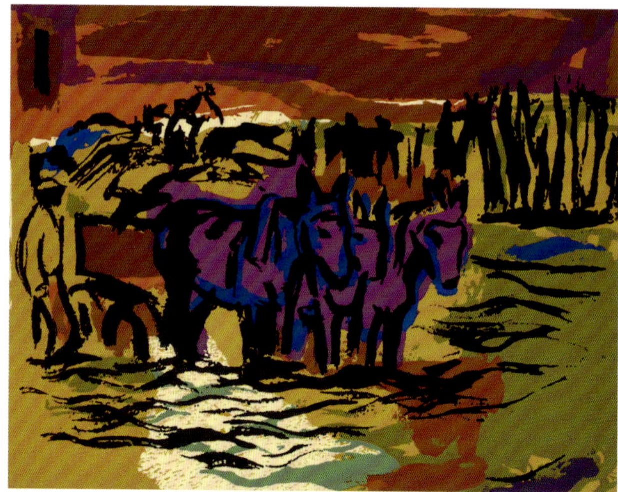

150
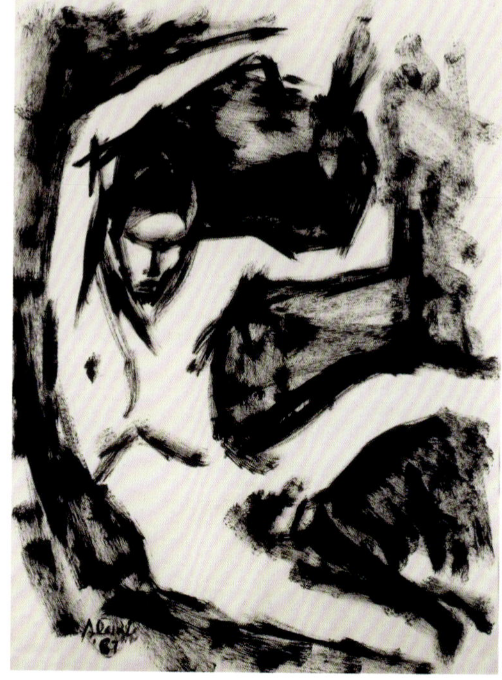

149
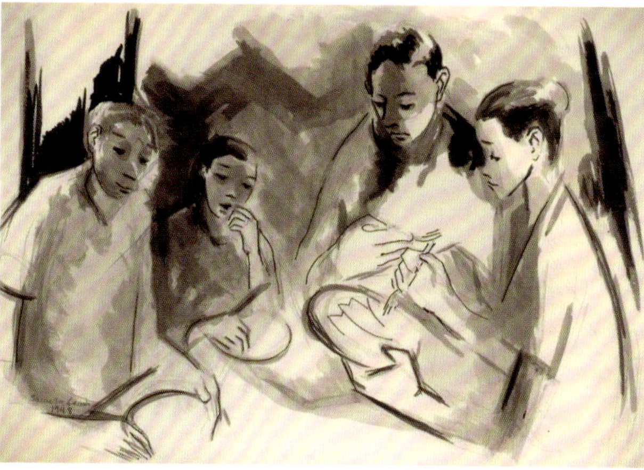

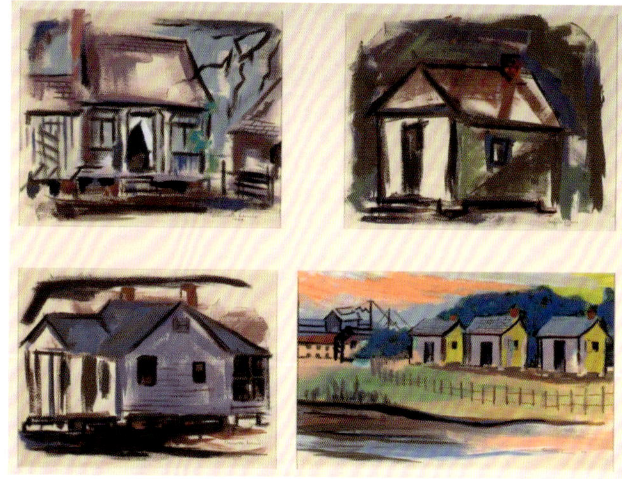
151

Cat. 148
Samella Lewis, *Creole Mules*, 1995, Screenprint on paper, 24¼" × 29", Courtesy of the Eric Key Collection, © 2023 Samella Lewis / Licensed by VAGA at Artists Rights Society (ARS), NY.

Cat. 149
Samella Lewis, *Family*, 1948, Watercolor on paper, 20" × 24⅛", Courtesy of the Eric Key Collection, © 2023 Samella Lewis / Licensed by VAGA at Artists Rights Society (ARS), NY.

Cat. 150
Samella Lewis, *Nude*, 1967, Watercolor on paper, 32" × 26", Courtesy of the Eric Key Collection, © 2023 Samella Lewis / Licensed by VAGA at Artists Rights Society (ARS), NY.

Cat. 151
Samella Lewis, *Plantation Houses*, 1949, Acrylic on paper, 26½" × 31½", Courtesy of the Eric Key Collection, © 2023 Samella Lewis / Licensed by VAGA at Artists Rights Society (ARS), NY.

152

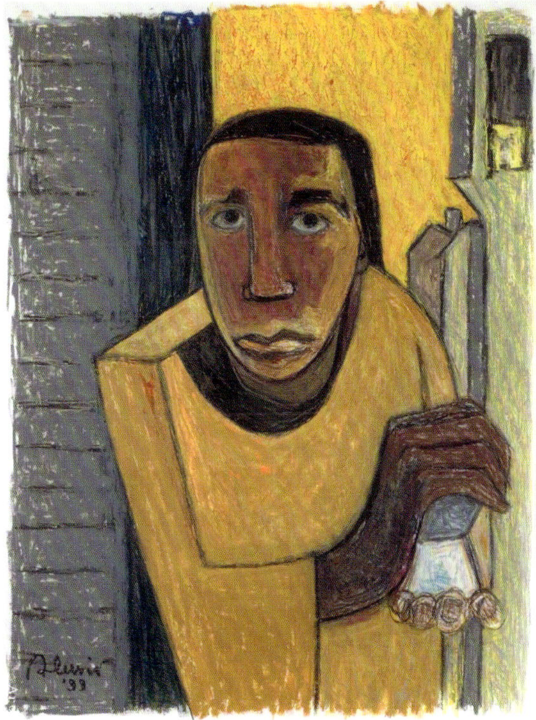

153

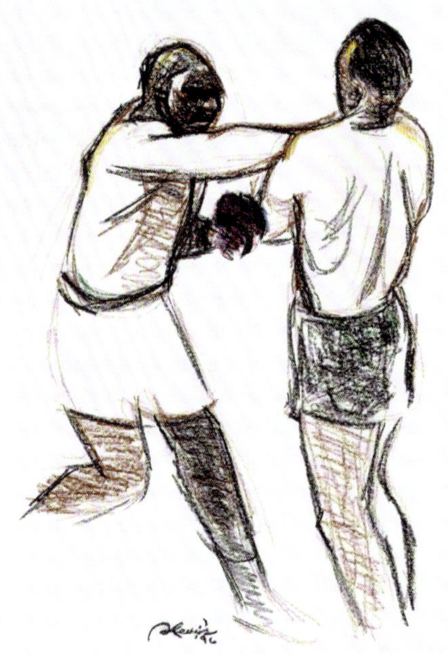

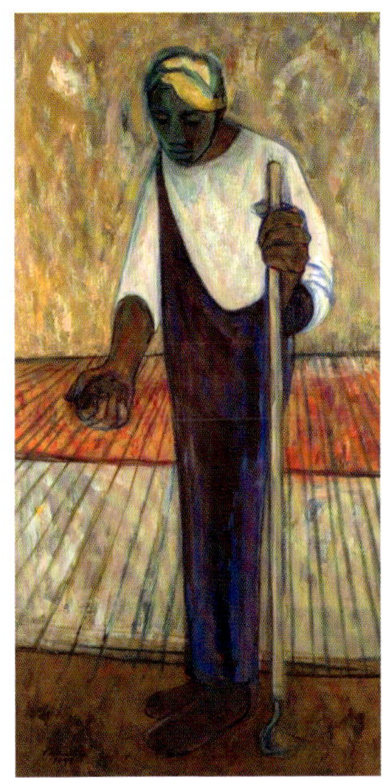

154

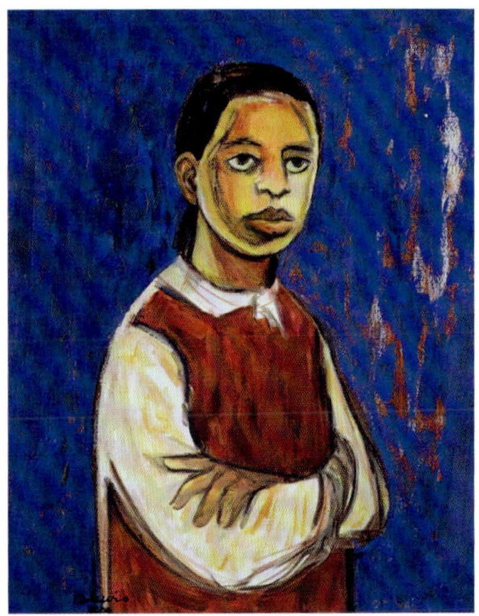

155

Cat. 152
Samella Lewis, *Special Delivery*, 1999, Oil stick on paper, 28" × 22", Courtesy of the Eric Key Collection, © 2023 Samella Lewis / Licensed by VAGA at Artists Rights Society (ARS), NY.

Cat. 153
Samella Lewis, *The Blow*, 1996, Oil stick on paper, 30" × 23¾", Courtesy of the Eric Key Collection, © 2023 Samella Lewis / Licensed by VAGA at Artists Rights Society (ARS), NY.

Cat. 154
Samella Lewis, *The Farmer*, 1999, Oil on canvas, 50" × 28" × 2", Courtesy of the Eric Key Collection, © 2023 Samella Lewis / Licensed by VAGA at Artists Rights Society (ARS), NY.

Cat. 155
Samella Lewis, *Untitled*, 1999, Mixed media, 32" × 26", Courtesy of the Eric Key Collection, © 2023 Samella Lewis / Licensed by VAGA at Artists Rights Society (ARS), NY.

156

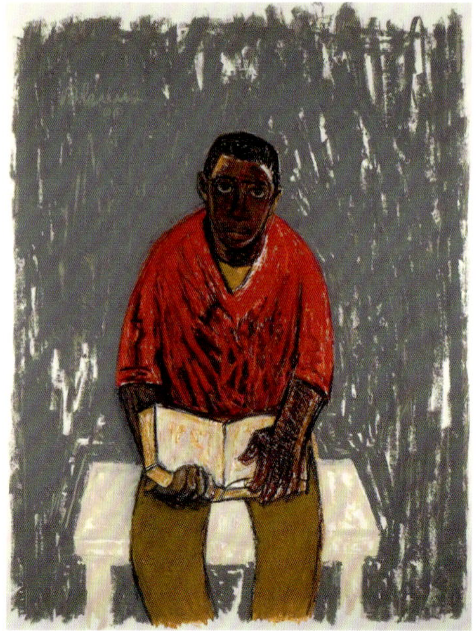

157

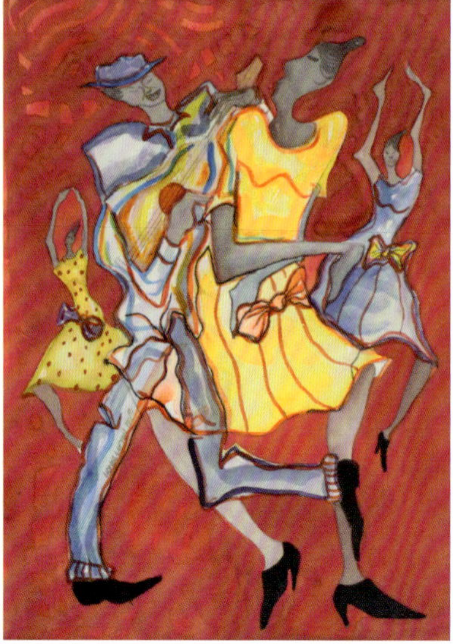

158

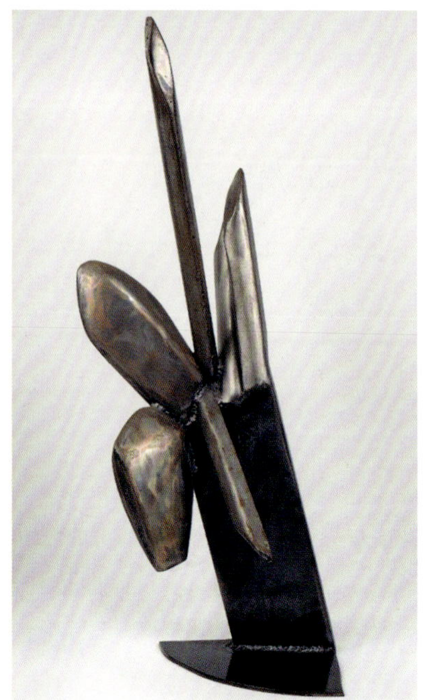

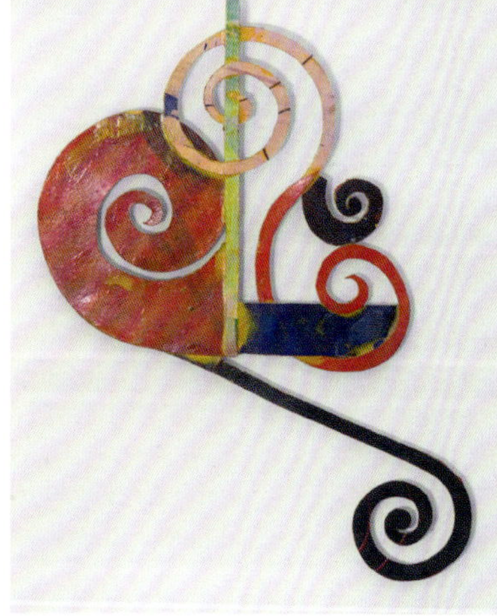

159

160

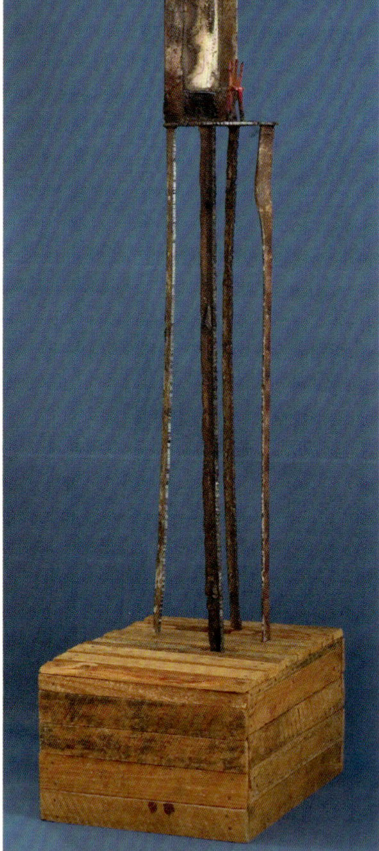

Cat. 156
Samella Lewis, *We've Always Wanted to Know How to Read and Write*, 2000, Oil stick on paper, 36" × 29" × 2", Courtesy of the Eric Key Collection, © 2023 Samella Lewis / Licensed by VAGA at Artists Rights Society (ARS), NY.

Cat. 157
Lionel Lofton, *Untitled (Dancers)*, 1988, Watercolor on paper, 21½" × 17½", Courtesy of the Eric Key Collection, © Lionel Lofton.

Cat. 158
Ed Love, *Monk*, 1982, Welded steel, 36" × 11" × 9", Courtesy of the Eric Key Collection, © Ed Love.

Cat. 159
Al Loving, *Whyte St. #15*, 1992, Mixed media, 36" × 27" × 2", Courtesy of the Eric Key Collection, the artist, and Garth Greenan Gallery, NY, © Garth Greenan.

Cat. 160
Faheem Majeed, *Grandma Chair*, 2009, Paint, metal, wood, 75¼" × 19⅝" × 26⅝", Courtesy of the Eric Key Collection, © Faheem Majeed.

161

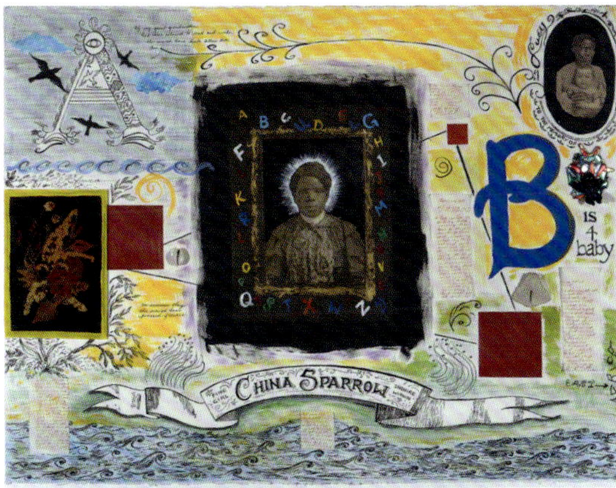

162

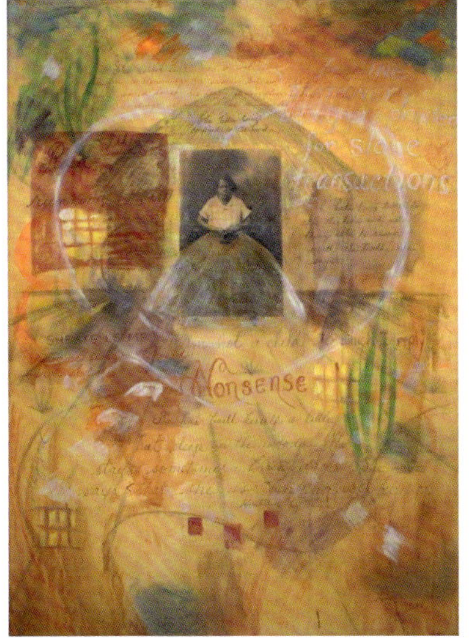

163

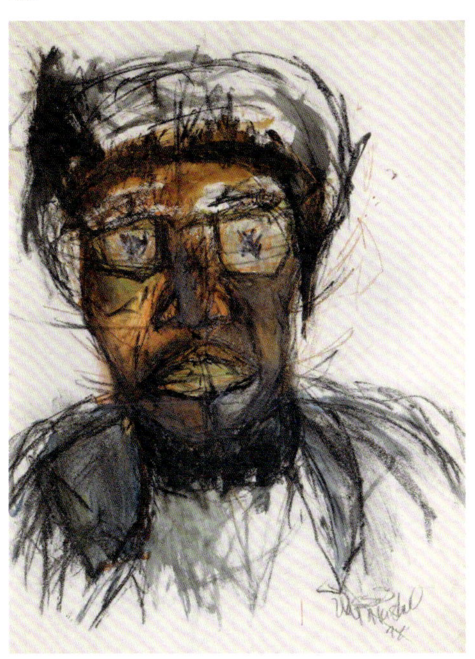

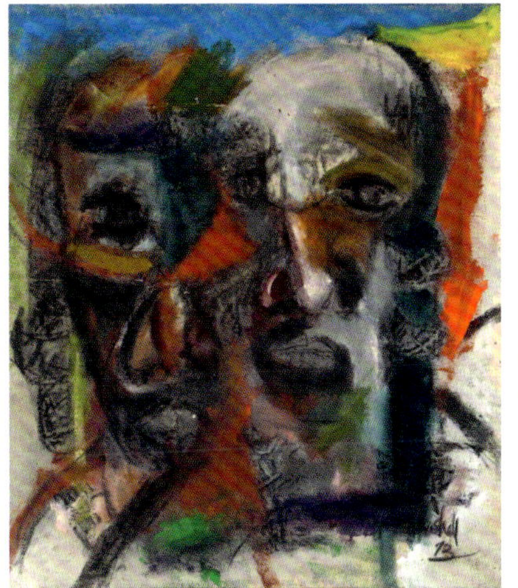

164

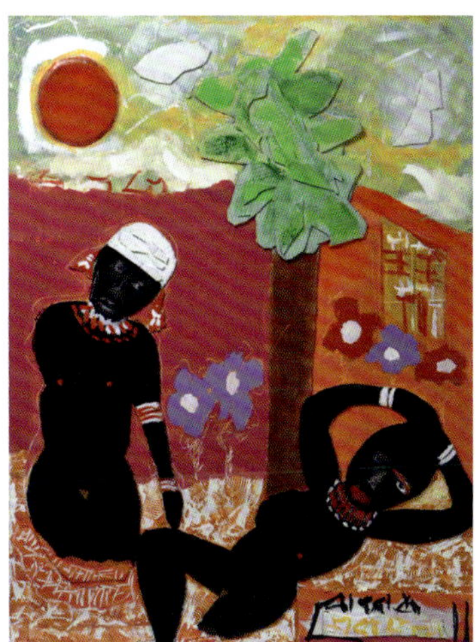

165

Cat. 161
Lynn Marshall Linnemeier, *Black Baby*, 2013, Mixed media, 24" × 32", Courtesy of the Eric Key Collection, © Lynn Marshall Linnemeier.

Cat. 162
Lynn Marshall Linnemeier, *Nonsense*, 2001, Watercolor and pencil on paper, 77" × 56¼" × 1½", Courtesy of the Eric Key Collection, © Lynn Marshall Linnemeier.

Cat. 163
Ulysses Marshall, *Man Child*, 1974, Acrylic on paper, 39" × 33⅜" × 1¼", Courtesy of the Eric Key Collection, © Ulysses Marshall.

Cat. 164
Ulysses Marshall, *Masks*, 1973, Acrylic on linen, 35" × 31", Courtesy of the Eric Key Collection, © Ulysses Marshall.

Cat. 165
Ulysses Marshall, *Untitled (two nudes under tree)*, 2008, Mixed media, 50" × 38", Courtesy of the Eric Key Collection, © Ulysses Marshall.

166

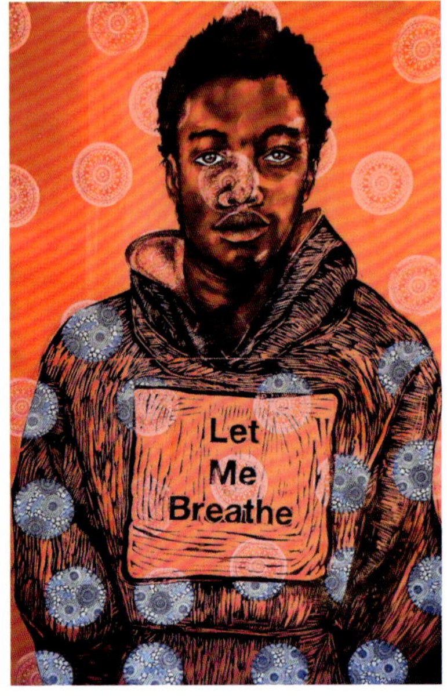

167

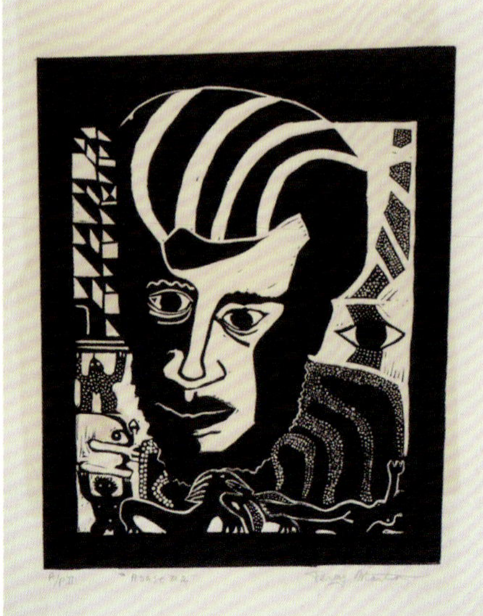

168

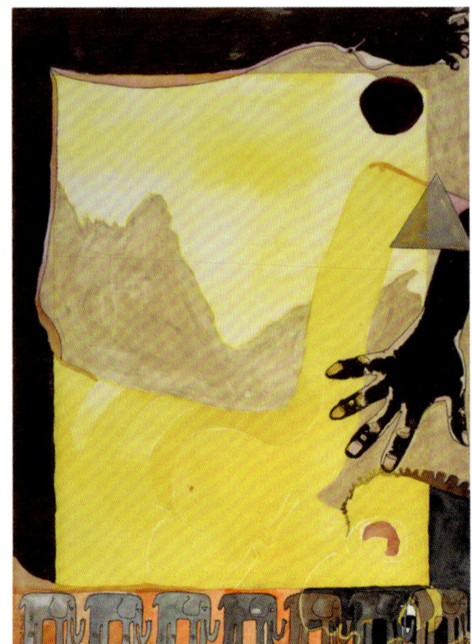

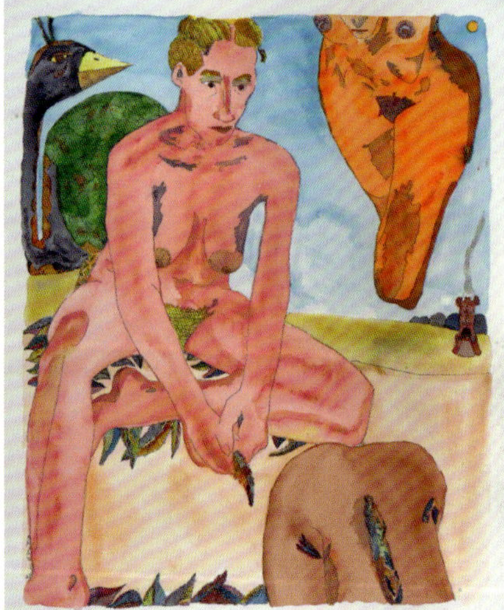

169

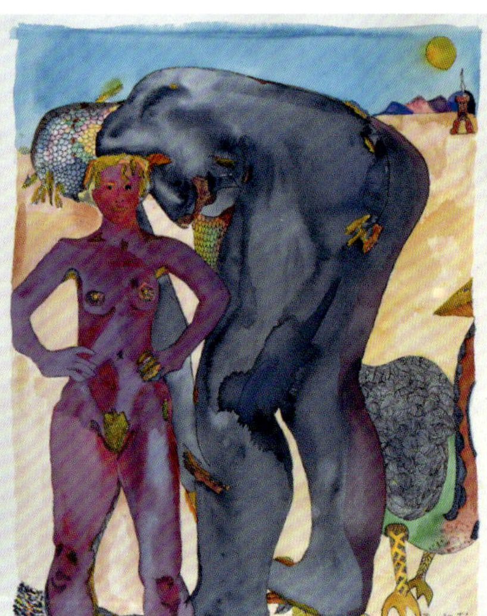

170

Cat. 166
Delita Martin, *Let Me Breathe*, 2020, Relief print on paper, 36" × 24", Courtesy of the Eric Key Collection, © Delita Martin.

Cat. 167
Percy Martin, *Asasa #2*, 1980, Medium undefined, 20" × 15", Courtesy of the Eric Key Collection, © Percy Martin.

Cat. 168
Percy Martin, *Bushman Series*, no date, Watercolor on paper, 43" × 35", Courtesy of the Eric Key Collection, © Percy Martin.

Cat. 169
Percy Martin, *Bushman Series (Pink Nude Figure)*, no date, Watercolor on paper, 33¼" × 29", Courtesy of the Eric Key Collection, © Percy Martin.

Cat. 170
Percy Martin, *Bushman Series (Purple Female Figure)*, no date, Watercolor on paper, 33¼" × 29", Courtesy of the Eric Key Collection, © Percy Martin.

171

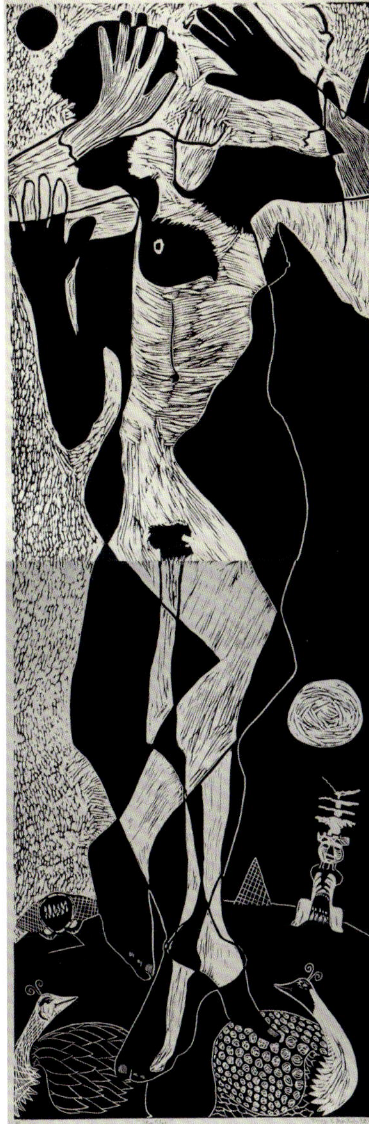

172

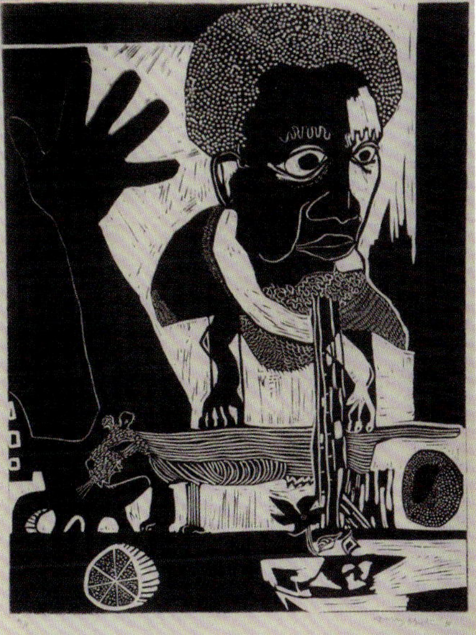

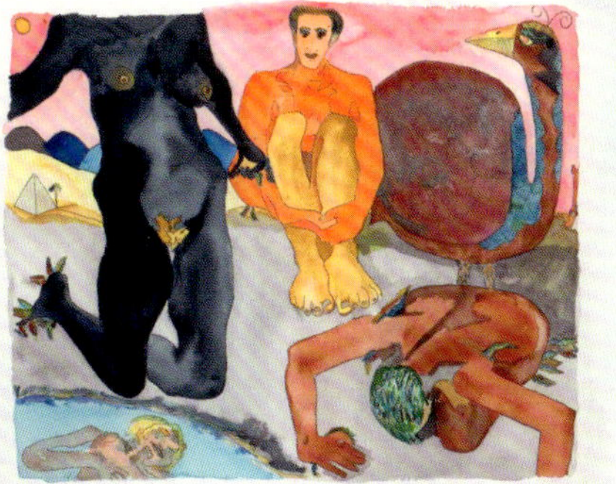

173

174

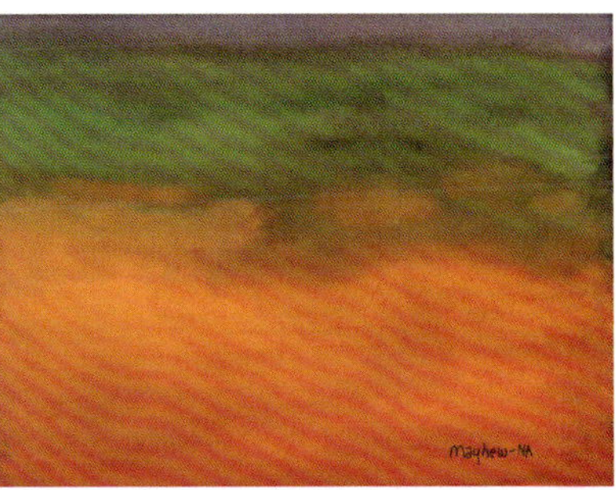

175

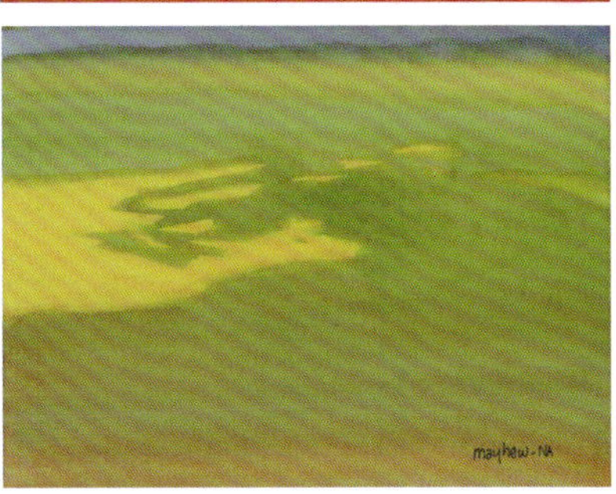

Cat. 171
Percy Martin, *Sky Step*, 1980, Linoleum, 74" × 25", Courtesy of the Eric Key Collection, © Percy Martin.

Cat. 172
Percy Martin, *Tere*, 1980, Linoleum on rice paper, 30½" × 22½", Courtesy of the Eric Key Collection, © Percy Martin.

Cat. 173
Percy Martin, *Three Bushwomen*, no date, Watercolor on paper, 30" × 33" × 2", Courtesy of the Eric Key Collection, © Percy Martin.

Cat. 174
Richard Mayhew, *Spring Mood Series #4 (Rust Green Landscape)*, 2018, Watercolor on paper, 9" × 12" × 2", Courtesy of the Eric Key Collection, © Richard Mayhew.

Cat. 175
Richard Mayhew, *Spring Mood Series #6, (Yellow Green Landscape)*, 2018, Watercolor on paper, 9" × 12" × 2", Courtesy of the Eric Key Collection, © Richard Mayhew.

176

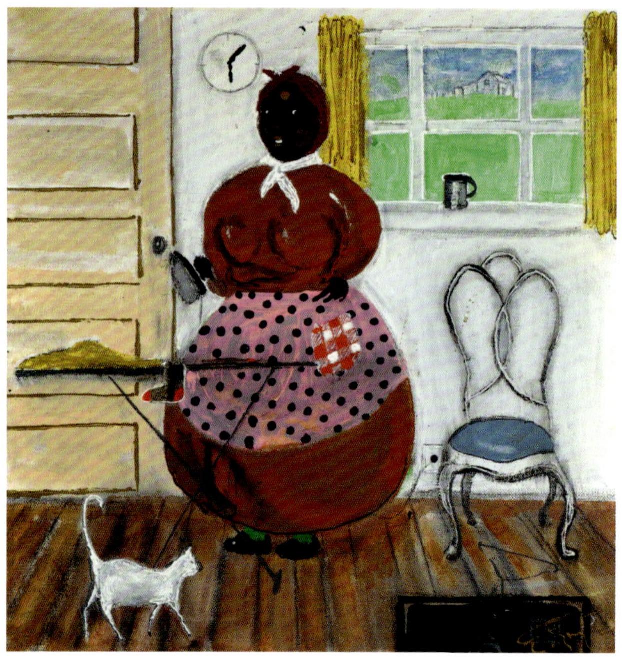

178

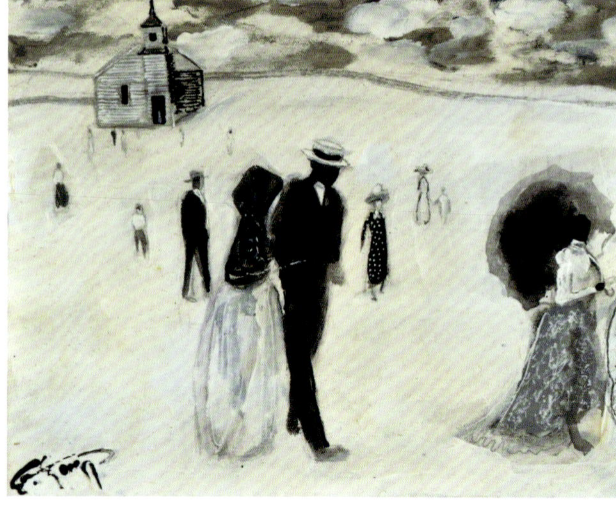

177

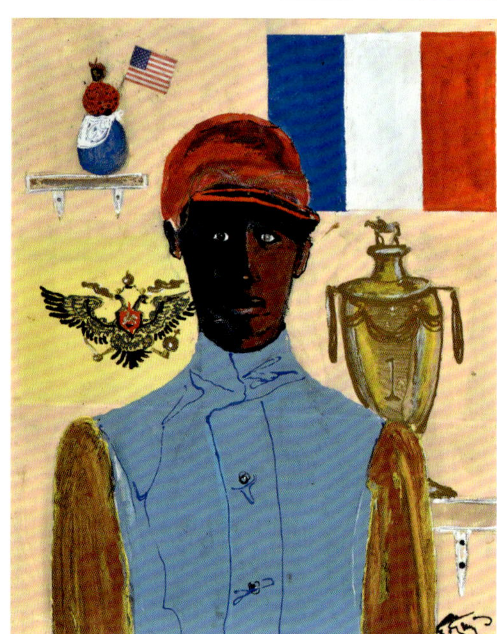

179

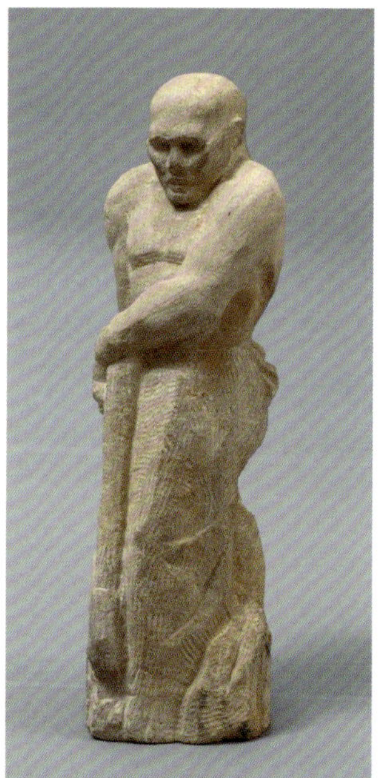

Cat. 176
Ealy Mays, *Angie Mama*, 2012, Oil on canvas, 17" × 17", Courtesy of the Eric Key Collection, © Ealy Mays.

Cat. 177
Ealy Mays, *Untitled*, 2013, Oil on canvas, 17" × 14", Courtesy of the Eric Key Collection, © Ealy Mays.

Cat. 178
Ealy Mays, *Walking in the Park*, 2015, Oil on canvas, 14" × 17¼", Courtesy of the Eric Key Collection, © Ealy Mays.

Cat. 179
James McMillan, *Untitled*, 1952, Stone, 17" × 5½" × 6¾", Courtesy of the Eric Key Collection, © James McMillan.

180

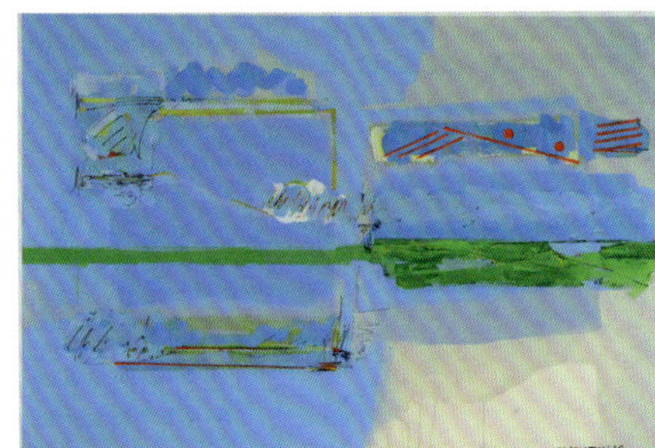

181

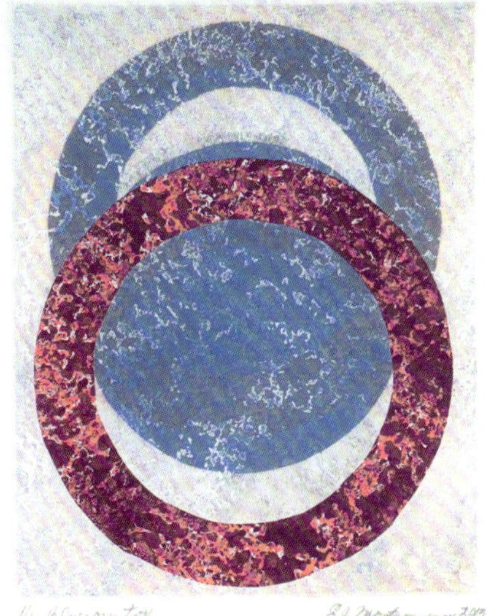

182

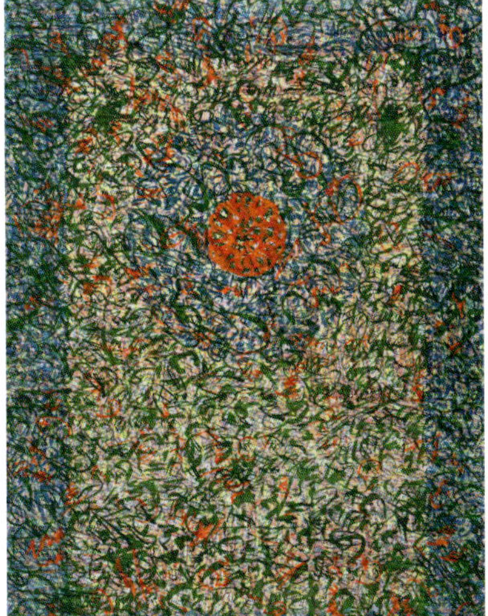

184

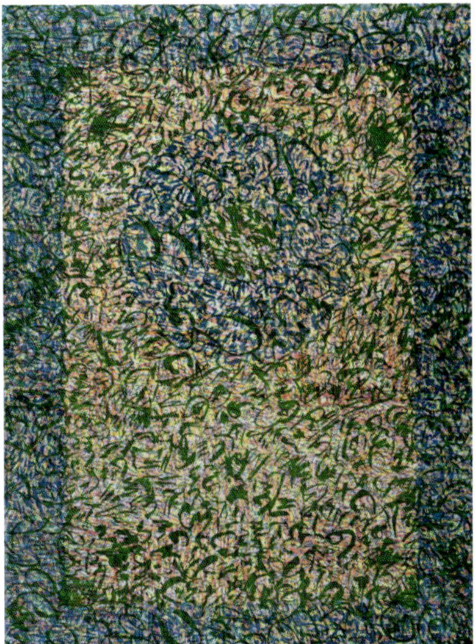

183

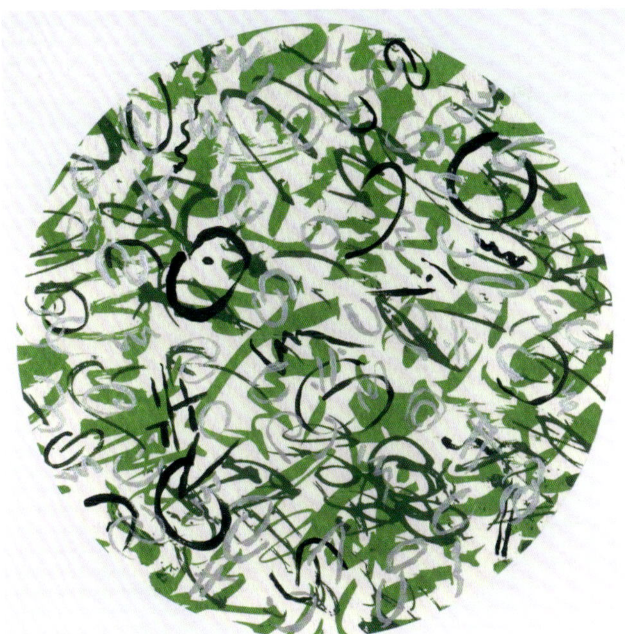

Cat. 180
Sam Middleton, *Polder Spring Two*, 1979, Mixed media, 19¾" × 28¾", Courtesy of the Eric Key Collection, © Sam Middleton.

Cat. 181
Evangeline "EJ" Montgomery, *Blues on Top*, 2013, Etching on paper, 23" × 17", Courtesy of the Eric Key Collection, © Evangeline "EJ" Montgomery.

Cat. 182
Evangeline "EJ" Montgomery, *Configuration*, 1991, Lithograph on paper, 30" × 22", Courtesy of the Eric Key Collection, © Evangeline "EJ" Montgomery.

Cat. 183
Evangeline "EJ" Montgomery, *Evergreen Park*, 2007, Screenprint on paper (2/5), 41" × 39" × 2", Courtesy of the Eric Key Collection, © Evangeline "EJ" Montgomery.

Cat. 184
Evangeline "EJ" Montgomery, *The Window*, 1991, Lithograph on paper, 30" × 22", Courtesy of the Eric Key Collection, © Evangeline "EJ" Montgomery.

185

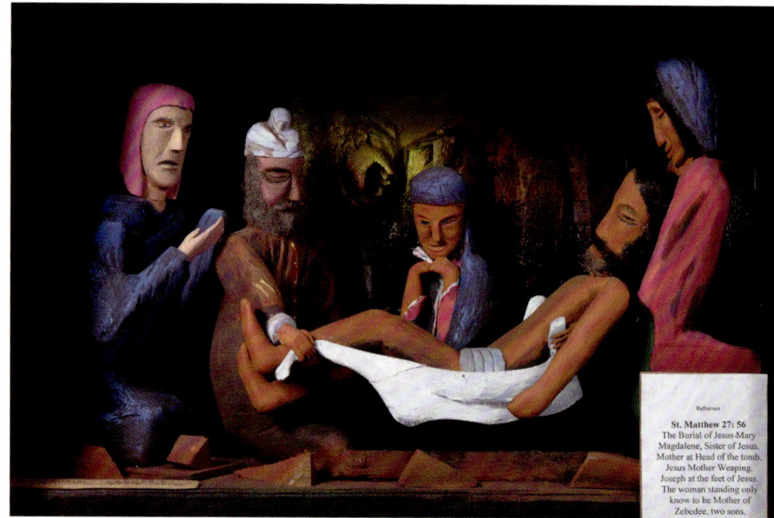

186

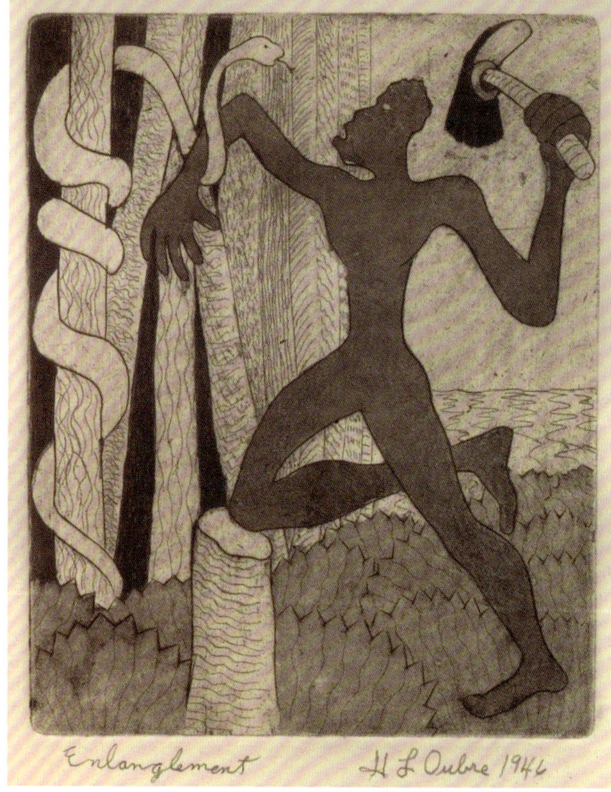

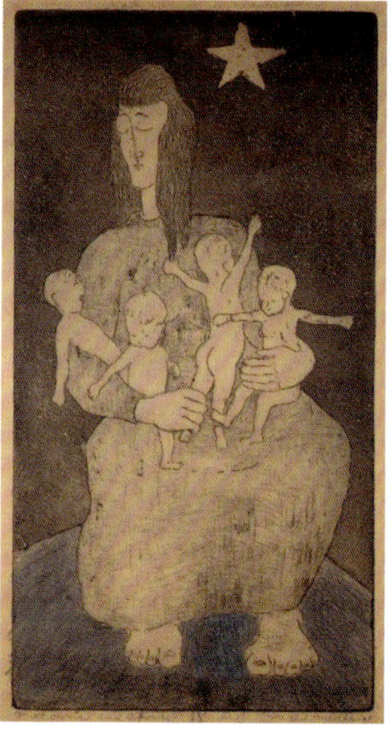

187

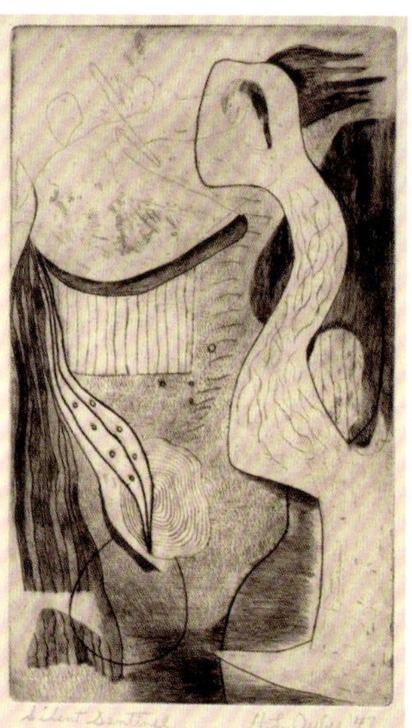

188

Cat. 185
Eddie Moore, *Jesus Burial*, 1995, Painted wood, 21" × 20" × 12", Courtesy of the Eric Key Collection, © Eddie Moore.

Cat. 186
Hayward Oubre, *Entanglement*, 1946, Etching on paper, 12" × 11", Courtesy of the Eric Key Collection, © Hayward Oubre.

Cat. 187
Hayward Oubre, *Madonna and Quads*, 1947, Mixed media, 25" × 17", Courtesy of the Eric Key Collection, © Hayward Oubre.

Cat. 188
Hayward Oubre, *Silent Sentinel*, 1947, Medium undefined, 22½" × 16½", Courtesy of the Eric Key Collection, © Hayward Oubre.

189

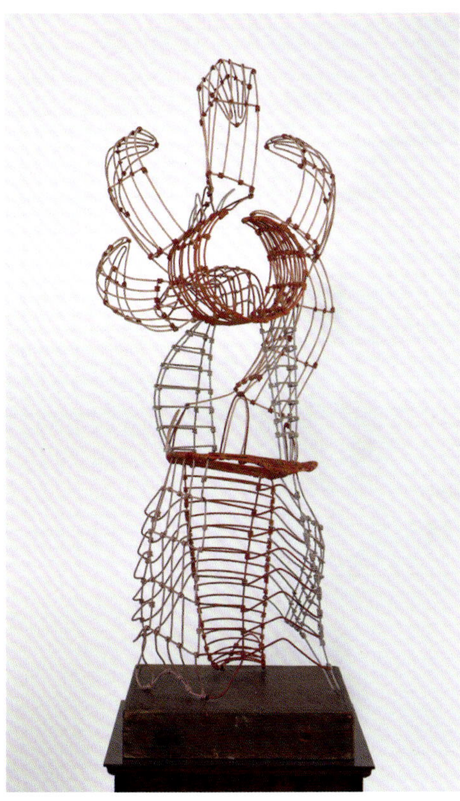

190

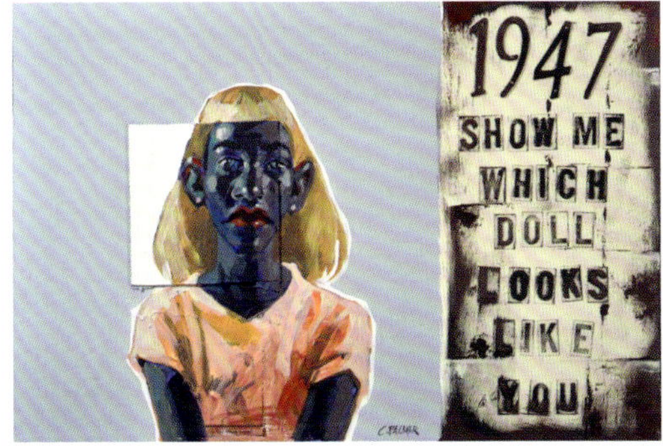

191

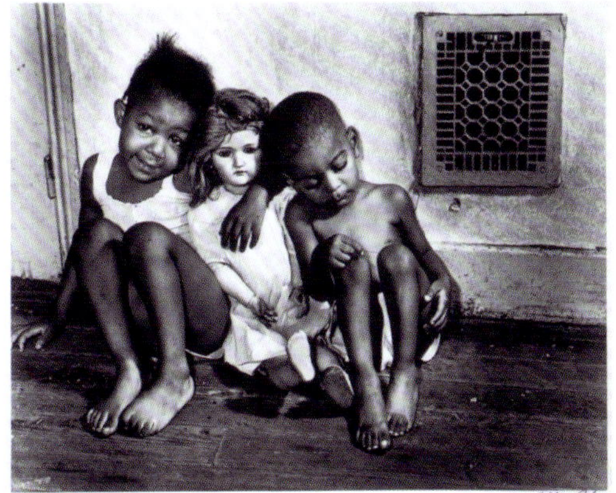

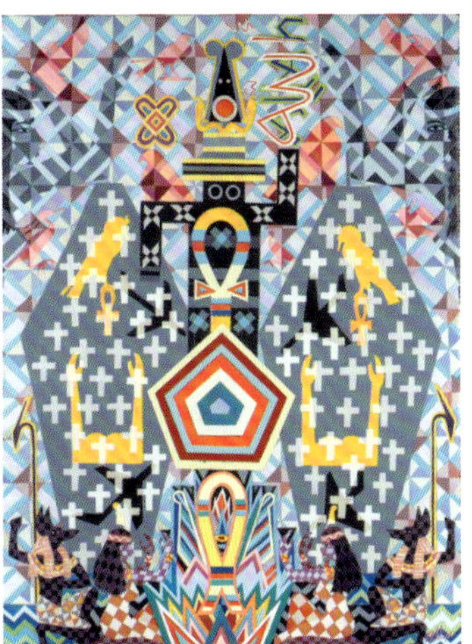

192

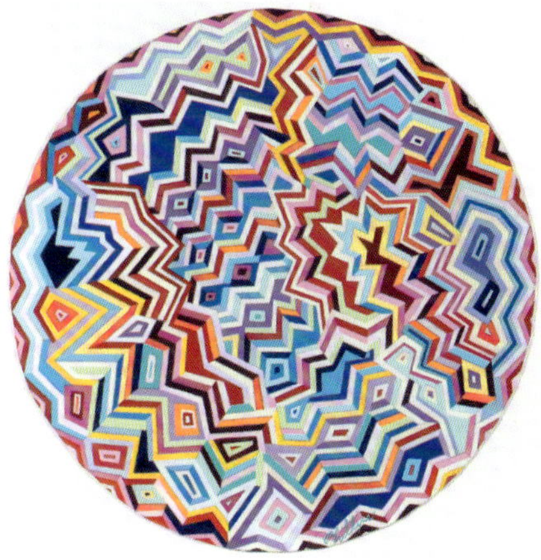

193

Cat. 189
Hayward Oubre, *Variation*, 1969, Wire and paint, 37½" × 14½" × 15½", Courtesy of the Eric Key Collection, © Hayward Oubre.

Cat. 190
Charly Palmer, *Identity Lost*, 2006, Mixed media, 24" × 36", Courtesy of the Eric Key Collection, © Charly Palmer.

Cat. 191
Gordon Parks, *Children with Doll, Washington, D.C.*, 1942, Photograph, 22" × 25", Courtesy of the Eric Key Collection, © Courtesy of and Copyright of The Gordon Parks Foundation.

Cat. 192
James Phillips, *911*, 2002, Acrylic on paper, 40" × 36", Courtesy of the Eric Key Collection, © James Phillips.

Cat. 193
James Phillips, *Katango: Lights on Another Satellite Series*, 2013, Acrylic on paper, 16" in diameter, Courtesy of the Eric Key Collection, © James Phillips.

194

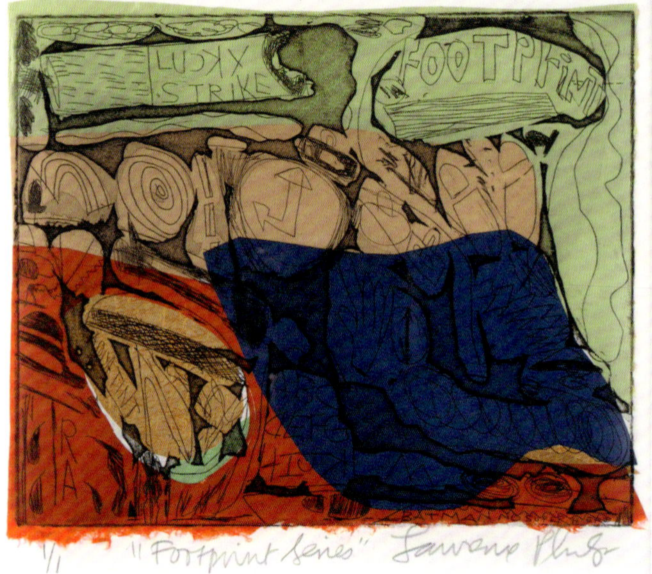

195

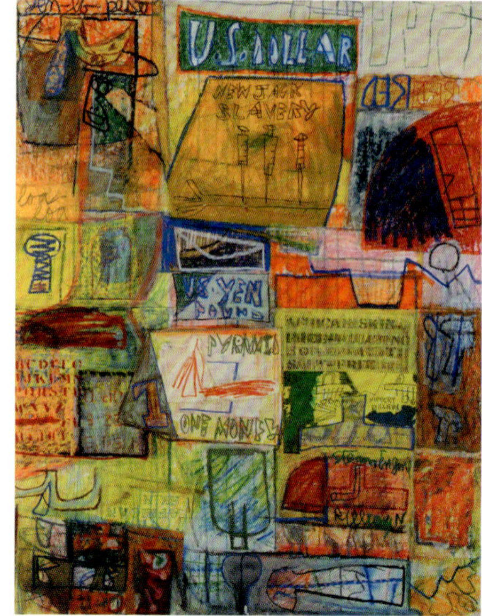

196

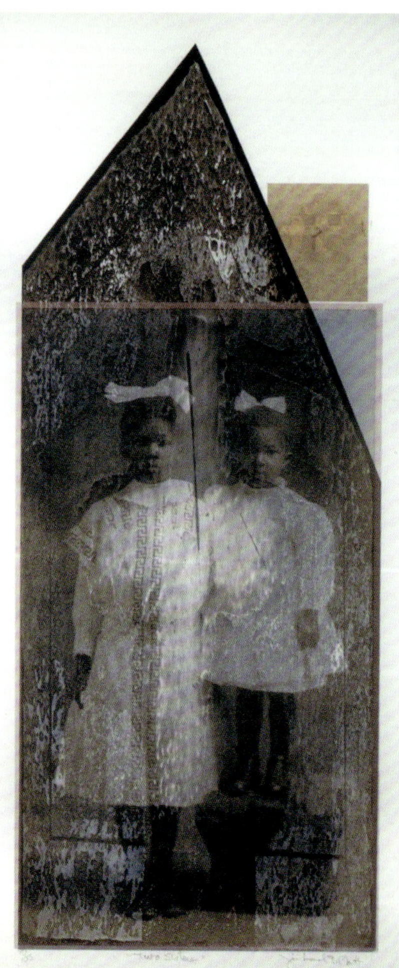

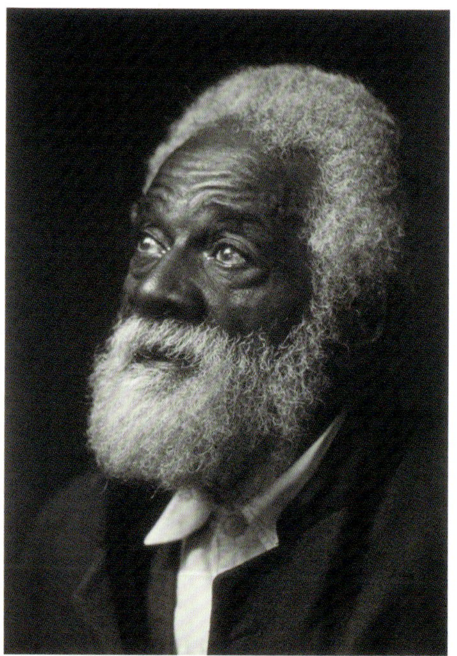

197

Cat. 194
Lawrence Philp, *Footprint Series*, no date, Print on paper, 8" × 10", Courtesy of the Eric Key Collection, © Lawrence Philp.

Cat. 195
Lawrence Philp, *US Dollar*, 1999–2000, Mixed media, 62" × 48" × 2", Courtesy of the Eric Key Collection, © Lawrence Philp.

Cat. 196
Michael Platt, *Two Sisters*, 2003, Print on paper, 32" × 16", Courtesy of the Eric Key Collection, © Michael Platt.

Cat. 197
Prentice H. Polk, *Henry Baker*, 1984, Photograph, 22½" × 16½", Courtesy of the Eric Key Collection, © Prentice H. Polk.

198

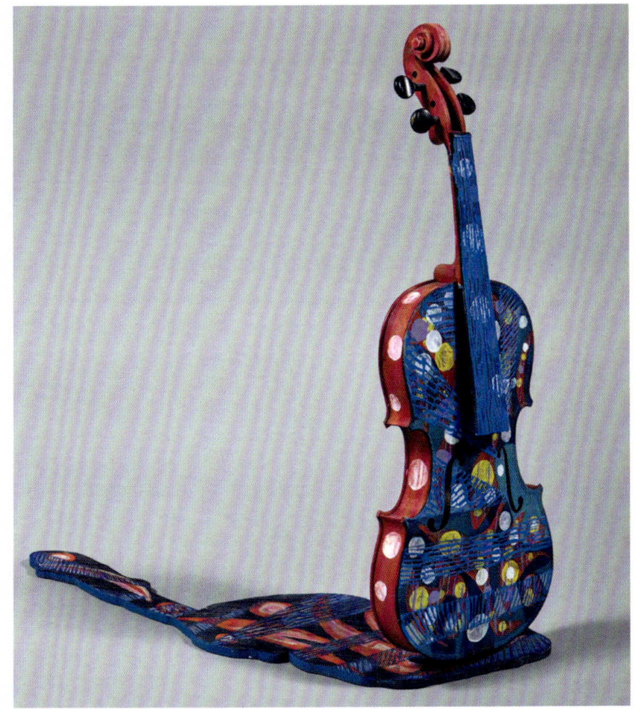

199

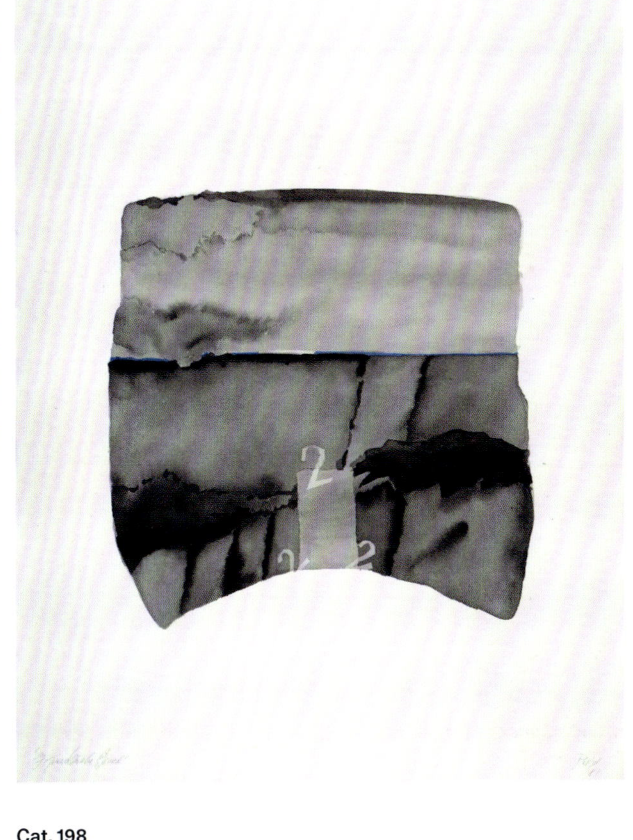

200

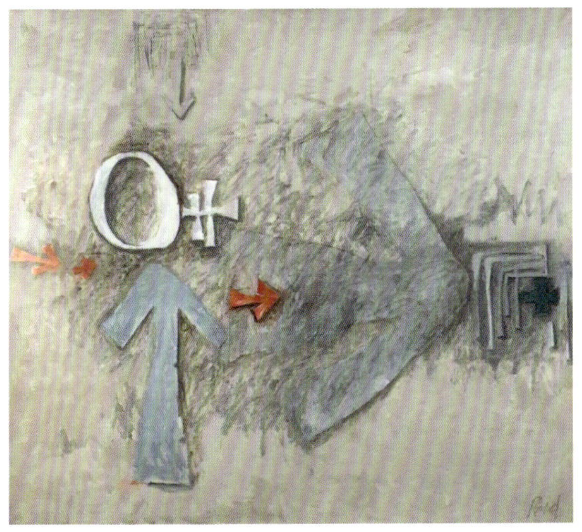

201

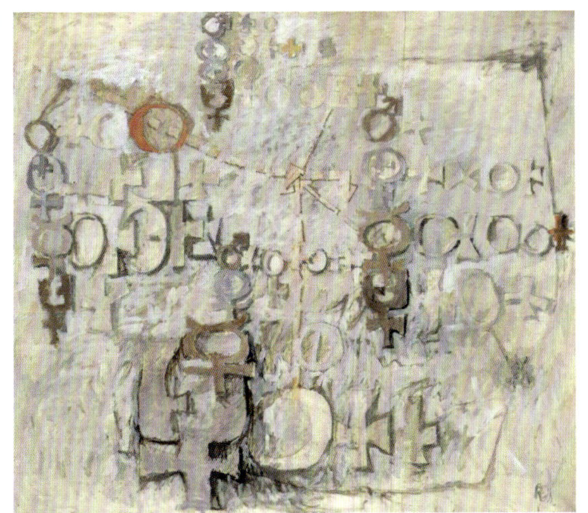

Cat. 198
Eric Pryor, *Shadow and Rhythm/ Untitled*, 2002, Paint on wood, 22" × 10" × 22", Courtesy of the Eric Key Collection, © Eric Pryor.

Cat. 199
Robert Reid, *Figure on the Beach*, 1981, Watercolor on paper, 30" × 22", Courtesy of the Eric Key Collection, © Robert Reid.

Cat. 200
Robert Reid, *Follow the Leader*, no date, Oil and collage on linen, 37½" × 41¼" × 1¾", Courtesy of the Eric Key Collection, © Robert Reid.

Cat. 201
Robert Reid, *West Wind*, 1965, Collage on canvas, 43½" × 49½", Courtesy of the Eric Key Collection, © Robert Reid.

202

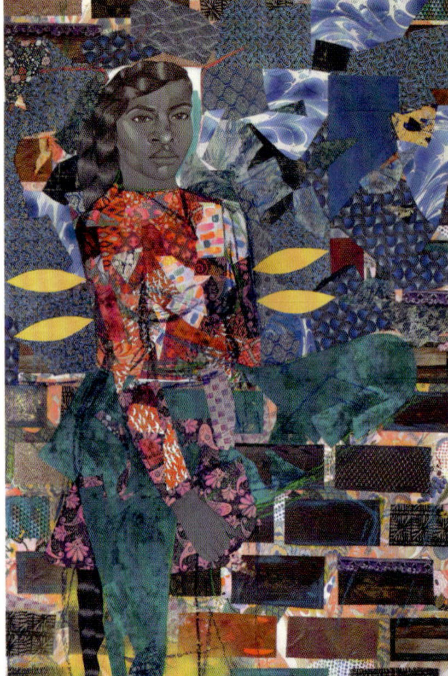

204

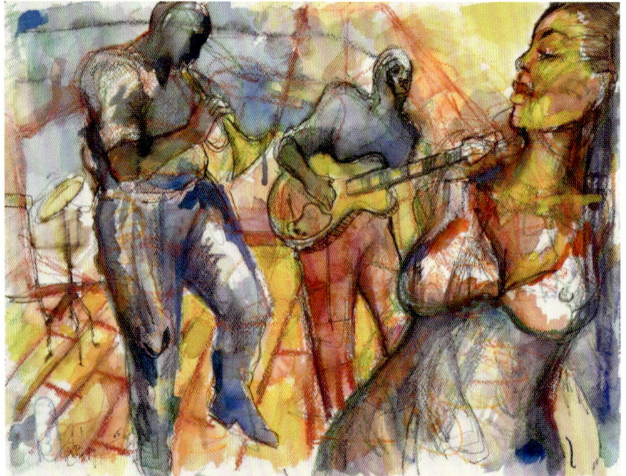

205

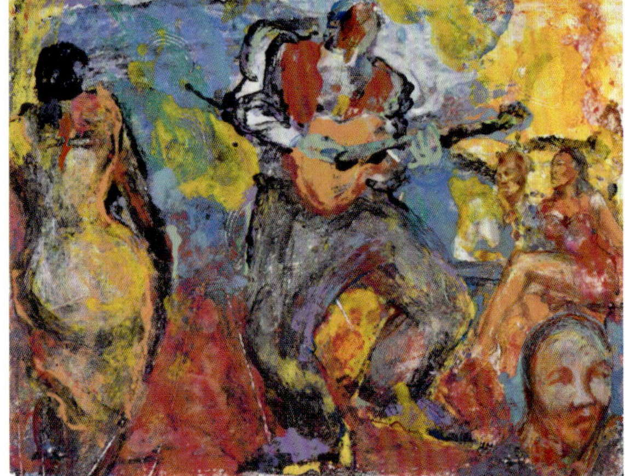

203

206

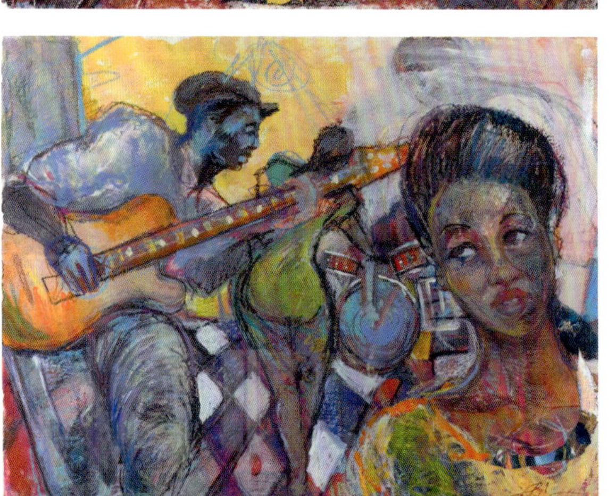

Cat. 202
Jamea Richmond-Edwards, *Easy Breezy Girl*, 2020, Mixed media, 72" × 48" × 2", Courtesy of the Eric Key Collection, © Jamea Richmond-Edwards.

Cat. 203
Preston Sampson, *Cabana Boy*, 2019, Encaustic on plywood, 18" × 8", Courtesy of the Eric Key Collection, © Preston Sampson.

Cat. 204
Preston Sampson, *Dancing*, 2005, Watercolor on paper, 22½" × 25½", Courtesy of the Eric Key Collection, © Preston Sampson.

Cat. 205
Preston Sampson, *Man Playing Guitar 1*, 2005, Watercolor on pulp paper, 41¾" × 49½", Courtesy of the Eric Key Collection, © Preston Sampson.

Cat. 206
Preston Sampson, *Man Playing Guitar 2*, 2005, Acrylic on canvas, 41½" × 49", Courtesy of the Eric Key Collection, © Preston Sampson.

207

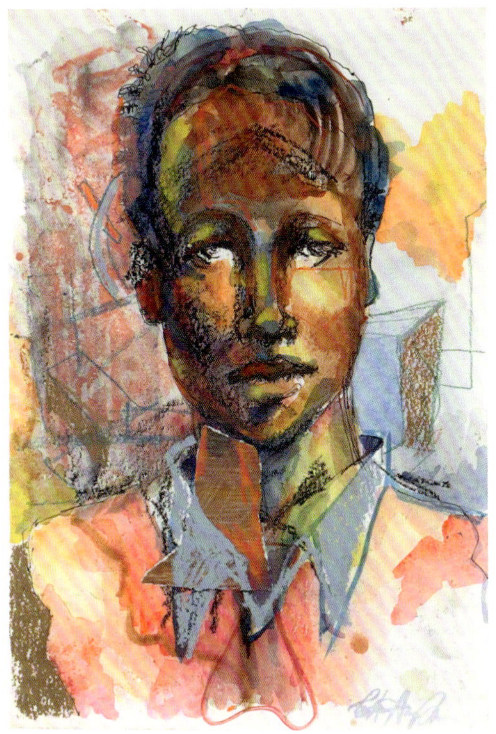

208

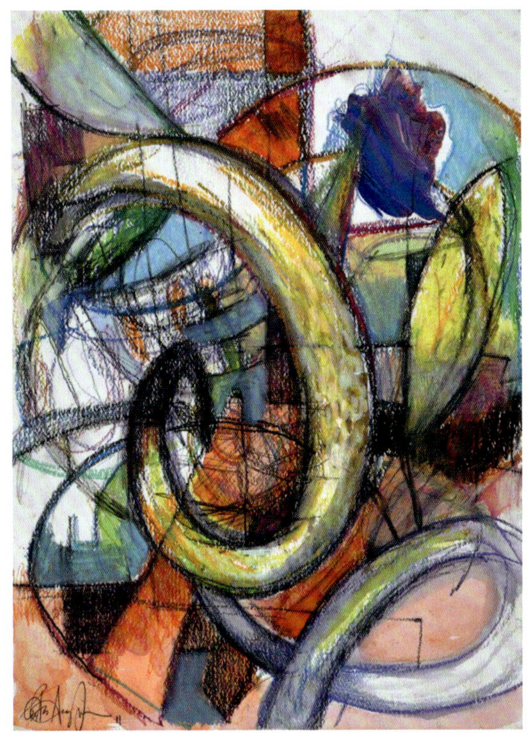

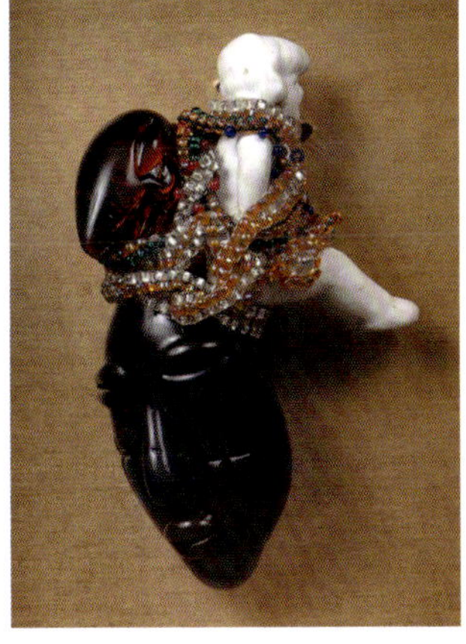

209

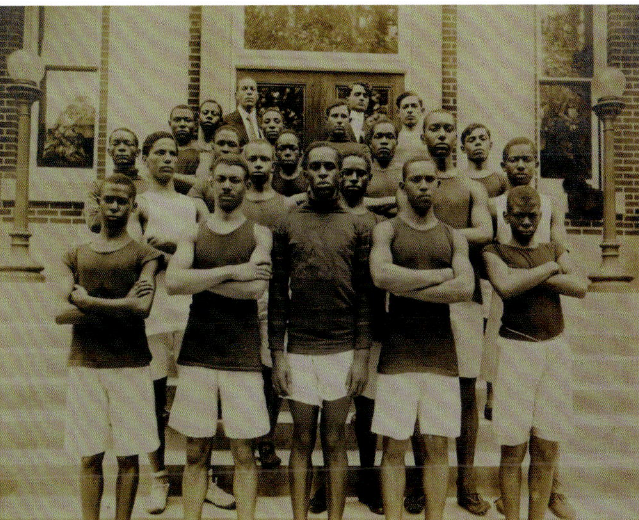

210

Cat. 207
Preston Sampson, *Portrait*, 2000, Watercolor with collage on paper, 18" × 12", Courtesy of the Eric Key Collection, © Preston Sampson.

Cat. 208
Preston Sampson, *Untitled (Yellow White Ribbon)*, 2011, Mixed media, 23" × 19", Courtesy of the Eric Key Collection, © Preston Sampson.

Cat. 209
Joyce Scott, *Untitled*, 2014, Porcelain, blown fused glass, beads, 10" × 8" × 3", Courtesy of the Eric Key Collection, © Courtesy of Goya Contemporary Gallery for Joyce Scott.

Cat. 210
Addison Scurlock, *West Virginia Basketball Team Visited Armstrong*, 1930, Photoprint, 6¾" × 8¾", Courtesy of the Eric Key Collection, © Addison Scurlock.

211

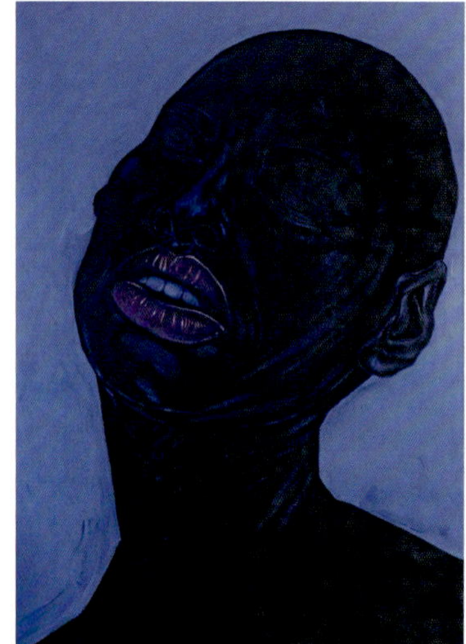

212

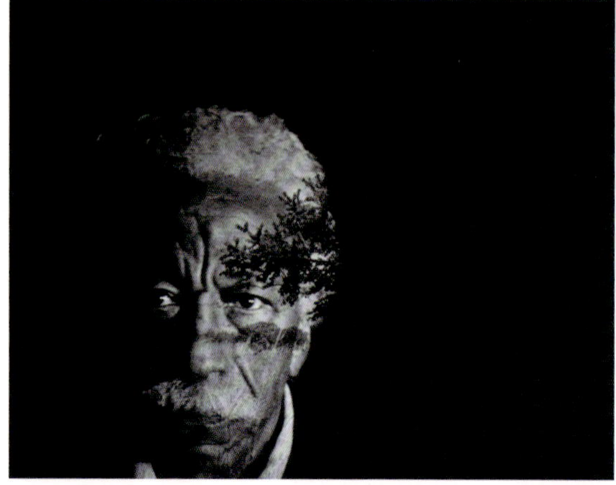

213

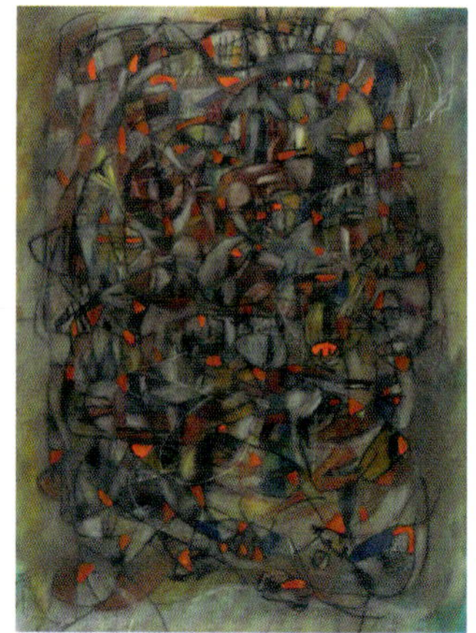

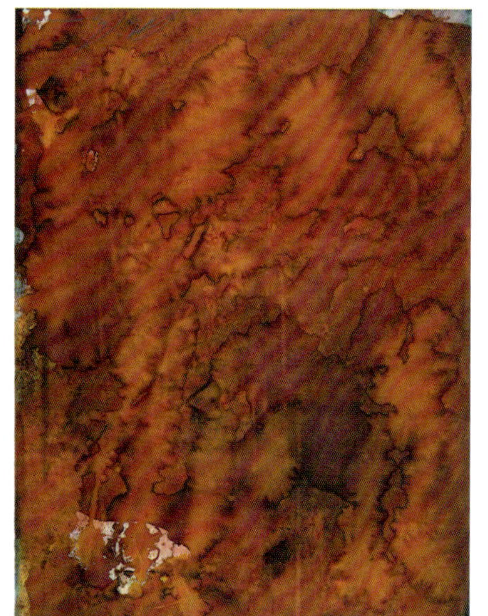

214

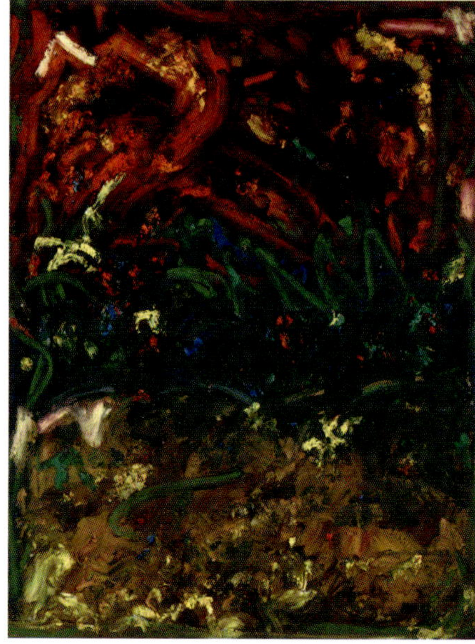

215

Cat. 211
Navel Seakamela, *Blue Fantasy II*, 2022, 79⅛" × 56 ¼", Acrylic and charcoal on canvas, Courtesy of the Eric Key Collection, © Navel Seakamela.

Cat. 212
Carl Sidle, *Gordon's The Learning Tree*, 2004, Photograph, 25" × 30", Courtesy of the Eric Key Collection, © Carl Sidle.

Cat. 213
Danny Simmons, *More Complicated Than May Seem*, 2007, Mixed media on Arch watercolor paper, 30¼" × 22¼", Courtesy of the Eric Key Collection, © Danny Simmons.

Cat. 214
Alec Simpson, *Autumn*, 1991, Monotype on paper, 30" × 22", Courtesy of the Eric Key Collection, © Alec Simpson.

Cat. 215
Alec Simpson, *Back Again III*, 1994, Oil on canvas, 45" × 37", Courtesy of the Eric Key Collection, © Alec Simpson.

216

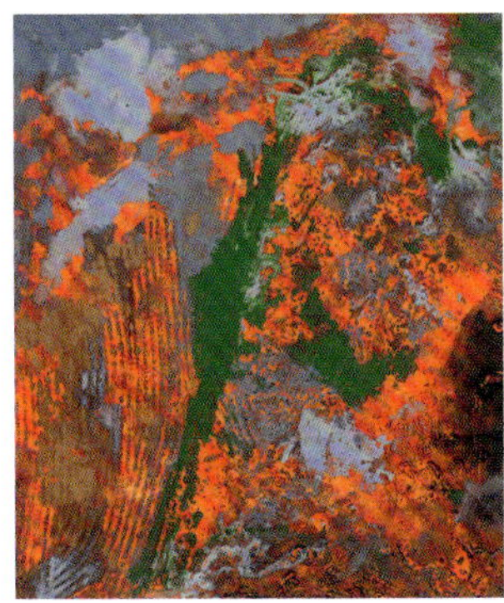

217

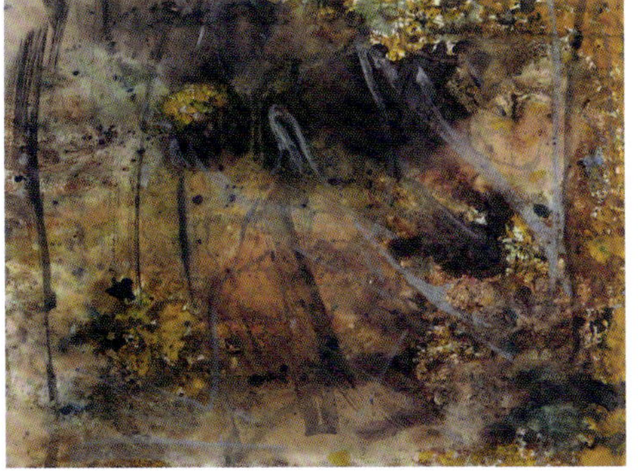

218

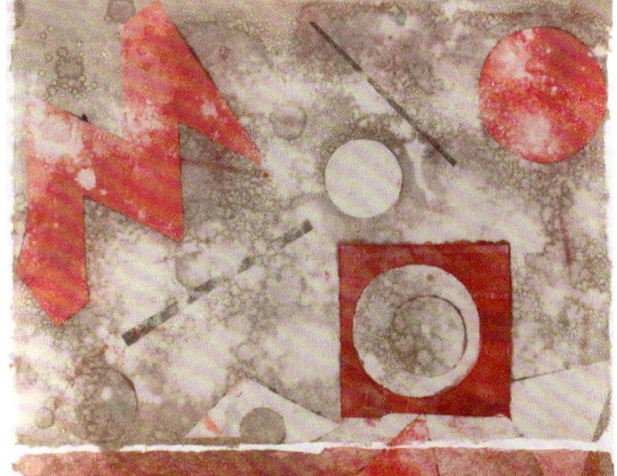

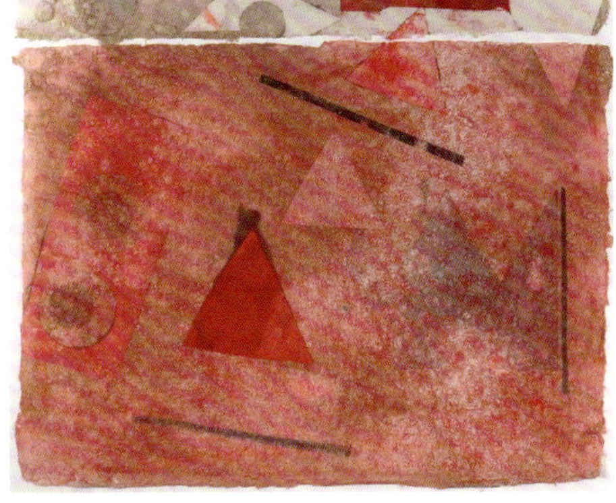

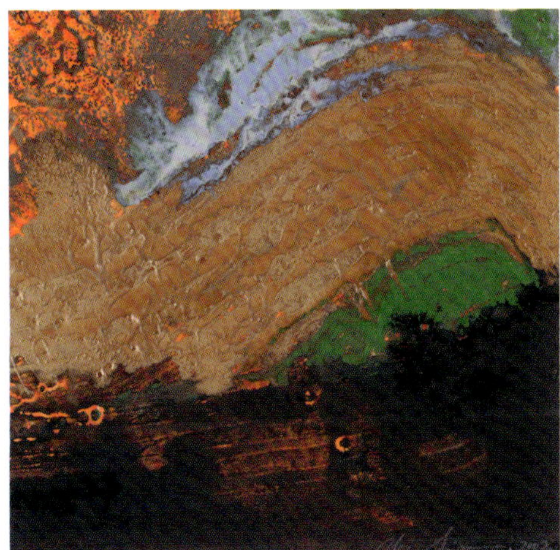

219

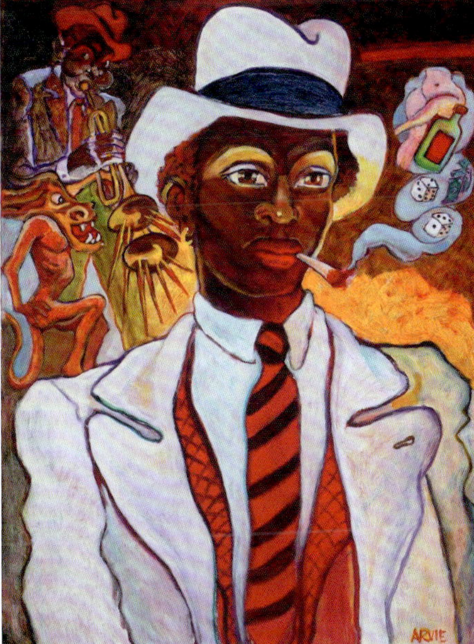

220

Cat. 216
Alec Simpson, *Moon Dance*, 2002, Monotype on paper, 17" × 15", Courtesy of the Eric Key Collection, © Alec Simpson.

Cat. 217
Alec Simpson, *Passion to Paradise*, 1991, Monotype on paper, 31 ½" × 23½", Courtesy of the Eric Key Collection, © Alec Simpson.

Cat. 218
Alec Simpson, *Topsy Turvy*, 1997, Monotype on paper, 46" × 33" × 2", Courtesy of the Eric Key Collection, © Alec Simpson.

Cat. 219
Alec Simpson, *Untitled*, 2002, Monotype on paper, 8½" × 8½", Courtesy of the Eric Key Collection, © Alec Simpson.

Cat. 220
Arvie Smith, *The Hustler*, 2019, Oil on canvas, 40" × 30", Courtesy of the Eric Key Collection, © Arvie Smith.

221

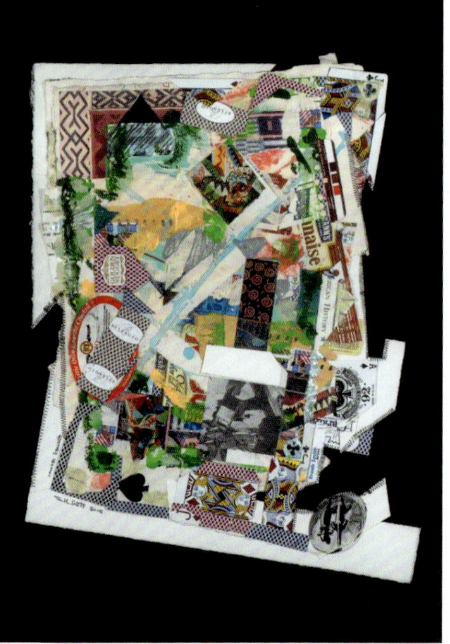

222

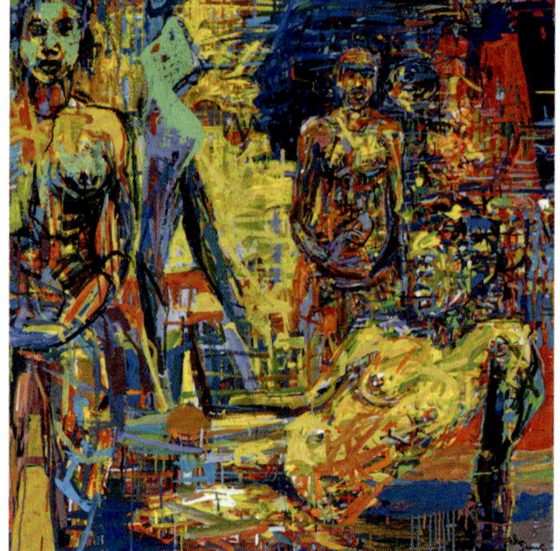

223

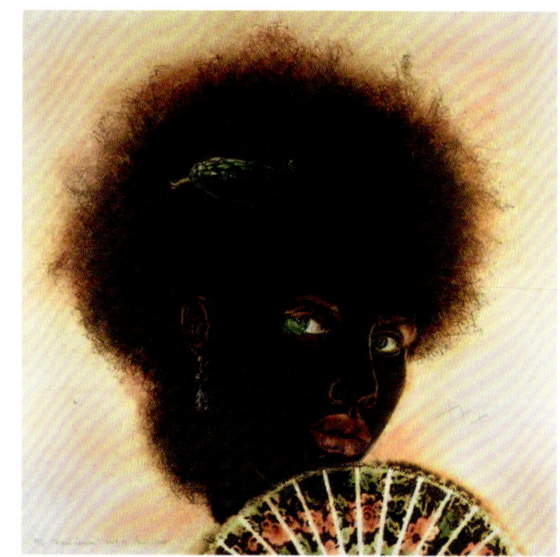

224

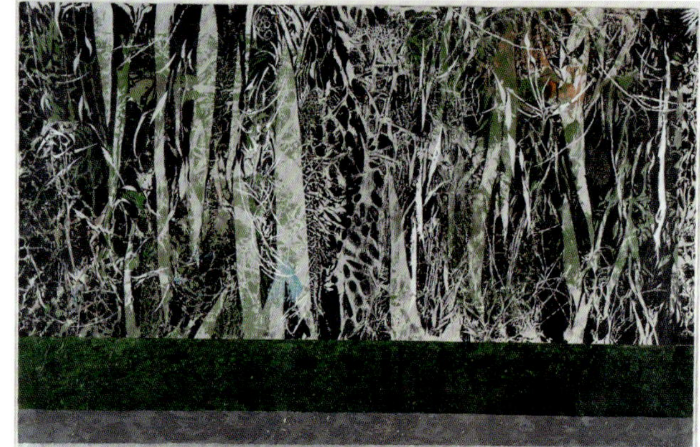

225

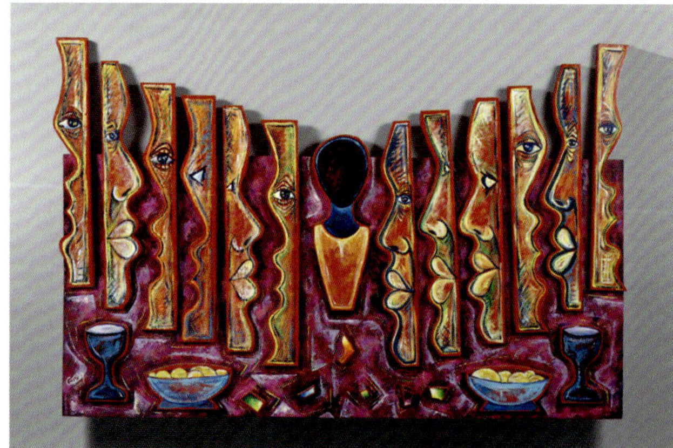

Cat. 221
Frank Smith, *History Lesson*, 2005, Mixed media, 24" × 20", Courtesy of the Eric Key Collection, © Frank Smith.

Cat. 222
Nelson Stevens, *Untitled (nude female)*, 1980, Oil on canvas, 42" × 42" × 2", Courtesy of the Eric Key Collection, © Nelson Stevens.

Cat. 223
Renée Stout, *Marie Laveau*, 2009, Color lithograph on paper (10/10), 24" × 24", Courtesy of the Eric Key Collection, © Renée Stout.

Cat. 224
Freddie Styles, *New Collage Series: Winter*, 2017, Paint and mud on paper, 33½" × 47¼" × 2⅜", Courtesy of the Eric Key Collection, © Freddie Styles.

Cat. 225
Clarence Talley, *Last Supper*, 1993, Painted wood, 31¼" × 42" × 3", Courtesy of the Eric Key Collection, © Clarence Talley.

226

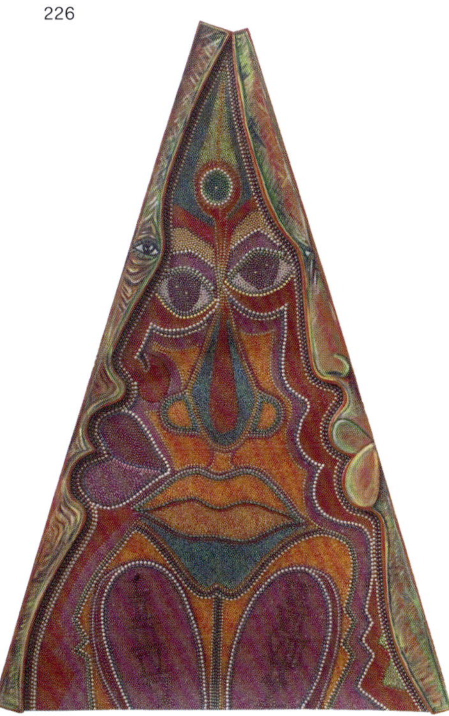

227

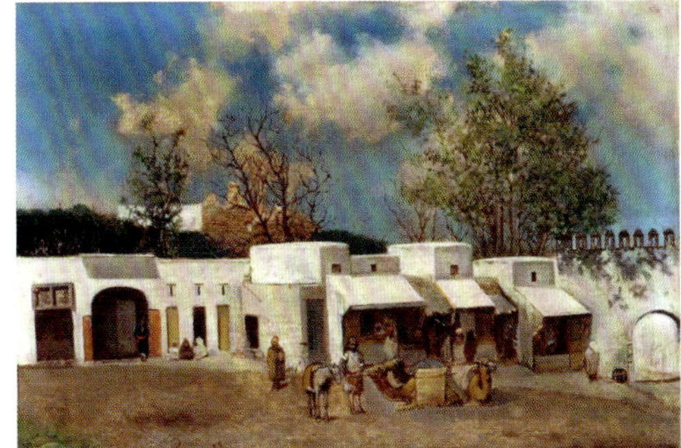

228

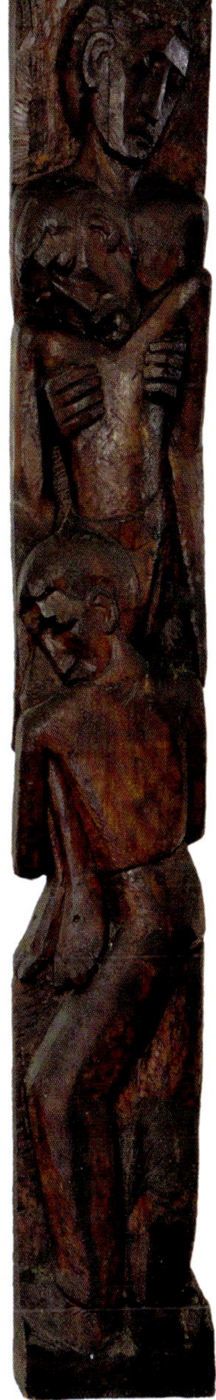

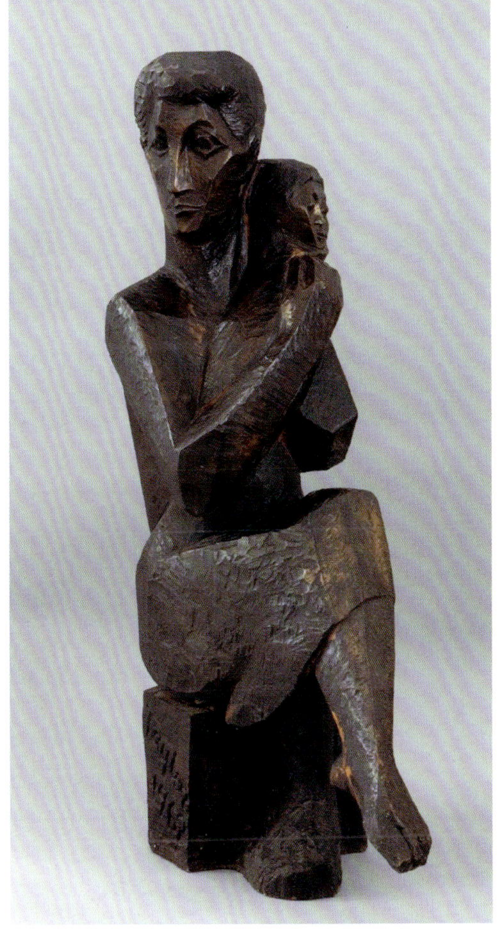

229

Cat. 226
Clarence Talley, *Moses and the Ten Commandments*, 1993, Mixed media with beads, 50" × 42" × 2", Courtesy of the Eric Key Collection, © Clarence Talley.

Cat. 227
Henry Tanner, *Tangier*, 1888, Oil on canvas, 12½" × 16½", Courtesy of the Eric Key Collection, © Henry Tanner.

Cat. 228
William "Bill" Taylor, *Christ*, 1961, Wood, 68" × 10" × 3½", Courtesy of the Eric Key Collection, © William "Bill" Taylor.

Cat. 229
William "Bill" Taylor, *Mother and Child*, 1969, Painted wood, 37" × 12" × 20", Courtesy of the Eric Key Collection, © William "Bill" Taylor.

230

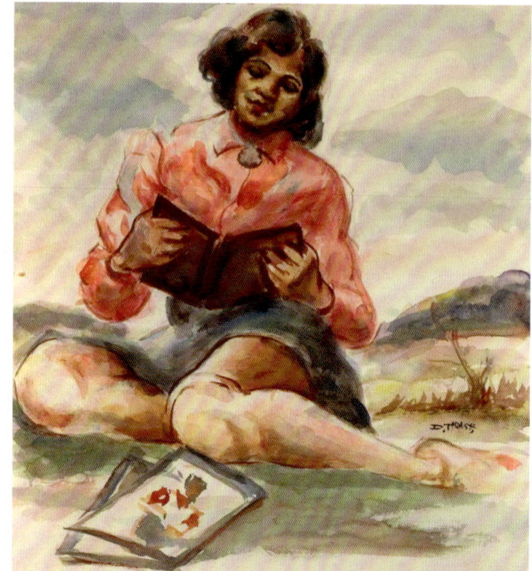

232

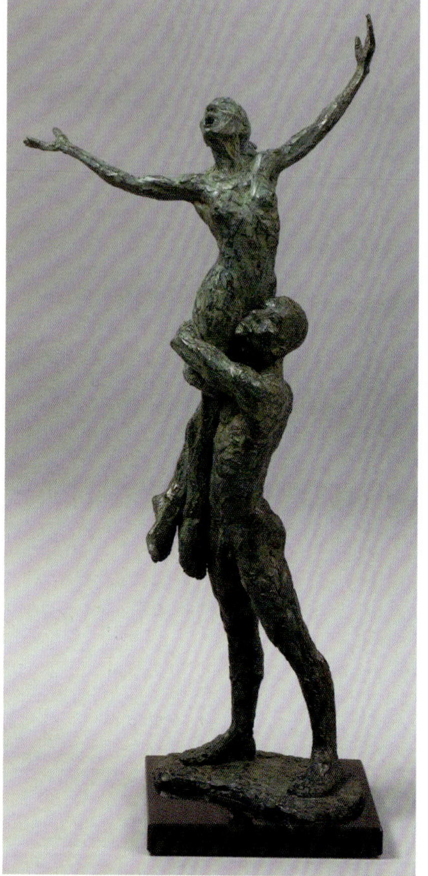

231

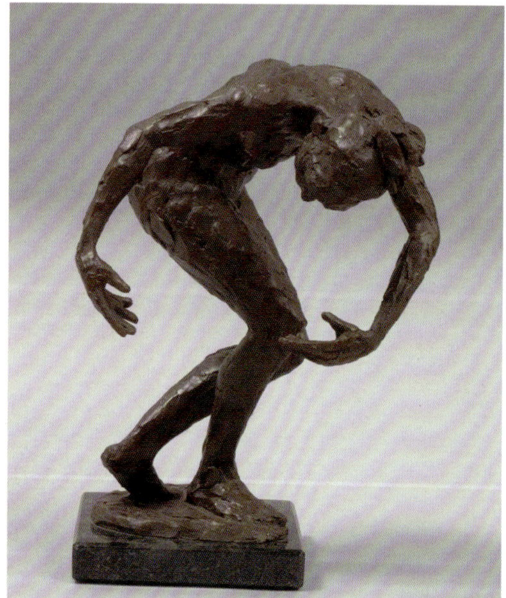

233

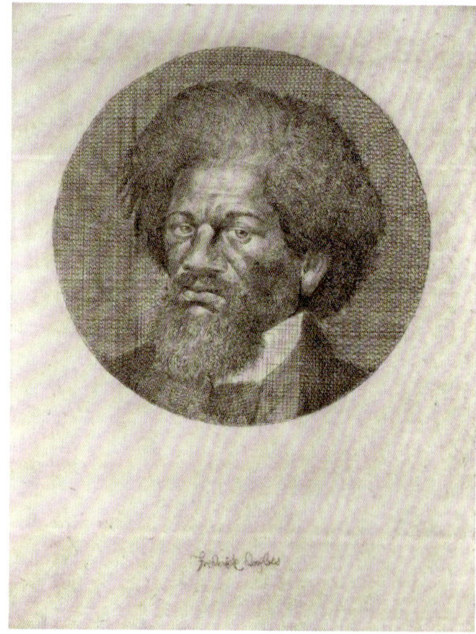

Cat. 230
Dox Thrash, *Untitled (Woman Reading)*, no date, Watercolor on paper, 22½" × 18" × 2", Courtesy of the Eric Key Collection, © Dox Thrash.

Cat. 231
Basil Watson, *Ballerina*, no date, Bronze, 13" × 9" × 9", Courtesy of the Eric Key Collection, © Basil Watson.

Cat. 232
Basil Watson, *Dancers*, 1995, Bronze, green patina, 28" × 13" × 8", Courtesy of the Eric Key Collection, © Basil Watson.

Cat. 233
Charles Wilbert White, *Frederick Douglass*, 1973, Etching on paper, 33" × 27" × 1", Courtesy of The Eric Key Collection, © Courtesy of The Charles White Archives.

234

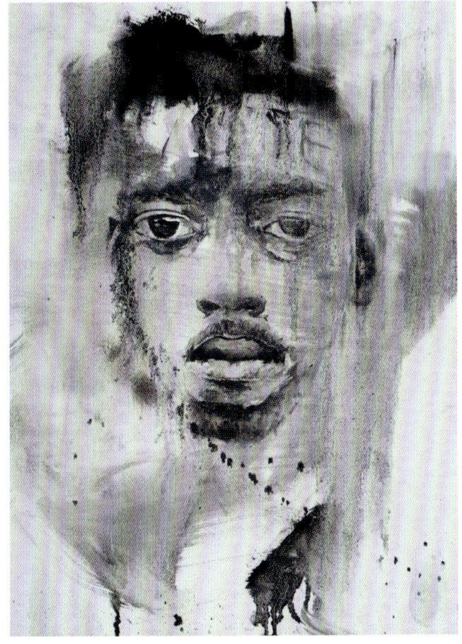

235

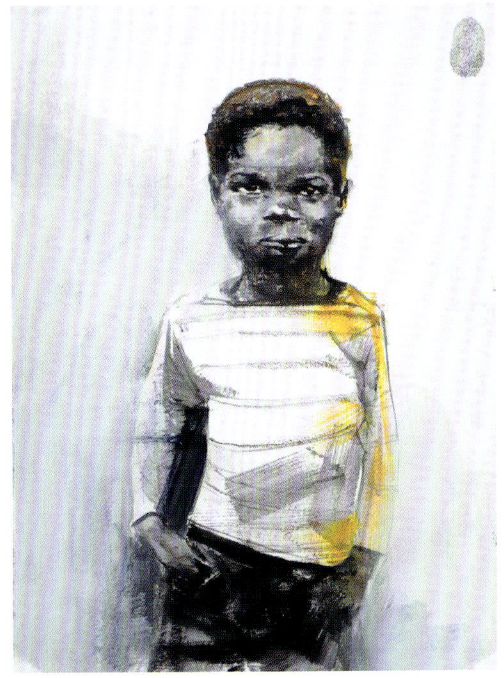

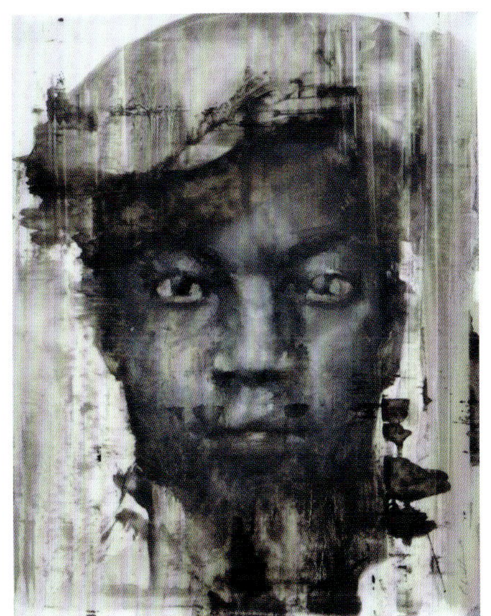

236

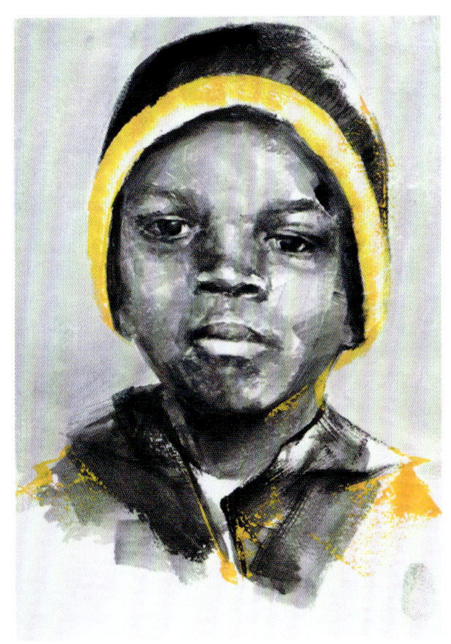

237

Cat. 234
Charles Edward Williams, *Hope*, 2016, Oil on watercolor paper, 12" × 9" × 2", Courtesy of the Eric Key Collection, © Charles Edward Williams.

Cat. 235
Charles Edward Williams, *Untitled (Boy in Shirt)*, 2017, Oil on watercolor paper, 12" × 9" × 2", Courtesy of the Eric Key Collection, © Charles Edward Williams.

Cat. 236
Charles Edward Williams, *Untitled (Boy with Cap)*, no date, Oil on Mylar, 12" × 9" × 2", Courtesy of the Eric Key Collection, © Charles Edward Williams.

Cat. 237
Charles Edward Williams, *Untitled (Boy with Skull Cap with Yellow Band)*, 2017, Oil on watercolor paper, 12" × 9" × 2", Courtesy of the Eric Key Collection, © Charles Edward Williams.

238

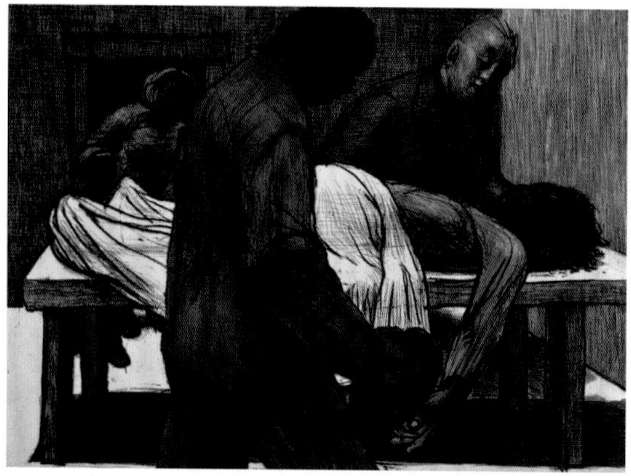

239

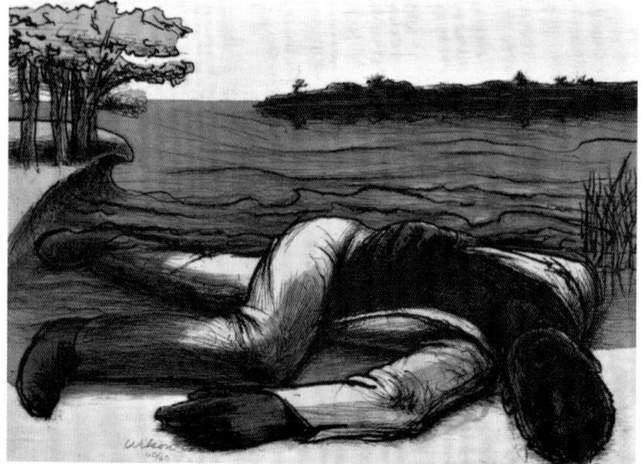

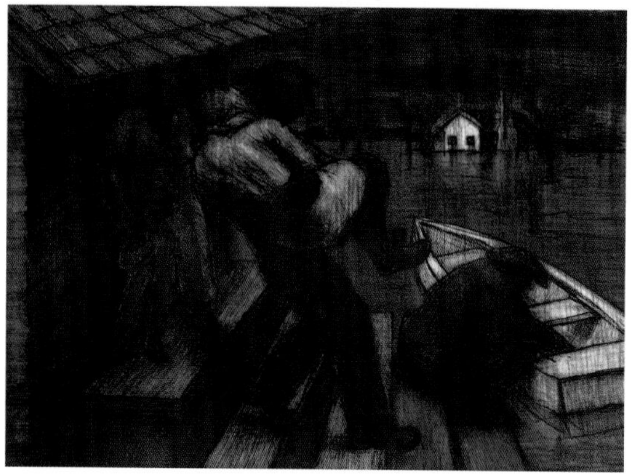

240

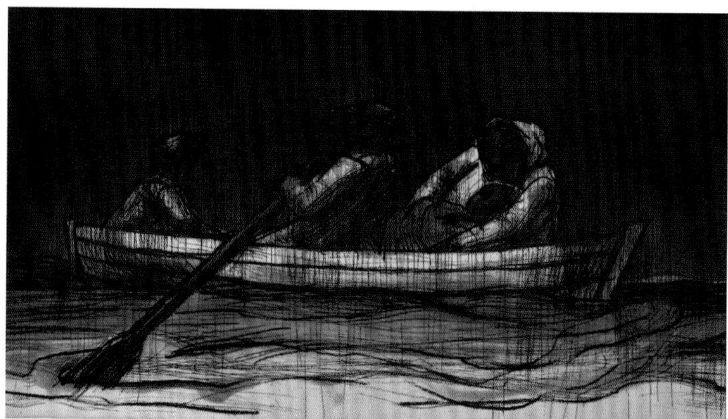

241

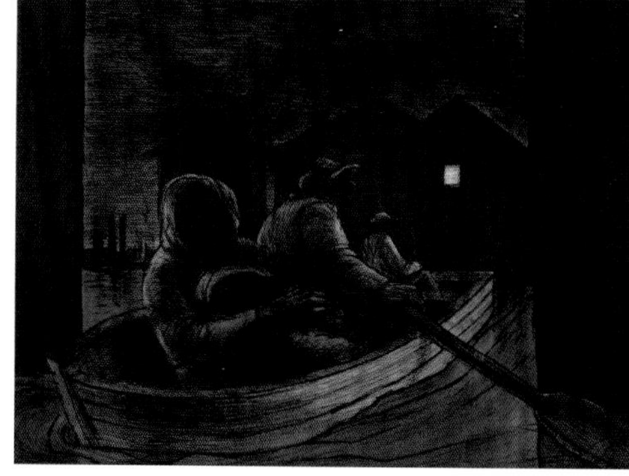

242

Cat. 238
John Wilson, *Portfolio "Down by the Riverside," Death of Lulu*, 2001, Etching and aquatint on wove paper, 12" × 16", Courtesy of the Eric Key Collection, © 2023 Estate of John Wilson / Licensed by VAGA at Artists Rights Society (ARS), NY.

Cat. 239
John Wilson, *Portfolio "Down by the Riverside," Death of Mann*, 2001, Etching and aquatint on wove paper, 12" × 16", Courtesy of the Eric Key Collection, © 2023 Estate of John Wilson / Licensed by VAGA at Artists Rights Society (ARS), NY.

Cat. 240
John Wilson, *Portfolio "Down by the Riverside," Embarkation*, 2001, Etching and aquatint on wove paper, 12" × 16", Courtesy of the Eric Key Collection, © 2023 Estate of John Wilson / Licensed by VAGA at Artists Rights Society (ARS), NY.

Cat. 241
John Wilson, *Portfolio "Down by the Riverside," Journey of Mann Family*, 2001, Etching and aquatint on wove paper, 12" × 16", Courtesy of the Eric Key Collection, © 2023 Estate of John Wilson / Licensed by VAGA at Artists Rights Society (ARS), NY.

Cat. 242
John Wilson, *Portfolio "Down by the Riverside," Light in the Window*, 2001, Etching and aquatint on wove paper, 12" × 16", Courtesy of the Eric Key Collection, © 2023 Estate of John Wilson / Licensed by VAGA at Artists Rights Society (ARS), NY.

243

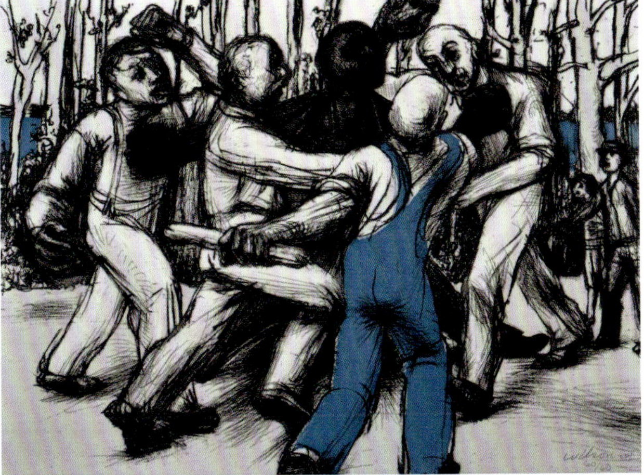

244

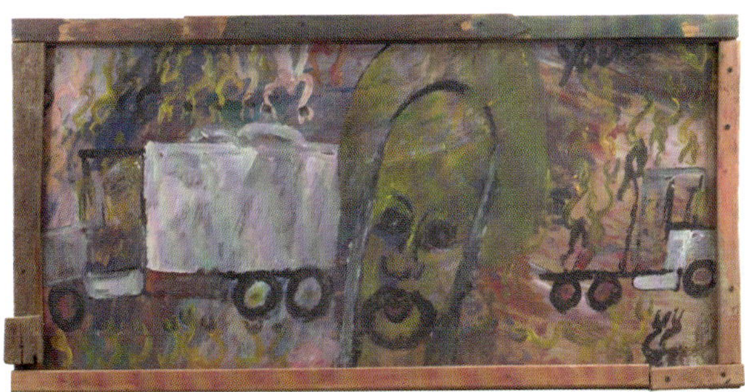

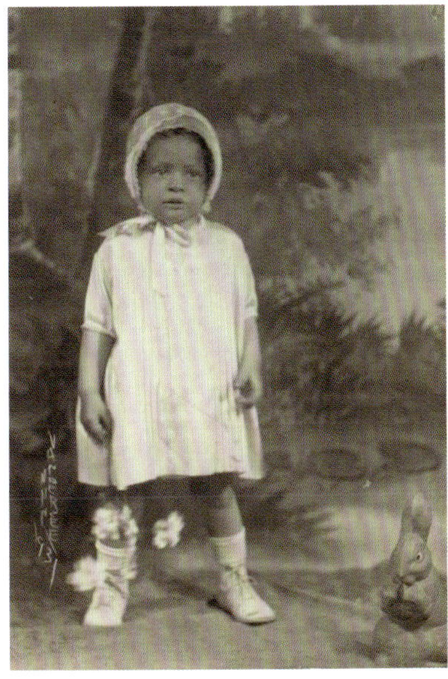

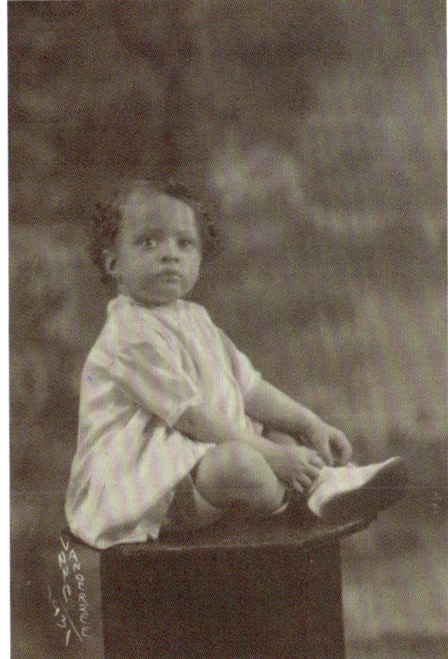

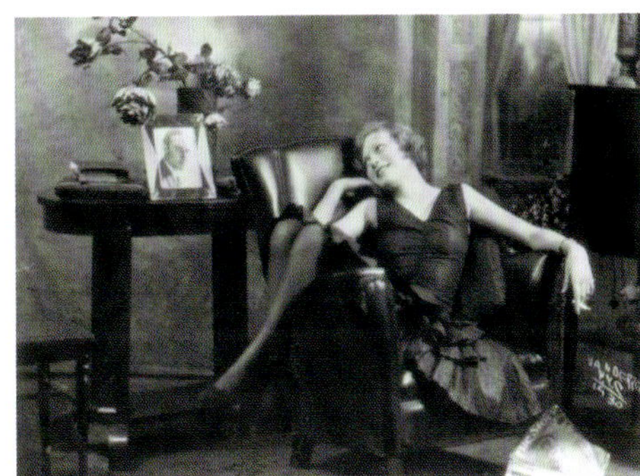

247

246

245

Cat. 243
John Wilson, *Portfolio "Down by the Riverside," Mann Attack*, 2001, Etching and aquatint on wove paper, 12" × 16", Courtesy of the Eric Key Collection, © 2023 Estate of John Wilson / Licensed by VAGA at Artists Rights Society (ARS), NY.

Cat. 244
Purvis Young, *Untitled*, no date, Oil on found wood, 24" × 48", Courtesy of the Eric Key Collection, © 2023 The Larry T. Clemons Collection / Artists Rights Society (ARS), NY.

Cat. 245
James Van Der Zee, *Untitled (Child Standing)*, 1931, Photograph, 8" × 6½", Courtesy of the Eric Key Collection, © James Van Der Zee.

Cat. 246
James Van Der Zee, *Untitled (Seated Baby)*, 1931, Photograph, 8" × 6½", Courtesy of the Eric Key Collection, © James Van Der Zee.

Cat. 247
James Van Der Zee, *Untitled (Woman in Chair)*, 1930, Photograph, 19" × 23", Courtesy of the Eric Key Collection, © James Van Der Zee.

BIBLIOGRAPHY

Brooks, Kinitra, and Kameelah L. Martin and LaKisha Simmons. "Conjure Feminism: Toward a Genealogy." *Hypatia 36,* no. 3: 452-461. doi:10.1017/hyp.2021.43.

Childs, Adrienne L. "A Conversation with Richard Hunt and Adrienne L. Childs." In *Richard Hunt,* 281-282. New York: Gregory R. Miller and Co., 2022.

English, Darby. *1971: A Year in the Life of Color.* Chicago: The University of Chicago Press, 2016.

Farrington, Lisa. *Creating Their Own Image: The History of African American Women Artists.* Oxford: Oxford University Press, 2005.

Greene, Nikki. "Rest: A Pedagogy of Art and Care." Keynote lecture at the Feminist Art History Conference, American University, Washington, DC, September 30, 2023.

Hersey, Tricia. *Rest in Resistance: A Manifesto.* First edition. New York: Little, Brown Spark, 2022.

hooks, bell. *Art on My Mind: Visual Politics.* New York: The New Press, 1995.

Jones, Kellie. "Swimming with E.C." In *We Wanted a Revolution: Black Radical Women, 1965-1985, New Perspectives.* Edited by Catherine Morris and Rujeko Hockley. Brooklyn, NY: Brooklyn Museum, 2018.

Kim, Christine Y. and Myrtle Elizabeth Andrews. *Black American Portraits: From the Los Angeles County Museum of Art.* Los Angeles, CA: Los Angeles County Museum of Art, 2023.

Locke, Alain. *The New Negro: An Interpretation.* Mansfield Centre, CT: Martino Publishing, 2015.

Martin, Kameelah L. "Black Feminist Voodoo Aesthetics, Conjure Feminism, and the Arts." In *In the Black Fantastic*, edited by Ekow Eshun, 137-144. Cambridge: The MIT Press, 2022.

Samella Lewis, interviewed by Karen Anne Mason, March 15, 1992, transcript page 32, UCLA Oral History, 1.2 Tape Number: I Side Two, University of California Los Angeles Oral History Library. https://oralhistory.library.ucla.edu/catalog/21198-zz0008zpm5.

Smalls, James. "Féral Benga: African Muse of Modernism." *Nka 41* (November 2017): 45-59.

Stauffer, John, Zoe Trodd, and Celeste-Marie Bernier. *Picturing Frederick Douglass: An Illustrated Biography of the Nineteenth Century's Most Photographed American.* New York: Liveright Publishing Corporation, 2015.

Tesfagiorgis, Freida High. "Afrofemcentrism in the Art of Elizabeth Catlett and Faith Ringgold (a View of Women by Women)." *Sage: A Scholarly Journal on Black Women 4*, no. 1 (1987): 25-32.

Woodruff, Hale. "The Black Artist in America: A Symposium." *The Metropolitan Museum of Art Bulletin 27*, no. 5 (January 1969): 253.

EXHIBITION TOUR SCHEDULE

as of July 2024

January 31, 2026 - April 26, 2026
Flint Institute of Arts
Flint, MI

May 24, 2026 - August 16, 2026
The Rockwell Museum
Corning, NY

September 25, 2026 - January 30, 2027
Museum of the Shenandoah Valley
Winchester, VA

February 13, 2027 - May 9, 2027
Dayton Art Institute
Dayton, OH

June 4, 2027 - August 20, 2027
El Paso Museum of Art
El Paso, TX

September 16, 2027 - December 18, 2027
Fairfield University Museum of Art
Fairfield, CT

February 4, 2028 - May 12, 2028
Northwest Museum of Arts & Culture
Spokane, WA

June 16, 2028 - September 17, 2028
Huntsville Museum of Art
Huntsville, AL

AUTHOR BIOGRAPHIES

Halima Taha
Writer, Curator
www.tahathinks.art

Halima Taha is best known for her groundbreaking bestseller, *Collecting African American Art: Works on Paper and Canvas*, the first book to validate the collection of fine art, printmaking, and photography by Americans of African descent as viable assets and commodities within the art market. Her book served as a choice PBS membership incentive, raising its fundraising goal three times. In addition, her work created the foundation, in conjunction with the National Black Fine Art Show (1997-2009), to cultivate and educate global markets, enabling Swann Galleries to establish the first African American auction category in 2008. Her work catalyzed prominent museums to pursue collections of African American Art for exhibition and acquisition within the first two decades of this century. Taha is an art professional and tireless advocate for Black visual culture; her curatorial, art advisory, and strategic planning develop corporate and not-for-profit programs and audiences.

Adrienne L. Childs PhD
Art historian, Curator

Adrienne L. Childs PhD is an independent art historian, curator, and Senior Consulting Curator at The Phillips Collection. She also served as curator at the David C. Driskell Center, where she curated numerous exhibitions on African American art. Childs co-curated the exhibition *The Colour of Anxiety: Race, Sexuality and Disorder in Victorian Sculpture* for the Henry Moore Institute, as well as *Riffs and Relations: African American Artists and the European Modernist Tradition*, (2020) for the Phillips Collection. Childs's current book project is *Ornamental Blackness: The Black Figure in European Decorative Arts*, forthcoming from Yale University Press. She has been awarded fellowships by many institutions, including the Hutchins Center at Harvard University and the Center for Advanced Studies in the Visual Arts at the National Gallery. In 2022, Childs was awarded the Driskell Prize by the High Museum of Art for her contributions to the field of African American Art.

INDEX

Page numbers in *italics* refer to the illustrations

PHOTO CREDITS

Unless otherwise noted, all photographs by Greg Staley and John Woo.